Wahlen und politische Einstellungen

Wahlen sind ein zentrales Element aller Demokratien. Daher hat die Untersuchung des Wahlverhaltens der Bürgerinnen und Bürger und seiner Erklärungsfaktoren eine lange Tradition in der politikwissenschaftlichen Forschung, insbesondere in ihrem quantitativ-empirischen Zweig. Die Buchreihe „Wahlen und politische Einstellungen", die vom Arbeitskreis „Wahlen und politische Einstellungen" der DVPW herausgegeben wird, bietet ein Publikationsforum für die deutsche und internationale Wahl- und Einstellungsforschung, in dem unterschiedliche Richtungen gebündelt und aktuelle Forschungsergebnisse vorgestellt werden. Die Reihe steht sowohl „klassischen" als auch interdisziplinären, vergleichenden sowie methodisch innovativen Arbeiten offen, um die Wahl- und Einstellungsforschung in ihrer gesamten Breite zu erfassen. Thematisch deckt die Reihe klassische Fragen der Politischen Soziologie bzw. der Wahlsoziologie, der Politischen Kommunikationsforschung, der Politischen Psychologie sowie der Politischen Ökonomie ab.

Lukas Antoine

The Subjective Value of Privacy

Assessing Individuals' Calculus of Costs and Benefits in the Context of State Surveillance

Springer VS

Lukas Antoine
Fachbereich Politik- und
Sozialwissenschaften
Freie Universität Berlin
Berlin, Germany

D 188—Dissertation Freie Universität Berlin, 2024

ISSN 2945-9591 ISSN 2945-9605 (electronic)
Wahlen und politische Einstellungen
ISBN 978-3-658-46461-5 ISBN 978-3-658-46462-2 (eBook)
https://doi.org/10.1007/978-3-658-46462-2

This Springer VS imprint is published by the registered company Springer Fachmedien Wiesbaden GmbH, part of Springer Nature.
The registered company address is: Abraham-Lincoln-Str. 46, 65189 Wiesbaden, Germany

Acknowledgements

In completing this work over the past 3.5 years, many people have played a significant role, and I would like to express my heartfelt gratitude to them. First and foremost, I would like to give thanks to my first supervisor, Heiko Giebler, who has been a constant source of guidance and support from day one. His mentorship has been invaluable, and I have had the privilege of learning a great deal, both personally and within his research group, over the past years. Thank you for your outstanding support, Heiko!

I would also like to sincerely thank my second supervisor, Thorsten Faas, who not only agreed to co-supervise my work but whose conversations with me and whose feedback have consistently motivated me. It is also thanks to his suggestion that I decided to apply for the doctoral position four years ago.

Special thanks are due to my colleagues Rasmus Ollroge, Ade Ajayi, Ana Karalashvili, Anna Kamenskikh, and Karoline Estermann for their support, especially in reading numerous earlier versions of individual chapters and providing assistance to the work on this thesis in various ways. I am also deeply thankful to Julian Götsch for revisiting the entire work and offering very helpful comments.

Last but not least, I would like to extend my warmest thanks to my family, my friends, and especially to Julia, whose support has been instrumental in completing this work. Thank you for standing by me throughout this journey!

Contents

Abbreviations

APCO	Antecedents–Privacy Concerns–Outcomes
CAPI	Computer-assisted personal interview
CAWI	Computer-assisted web interview
CCTV	Close-circuit television
CD	Coefficient of determination
EU	European Union
ICC	Intraclass correlation coefficient
ISSP	International Social Survey Programme
ML	Maximum likelihood estimation
NSA	National Security Agency (USA)
PALS	Public Attitudes towards the Liberal Script
REML	Restricted maximum likelihood estimation
RWA	Right-wing authoritarianism
SCRIPTS	Cluster of Excellence "Contestations of the Liberal Script"
SNS	Social networking site
SRMSR	Standardized root mean squared residual
USA	United States of America
V-Dem	Varieties of Democracy Project

List of Figures

List of Tables

Introduction 1

When in June 2013, the Washington Post and the Guardian published the initial details of the extensive state surveillance programs of the United States and its partners, obtained through the then-contractor for the National Security Agency (NSA), Edward Snowden, public outcry was significant. The revelation that states had the capability to monitor entire internet and cellphone communications and were actively doing so seemed unimaginable to many. State surveillance was associated with authoritarian regimes such as China or the Soviet Union (Frohman 2020) but appeared incompatible with liberal democracies.

However, the activities of the NSA were by no means a new development. Surveillance of citizens has always been always been closely linked to the nation-state (Giddens 1987: 181; Keiber 2015: 171). Technological progress merely allowed state institutions to collect, store, and process larger amounts of data. Especially since the events of September 11, 2001, states justified their surveillance measures as necessary for (national) security. The monitoring of citizens and the collection of data were deemed crucial to protect citizens from the dangers of terrorism. This argument, that states provide security to citizens in exchange for relinquishing certain freedoms, was already articulated by Thomas Hobbes in his *Leviathan.* Today's understanding of security is largely based on the idea of preventive justice: State institutions aim to identify crimes and criminals based on probabilities before they can occur (Ashworth & Zedner 2014). The collateral damage of restricting not only the freedoms of potential wrongdoers but also of the innocent is seen as unavoidable—security takes precedence.

One of these freedoms is privacy. It is often relegated to being considered something "nice to have," potentially less important than security. However, privacy plays a crucial role in individuals' lives and their coexistence. Privacy allows for example for the exclusivity of certain information/behavior, distinguishing

L. Antoine, *The Subjective Value of Privacy*, Wahlen und politische Einstellungen,
https://doi.org/10.1007/978-3-658-46462-2_1

intimate relationships from other human interactions (Gavison 1980; Rosen 2000: 410; Schoeman 1984). It is also considered essential for individual opinion formation and, consequently, democracy as a whole (Gavison 1980; Lever 2005: 15; Regan 1995: 225; Roberts 2015: 339; Simitis 1987: 734). Meanwhile, in recent decades, many everyday behaviors and interactions have become digital. We shop online, work online, or even search for our next partner online, leaving digital traces everywhere. Simultaneously, an increasing number of people generously share information about themselves on social networks or with institutions and companies, leading some commentators to argue that "privacy is dead" (Dienlin & Breuer 2023).

Does the fact that nearly all individuals worldwide find themselves subjected to state surveillance while simultaneously many willingly share private information with companies and on social media imply that individuals do not care about privacy? Probably not, but we do not really know, as surprisingly, research on the subjective appreciation of privacy is relatively limited. To contribute to changing this, the present work analyzes the subjective value of privacy in the context of state surveillance and addresses the question of when and to what extent people are willing to sacrifice privacy when offered something else in return.

The introduction proceeds as follows: Firstly, I provide a brief overview of the existing research regarding privacy attitudes, followed by a description of the main model underlying this work—the privacy calculus model. Subsequently, I elucidate the contribution the thesis makes to the existing literature, concluding with an explanation of its structure.

1.1 Privacy Attitudes

Historical roots of the concept of privacy can be traced back up until 400 BC (B. Moore 1984). Modern interpretations emerged from changes in philosophy, technological advancements, and economic growth (C. Berg 2018: 75). The systematic discussion on privacy began with Samuel D. Warren and Louis D. Brandeis' (1890: 193) definition of the right to privacy as "the right to enjoy life—the right to be let alone." Initially a legal concept, privacy affirms personal freedom, property rights, and connects with liberty, autonomy, and human dignity (Koops et al. 2017: 493; Lever 2006). The unified right to privacy is a relatively recent development, replacing and merging earlier settlements on home inviolability or confidentiality of correspondence. Privacy discussions involve philosophical, ethical, moral, and legal perspectives. In the literature, there is significant disagreement about the optimal conceptualization of privacy, with a multitude of proposals. Scholars engage in debates over privacy's definition, protected interests, invasion criteria, and its intrinsic or instrumental value. Unitary theories aim for universal definitions, while typological approaches provide descriptive insights into legal protections and various forms of privacy.

Regardless of prominent (normative) debates on privacy, studies examining individual attitudes and factors explaining them have been relatively scarce. This is particularly true for state surveillance, while in the field of consumer research, there is a plethora of studies addressing consumer decision-making regarding data disclosure. Existing studies primarily focus on specific cases in particular country contexts, predominantly the United States of America (USA), and often lack interconnection (H. Watson et al. 2017). This is partly due to the absence of a universally accepted definition of privacy. Consequently, the research field is relatively unstructured, leading to a limited understanding of public attitudes towards state surveillance. Even if we know from previous findings that people's willingness to accept government measures depends, for example, on context factors, such as a salient threat (Ziller & Helbling 2021), our understanding of how the design of security policies influences individuals' acceptance remains incomplete. Also, from a methodological perspective, approaches to understanding the subjective appreciation of privacy have been relatively limited thus far. Notwithstanding significant progress in the development of survey instruments in recent years, enabling researchers to explore more intricate individual decision-making processes, this advancement is not extensively reflected in the field of privacy and surveillance studies (Baele & Thomson 2017; Preibusch 2013).

This is despite the fact that there is a clear need to better understand citizens' attitudes. The degree of public support can provide insights into the (perceived) legitimacy of policies. At the same time, it is known that citizens' attitudes can also influence political decision-making. There is the conventional perspective on representation according to which governments implement citizens' preferences in order to be re-elected (Burstein 2003). Several studies have shown that public support increases the probability of a policy's implementation (Gilens 2012; Schakel 2021) and decreases the time until it is adopted (Toshkov et al. 2020). In the eye of the slippery slope and normalization arguments that increasing surveillance may contest the nature of liberal societies (Selinger & Rhee 2021), understanding when and why citizens accept surveillance is of salient importance.

1.2 Privacy Calculus

The predominant theoretical framework to analyzing attitudes towards privacy invasions is the "privacy calculus." This conceptual lens, rooted in the notion of "homo oeconomicus," posits that individuals engage in a strategic evaluation of the costs and benefits associated with divulging personal data (Laufer & Wolfe 1977). Drawing on the foundations of social exchange theory (Homans 1961), this calculus asserts that individuals partake in a transactional give-and-take, sharing data when they anticipate a positive net outcome, meaning the expected benefits of disclosure outweigh the associated costs (N. Lee & Kwon 2015).

Privacy risks and costs emanate from perceived potential negative consequences linked to sharing information (Dinev & Hart 2006). It is assumed that individuals attribute different levels of intimacy to various types of information, with more intimate information posing greater risks upon disclosure. Potential losses due to information disclosure can be material (e.g., loss of financial or other assets), physical (e.g., loss of life or health), or psychological (e.g., loss of social status or relationships) (Mothersbaugh et al. 2012: 77). Concerns about sharing personal information revolve around the perceived risk of information misuse by surveillance agents, such as the state or corporations, creating a principal-agent problem due to information asymmetry (Li 2012). This asymmetry impedes individuals (the principal) from adequately monitoring the behavior of surveillance agents. Consequently, lacking knowledge about how surveillance agents utilize their information may lead individuals to hesitate in granting excessive control or withholding personal data (Yu et al. 2020). Perceived benefits or gratifications can be conceptualized as an individual's perception of the value derived from disclosing personal information. In the realm of online consumer research, where the application of privacy calculus is prevalent (Trepte et al. 2020), it is assumed that online consumers seek timely and inexpensive access to products or services, while the hedonistic value of a commercial exchange lies in its ability to fulfill needs for escapism, diversion, or emotional relief (Sun et al. 2015).

In the domain of state surveillance, research predominantly centers on utilitarian benefits (Fox et al. 2021), with individuals often (being asked to) accepting surveillance for enhanced security (Dinev et al. 2008; Thompson et al. 2020). Fundamental changes, unfolding rapidly and simultaneously, are considered a crucial characteristic of modernity, giving rise to both actual and perceived insecurities for many people (Beck 1992). Public opinion research shows that individuals are especially anxious concerning current events, such as the COVID-19 pandemic or consequences of the war in Ukraine (European Parliament 2022). In addition, studies find that people are increasingly concerned about societal cohesion or climate change (Kinnvall et al. 2018). However, fear of crime and terrorism prevails as one of the most frequently mentioned fears—even though crime numbers have dropped in many countries (Feltes et al. 2018: 606–8). As one response to security threats, governments around the globe, albeit in different magnitude, have implemented measures of mass surveillance. The governments' basic promise is that they can increase public security by watching over individuals (Lyon 2015b)—even though evidence for this is scarce. In the course of ongoing technological developments, applications of surveillance expand, ranging from increasingly "smart" camera surveillance in public places to the interception, storage, and processing of electronic communication. In this context, the phenomenon of *securitization* plays a prominent role in the literature (Buzan et al. 1997). It describes the perception or construction of an issue as a security problem. This securitization, placing it on the security agenda, may be aimed at gaining greater latitude in addressing the issue and politically enforcing broader measures. Securitization is contingent upon the audience, e.g., a country's population, accepting the move as valid, thereby conferring an intersubjective status to the perceived threat. Considering the intricacies of cost-benefit assessments, the privacy calculus in the literature is also denoted as a deliberate trade-off (Harborth & Pape 2023: 2). Despite some authors convincingly arguing that there is no *inherent* objective trade-off between security and freedom or privacy (e.g., Chandler 2009), subjective trade-offs are believed to be inherent in individual decision-making (Shaddy et al. 2021).

Privacy is attributed an objective value in various respects: At the individual level, privacy serves as a refuge from societal pressures, fostering emotional well-being and supporting creativity. In interpersonal relationships, privacy enables authenticity and intimacy, while at the societal level, it acts as a common good crucial for democracy, political participation, and safeguarding against the negative impact of surveillance on political processes and historically neglected groups (Inness 1996: 44–45). However, we know, not only from privacy research specifically but from values research in general, that there is not always congruence between objective and subjective values—only because something is objectively beneficial does not mean individuals perceive it as subjectively valuable. The incongruence between subjective and objective values is a multifaceted phenomenon with roots in diverse determinants (Acquisti et al. 2016; Adjerid et al. 2016; M. Lee 2007). Individual perspectives, shaped by personal experiences and cultural nuances, inherently introduce subjectivity into value interpretations. Cultural norms and societal priorities amplify this complexity, emphasizing different facets of human existence across societies. Personal experiences play a crucial role, significantly impacting individuals' perceptions and judgments. Cognitive biases, emotive dimensions, and informational deficiencies contribute to unintentional distortions in subjective valuations (Acquisti & Grossklags 2005; Acquisti 2009). Additionally, temporal dynamics, such as changing circumstances and personal maturation, introduce an evolutionary dimension, leading to shifts in individual perspectives and potential misalignments between subjective and objective values over time.

1.3 Contributions

While understanding privacy attitudes is crucial for a better comprehension of the functioning of surveillance, the current state of the literature on this topic is notably incomplete. In the exploration of the *subjective* value of privacy, this thesis aims to address critical gaps in the existing literature through a comprehensive analysis that spans theoretical, methodological, and empirical dimensions. The following contributions are intended to be provided by the thesis:

Firstly, the literature on attitudes towards surveillance recognizes a notable absence in systematic inquiry into state surveillance attitudes, despite the increasing scope of surveillance. Existing studies highlight challenges such as limited cross-referencing due to varying conceptual definitions, overgeneralization of findings, and divergent interpretations of key meta-concepts like the privacy-security trade-off (H. Watson et al. 2017). These challenges hinder a clear understanding of individuals' acceptance of state surveillance. This thesis endeavors to address these gaps by presenting a more coherent and comprehensive analysis. To achieve this goal, I systematically identify and scrutinize the most influential definitions and conceptualizations of privacy, aiming to distill an understanding widely acknowledged within scholarly circles. A thorough examination of the existing literature underscores the ubiquity of the *informational* dimension of privacy in all pertinent conceptualizations, with several authors emphasizing its pivotal significance (e.g., Koops et al. 2017; Parent 1983a; 1983b; Solove 2006). The deliberate focus on the informational aspect is designed to enhance the accessibility of the analyses and findings for both current and future research. Concurrently, this approach serves as a model for fostering increased interconnectivity within the research field, an imperative advancement for the discipline.

Secondly, the research focuses on the dearth of cross-national studies, emphasizing the contextual dependence of attitudes toward surveillance. While European Union (EU)-funded projects like PRISMS, PACT, and SurPRISE have broadened the scope, reliance on single-country samples persists. This approach is critiqued, and the call is made for a truly global perspective, recognizing variations in privacy concerns between cultural regions and between the Global North and Global South (Zureik & Harling Stalker 2010). Acknowledging the scarcity of cross-national studies in the field, this thesis employs robust datasets from two extensive cross-national surveys. By encompassing responses from over 20,000 and 50,000 participants across 30 and 26 countries, respectively, this research unfolds within a rich tapestry of global perspectives, encompassing varied political and cultural landscapes. In contrast to the reliance on convenience samples such as student samples in most other studies, each of the three studies featured in this thesis strives for a representative portrayal of selected characteristics within populations.

Thirdly, the thesis scrutinizes limited methodological approaches within survey research on privacy attitudes (Baele & Thomson 2017; Preibusch 2013). Recognizing the predominant use of correlational survey data in prior research, I make use of survey experiments in an effort to deepen the understanding of attitudes towards state surveillance, emphasizing the advantages of experimental methodologies, particularly in illuminating multidimensional choices and evaluations. Classical surveys are critiqued for their inability to establish causality, and the thesis advocates for more sophisticated analyses to unravel causal interactions, providing a nuanced understanding of the subjective value of privacy.

The fourth contribution pertains to securitization theory's omission of the role of the audience—acceptance of which is considered necessary for a securitization move to be successful (Côté 2016). To justify surveillance measures and gain them public support, governments often use the promise of security. It is usually claimed that individuals are more willing to have freedom and privacy restricted than waiving a promise of increased security. However, empirical evidence to support this claim has been scarce—especially from a comparative perspective. While the security-privacy trade-off is often emphasized as important, its actual function is not well explored. The research emphasizes the underdeveloped understanding of the audience within securitization processes and calls for exploration of groups more susceptible to accept securitization moves. This thesis seeks to contribute to a more precise understanding of the determinants of securitizing move success or failure based on the analysis of public attitudes.

Moving forward, the thesis delves into the role of the privacy calculus within a broader framework of understanding attitudes towards privacy, namely the Antecedents–Privacy Concerns–Outcome model (H. J. Smith et al. 2011), whose basic message is that there are antecedents that influence the degree to which individuals are concerned about privacy, which in turn manifests in behavior, and which has proven to be particularly relevant since almost all positivist empirical assessments of privacy can be grasped through it (Benamati et al. 2017). The thesis highlights the lack of theorization concerning the positioning of the privacy calculus within the model, leading to an incomplete understanding of its influence on privacy decision-making. While people in general prefer living in a secure environment, I argue that it is not only the imminent trade-off between security concerns and protecting one's privacy and freedom that ultimately persuades citizens to support surveillance measures. While the literature often emphasizes the narrow focus on privacy and security goods, it neglects consideration of other monetary or non-monetary costs and benefits as well as variations in individual or group engagement in the privacy calculus.

The sixth and final contribution revolves around the question of whether privacy is a stable personality trait or a context-dependent variable. Engaging with the theoretical debate on cognate-based and value-based definitions, the research aims to explore how individuals perceive and evaluate state surveillance measures. By investigating whether privacy is a latent personality trait or context-dependent, the thesis seeks to contribute to the broader discourse on privacy in both academic and political arenas (Nissenbaum 2015).

The empirical investigation of the identified blind spots is structured into three studies. In the first study, I use data from the *International Social Survey Programme* (ISSP) and its 2016 *Role of Government module* (Edlund & Lindh 2019; ISSP Research Group 2018), involving more than 20,000 survey participants across 30 countries. The second study uses data from an original factorial survey experiment which was part of the *Conflict of Values in Germany survey* (Giebler et al. 2024) with around 5000 respondents in Germany conducted in 2021. The third study is based on data from another original survey experiment which was part of the *Public Attitudes towards the Liberal Script* (PALS) survey (Giebler et al. 2023a; 2023b) with over 50,000 respondents across 26 countries surveyed in 2021 and 2022.

1.4 Structure of the Thesis

The thesis proceeds as follows: *Chapter 2* seeks to systematically summarize and present the extensive literature available on the complex topics of privacy and security. It introduces the theoretical underpinnings of the privacy-security nexus, delving into the ongoing debate within privacy research regarding its definition. This debate primarily centers on the distinction between unified definitions and pluralist conceptualizations. The informational nature of privacy emerges as particularly relevant and as the overarching common denominator among various conceptualizations. The chapter then explores the primarily beneficial nature of privacy before turning towards privacy invasions and the questions how states justify and why citizens would accept these. Acceptance of privacy invasions is studied through the privacy calculus theory, which suggests individuals weigh benefits and costs. Thereafter, I give an overview on the concept of security, especially focusing on the distinction between objective and subjective security, securitization as a social and political practice, and critiques of securitization theory. The subsequent and final subchapter investigates the interplay between privacy and security, presenting two perspectives: a hierarchical arrangement where security is foundational—as in Abraham Maslow's (1943) pyramid of values—and the idea of a trade-off between privacy and security.

In *Chapter 3*, the thesis addresses the evident lack of a systematic understanding of citizens' perspectives on state surveillance. This chapter undertakes a thorough analysis of existing literature concerning the interplay between attitudes toward privacy and security. Thereby, the prevailing trade-off paradigm between privacy and security is critically examined, with a specific focus on how citizens navigate conflicting values in decision-making processes. Contrary to the widely assumed trade-off, the findings reveal a nuanced relationship that challenges the notion of an *inherent* zero-sum game. The research sheds light on individuals' willingness to exchange privacy and security for convenience, relationships, and monetary rewards. This nuanced nature of privacy preferences underscores the dynamic relationship between perceived risks and benefits, extending beyond the conventional privacy versus security dichotomy.

Chapter 4 presents the conceptual framework and research strategy. Firstly, it identifies gaps in the literature outlined in the previous two chapters, aiming to contribute to their closure through the thesis. Concrete research questions are derived for this purpose. Before delving into how these questions will be addressed through the three empirical studies, theoretical considerations are presented to guide this process. This includes an exploration of the understanding of value and considerations regarding the concept of privacy for the subsequent studies. Finally, methodological considerations for researching privacy attitudes are explained, and the analytical approach is outlined. The analysis of the sensitive issue of privacy makes additional considerations necessary.

Chapters 5 to 7 encompass the three empirical studies. *Chapter 5* addresses the question: *To what extent does the susceptibility to accepting security frames differ between individuals and contexts?* Building on securitization theory, I previously argued that the role of the audience, whose acceptance is necessary to make an issue as a security problem, has been undertheorized and empirically underexplored. Utilizing data from the ISSP, I attempt to discern a potential effect of security frames and test the extent to which this varies between individuals and contexts.

Chapter 6 tackles the question: *To what extent do individuals consider costs and benefits when forming their privacy attitudes?* The focus is expanded to include other monetary and non-monetary costs and benefits that individuals might consider in their privacy calculus. Additionally, the context question is revisited, as the dataset from the *Conflict of Values in Germany survey* allows me to determine a proxy for subjective and objective security for each respondent and explore the effects of these on the acceptance of privacy invasions.

Chapter 7 addresses the question: *Is privacy a stable personality trait or a context-dependent variable?* Based on the assumption that individuals face considerations between privacy and security not only in the crime/terror context, but also in other areas such as health and financial fraud, I explore this calculus based on PALS data. The debate revolves around whether privacy is purely context-dependent or if individuals, to some extent, have certain predispositions guiding their context-specific privacy preferences.

In *Chapter 8*, the conclusion, the findings of the dissertation are synthesized. In light of the research questions outlined in Chapter 4, the central results of each part of the work are summarized and then condensed into a few key insights. Following this, the implications of these key insights for research are elucidated. The work concludes with a discussion of the limitations inherent in this study, followed by a look ahead to possible future research directions.

Theoretical Foundation

2

While the present work is primarily empirical in nature, this does not absolve me from establishing a robust theoretical foundation upon which the empirical studies can build. This chapter serves this purpose. At the same time, the review of the substantive implicitly reveals research gaps, which will be explicated in Chap. 4, guiding the subsequent empirical work. In addition to privacy as the theoretical cornerstone of this work, the following chapter focuses on security—a construct that assumes a prominent role in surveillance studies overall and specifically in the context of state surveillance. Security not only constitutes the primary assurance governments offer their citizens to justify state interventions but also stands as a pivotal consideration in individuals' privacy calculus.

2.1 Privacy

In this chapter, various approaches to defining privacy are examined, highlighting the multitude and diversity of proposals and elucidating the prevailing understanding that will be adopted for this thesis. Following this, before delving into the subjective component, the diverse objective value of the private realm is delineated, emphasizing its significance for individuals and collectives. Finally, attention is directed towards encroachments on privacy, specifically, the invasion thereof. This exploration encompasses not only definitional considerations but also delves into aspects of justification for privacy invasions by those conducting surveillance, as well as reasons contributing to the acceptance of such invasions by those under surveillance.

L. Antoine, *The Subjective Value of Privacy*, Wahlen und politische Einstellungen,
https://doi.org/10.1007/978-3-658-46462-2_2

2.1.1 Defining Privacy

Before I can address the question of what value privacy has, I need to clarify what privacy means in the first place. Ideas of privacy can be traced back to ancient Roman and Greek philosophy (Arendt 1998: 58–59), the Chinese Qin dynasty (221–206 BC), and the Indian Maruya Empire (322–187 BC) (B. Moore 1984). Changes in philosophical ideas, technological advancements, and economic growth led to modern interpretations (C. Berg 2018: 75). Warren and Brandeis' essay titled "The Right to Privacy" (1890) marks the systematic discussion's start, prompted by technological shifts invading private lives through media dissemination. According to Warren and Brandeis (1890: 193), the right to privacy describes "the right to enjoy life—the right to be let alone." Originally a legal concept, the right to privacy affirms personal freedom and property rights, intertwining with liberty, autonomy, and human dignity (Koops et al. 2017: 493; Lever 2006). The recognition of a unified right to privacy is a relatively recent phenomenon. Previously, privacy-related issues were settled by provisions on the inviolability of the home or, for example, the confidentiality of correspondence. An "umbrella right" to privacy emerged only later, by subsuming or supplementing previous provisions (Koops et al. 2017: 493). Privacy discussions stem from philosophical, ethical, moral perspectives, and legal implications. Policymakers and professional organizations have shaped privacy principles, particularly regarding informational privacy and data protection since the 1960s.

Scholars debate privacy's definition, protected interests, invasion criteria, and whether it has intrinsic or merely instrumental value. Some propose unitary theories seeking universal definitions. Others argue privacy resists clear definition, presenting it as "clusters of problems". Privacy's discourse in social sciences and law reveals diverse conceptualizations and theories. This subchapter outlines debates and conceptualizations, distinguishing between unitary accounts, which offer normative definitions (Solove 2002: 1095–99), and typological approaches, which provide descriptive insights into legal protections and various forms of privacy (Koops et al. 2017: 487; A. D. Moore 2008: 412–13).[1]

[1] In addition, recurring debates arise from *reductionist* perspectives, challenging the notion that privacy is a fundamental and distinctive concept. Reductionists argue that privacy issues are often derivatives of other values, such as negative freedom or autonomy, and may not warrant distinct categorization (A. D. Moore 2008: 413). Conversely, *coherentists* assert that privacy theories overlapping with other concepts can still be valuable for analysis, considering the shared interests and values individuals hold across various contexts (Inness 1996; A. D. Moore 2008; Scanlon 1975). As they do not recognize privacy as a distinct concept, reductionist approaches are largely excluded in this thesis.

2.1.1.1 Unified Conceptions of Privacy

In exploring unified—that means universal, all-encompassing—conceptions of privacy, several foundational perspectives emerge. Firstly, privacy is often defined by the *distinction between private and public spaces*, rooted in ancient Roman and Greek philosophy, notably articulated by Aristotle's differentiation between the public political *polis* and the private domestic *oikos* (see e.g., Arendt 1998: 58–59; Kymlicka 1990: 248–50). The demarcation typically involves the household, reproductive matters, and biological necessities categorized as private, while everything else falls into the public domain. This division, as argued by scholars, is inherently socially constructed and therefore difficult to generalize across time and space (Rössler 2005: 9).

A second perspective, notably presented by Warren and Brandeis in 1890, emphasizes the *right to be left alone.* While influential in academic, political, and legal discourse (Solove 2002: 1101), this concept raises questions about the specifics of what warrants protection, leading to discussions about the generalization of this right resembling a notion of negative civil liberty (Allen 1988; Parent 1983c). Critics argue that interpreting "left alone" as "non-interference" might be misleading, as the typical privacy claim often involves a desire *for* legal protection against external individuals or entities (Gavison 1980: 438).

A third category views privacy in terms of *limited access to the self*. This conceptualization revolves around individuals' yearning for seclusion and distance from others, closely related to the "right to be left alone" idea. Definitions in this category assert that an individual enjoys perfect privacy when completely inaccessible to others (Allen 1988: 11; Gavison 1980: 428), involving a state of existence where personal information and mental states remain beyond the reach of external observation or surveillance devices (D. M. O'Brien 1979: 16). Critics argue that limited access definitions lack a crucial element of "control." For instance, situations like being trapped in a crevasse or stranded on a deserted island meet the condition of inaccessibility but fall short of being deemed "private." This is because the state of isolation, seclusion, or secrecy in such cases is imposed rather than being a voluntary choice (Rössler 2005: 7; Schoeman 1984: 3; see also Westin 1967: 40). Adam D. Moore (1984: 73) and Daniel J. Solove (2002: 1104) posit that privacy inherently involves one's relationship to others, emphasizing its societal dimension.

The fourth perspective places *control* at its core, where privacy is defined as "the claim of individuals, groups, or institutions to determine [...] when, how, and to what extent information about them is communicated to others" (Westin

1967: 7).[2] This perspective also links privacy to intimacy, arguing that control over personal information enables varying degrees of intimacy in relationships, referred to as "relational privacy" (J.-L. Cohen 2004; Fried 1968; Gerety 1977; Gerstein 1978; Inness 1996; Schoeman 1984). Many control-based definitions of privacy are criticized for their narrow focus on specific aspects, often excluding fundamental decisions, as for example reproduction or child-rearing (Rössler 2005: 7–8; Solove 2002: 1110).[3] Several authors thus suggest to combine the third and the fourth perspective and argue that claims to privacy are *claims to control access* (Bok 1984: 10–11; see also A. D. Moore 2003; van den Haag 1971). However, defining privacy as control over access faces criticism as it could encompass voluntarily disclosing intimate details (Parent 1983b: 273).

Another significant viewpoint regards privacy as *personhood*,[4] focusing on protecting an individual's right to make autonomous decisions about their life without external interference. This theory is constructed around the normative end of privacy: the protection of the integrity of the personality (Warren & Brandeis 1890: 205). For Stanley I. Benn (1971), privacy means that individuals have infinite, indeterminate possibilities to choose (especially vis-à-vis the state). This view is reflected in several privacy rulings of the United States Supreme Court[5] (DeCew 1997: 42–45; Solove 2002: 1117). Critics question whether personhood theories truly address privacy or are more concerned with liberty and autonomy (Henkin 1974; Parent 1983b; Sandel 1998), potentially neglecting considerations of the private sector (Solove 2002: 1118).

This chapter explored a selection of unified conceptions. We see that there are diverse perspectives on privacy, from ancient philosophy to contemporary debates, and through distinctions like public versus private spaces, the right to be left alone, limited access to the self, and the centrality of control. This emphasizes the complex nature of privacy and makes me question whether privacy can be grasped sufficiently when defined as *one* unified concept.

[2] For an overview of the numerous scholars that have articulated similar theories, see A. D. Moore (2008: 414) and Solove (2002: 1109–10).

[3] For critiques of privacy as intimacy accounts, see e.g., Reiman (1976: 33–35).

[4] The term "personhood" was originally used by Freud to refer to "those attributes of an individual which are irreducible in his selfhood" (quoted in Craven 1976: 702).

[5] In 1973, for example, the US Supreme Court ruled in *Roe v. Wade*, which gained renewed notoriety when it was overturned in 2022, that the constitutional right to privacy included the decision to procure an abortion.

2.1.1.2 Typologies and Pluralist Conceptualizations of Privacy

Given the disunity on privacy definitions, scholars offer typologies and pluralist approaches, acknowledging the multifaceted nature of privacy. Drawing inspiration from Ludwig Wittgenstein's (1958: 31–36) idea of "family resemblances," Solove (2008b: 37) contends that privacy comprises a cluster of distinct yet interrelated dimensions. This section explores influential conceptualizations in the literature.

Westin's four states of privacy

Alan F. Westin (1967: 31) defines privacy through four basic states, each varying in the degree of integration into the public sphere:

(1) *Solitude:* Complete separation from the group, representing the most comprehensive form of privacy.
(2) *Intimacy:* Participation in a small unit, fostering closed and relaxed relationships.
(3) *Anonymity:* Public presence while seeking freedom from identification and surveillance.
(4) *Reserve:* Creating a psychological barrier against unwanted intrusion, involving the selective disclosure or withholding of information.

R. Clarke's four dimensions of privacy interest

Roger Clarke (1999; 2006) proposes a typology rooted in Maslow's (1943) pyramid of values, transforming life-needs into privacy-values.

(1) *Privacy of the Person:* Physical and bodily privacy. R. Clarke mentions compulsory immunization or blood transfusion without consent as interventions in this sphere.
(2) *Privacy of Personal Behavior:* Private actions without surveillance and recording.
(3) *Privacy of Personal Communication:* Uninterrupted communication without interception.
(4) *Privacy of Personal Data:* Protection of personal data. This form is closely related to ideas of record-keeping and bureaucracy.
(5) *Privacy of Personal Experience:* Added later, emphasizing freedom to experience unobserved activities (with a special focus on web 2.0 and mobile media) (R. Clarke 2015).

Rössler's three dimensions of privacy

Beate Rössler (2005; 2018) advocates for a freedom-oriented account, explicitly building upon "control over access" approaches (Rössler 2005: 8–9), and differentiating between three privacy dimensions:

(1) *Decisional Privacy:* Focus on self-determination, safeguarding actions affecting intimate spheres.
(2) *Informational Privacy:* Right to self-presentation, crucial for individual autonomy amid information technologies as well as for the constitution and gradual differentiation of social relationships.
(3) *Local Privacy:* Encompasses the protection of personal spaces, family communities, and relationships. Referring to the distinction between negative and positive freedom, Rössler (2005: 142–68) argues that this dimension includes protective aspects as well as the precondition for the possibility of self-discovery and an authentic life.

Solove's four groups of privacy problems

Solove (2006: 488–91) categorizes privacy problems into four groups, primarily focused on personal information:

(1) *Information Collection:* Gathering information about the data subject. Solove notes that not all forms of information collection are necessarily harmful.
(2) *Information Processing:* Storage, manipulation, and use of collected information. According to Solove, aggregation, identification, insecurity, secondary use and exclusion play a role here.
(3) *Dissemination of Information:* Transfer or publication of information.
(4) *Invasions:* Direct impingements on the individual, involving disruptions or decisional interference.

Since Solove's framework is strictly speaking not a classification of privacy but of privacy *harms*, it is often omitted in compilations of privacy conceptualizations (e.g., Koops et al. 2017).

Allen's five forms of privacy

Anita L. Allen (2011) derives privacy from moral and social values, proposing governments to treat privacy as a common good[6]—even if this means that some people

[6] See also the debate on the inalienability of privacy (Rössler 2015; Schwartz 2005), e.g., when an individual ' s privacy is compared to their human organs.

would be forced to have privacy (following the discussion about the meaningfulness of "control over access" definitions that also define the complete surrender of privacy as privacy). She differentiates five forms of privacy (Allen 2021):

(1) *Physical or spatial privacy* includes privacy expectations in or around one's home.
(2) *Informational privacy* includes information, data, and facts about individuals and their communications. Allen thus applies this category relatively broadly.
(3) *Decisional privacy* refers primarily to the protection of individuals against state interference when making certain intimate decisions concerning their own lives, such as same-sex marriage or assisted suicide.
(4) *Proprietary privacy* concerns one's reputation or the "right to one's honor." This includes protection from identity theft, but also control over photographs.
(5) *Associational privacy* includes both the ability to join groups and the values and criteria of groups, for example, in terms of inclusion and exclusion of members.

Allen (2011: 4) notes that there are certain "hybrid forms" of privacy that result from the overlap of several of their types (such as *locational privacy*—the privacy of information about someone's physical location—as a combination of physical and informational privacy, or *intellectual privacy* as a hybrid of associational and informational privacy).

Finn et al.'s seven types of privacy

Rachel L. Finn et al. (2013) present a typology based on EU legislation, expanding R. Clarke's (1999) dimensions:

(1) *Privacy of the person* is supplemented by aspects of bio informatics.
(2) Privacy of personal behavior is supplemented to *privacy of behavior and action* and thus no longer limited to private spaces but also includes the freedom to act in semi-public and public spaces without being recorded.
(3) *Privacy of communication* is supplemented by access to stored communication.
(4) *Privacy of data and image* adds the image aspect to R. Clarke's category as well as automated forms of data and image sharing.
(5) *Privacy of thoughts and feelings* addresses concerns about reading and influencing thoughts—especially in view of potential future technology.
(6) *Privacy of location and space* describes the right to move in public and semi-public spaces without being identified, tracked, or observed.
(7) *Privacy of association* includes the individual right to associate freely.

Koops et al.'s eight plus one forms of privacy
Bert-Jaap Koops et al. (2017) criticize that the existing typologies are rather enumerations and that in each case it is not clearly explained what the basis for the formation of the categories is and what the authors understand by privacy or the forms of privacy. They offer a more systematic approach, analyzing constitutional protections across nine countries, resulting in a typology with three dimensions:

(1) *Degree of Privateness:* Ranging from personal to public zones.
(2) *Negative and Positive Freedom:* Distinguishing between being let alone and self-development.
(3) *Restricted Access and Control:* Differentiating between limited access and subsequent control.

Based on the combinations of these three dimensions, they define eight forms of privacy, which are fundamentally modeled on existing accounts by other authors (notably Allen and Finn et al.). As an addition, the authors define *informational privacy* as an overarching aspect of each underlying type. They argue that informational privacy is best understood as "the other side of the coin" (Koops et al. 2017: 554) and is thus reflected in every other form of privacy of the individual's interest in limiting access to and control over the use of information about their own life. Informational privacy is thus a derivative, an additional layer or precondition for other forms of freedom (Koops et al. 2017: 568–69).

Conclusion
Diversity in privacy conceptualizations arises from different scholarly perspectives: R. Clarke's and Rössler's focus is on privacy *interests* which is conceptually different from *rights* (Finn et al.), *harms* (Solove), *protections* (Koops et al.) or Westin's and Allen's rather descriptive notion of *states* or *types.* The authors disagree on whether privacy is a single common denominator with various manifestation (Finn et al.) or whether there are different privac*ies* (Solove). Remarkable is the emphasis on the multifaceted nature of privacy, reflecting its complexity and the evolving landscape of digital technologies.

2.1.1.3 Synthesis of Understanding Privacy

The preceding subchapters have presented a diverse array of definitions and conceptualizations, underscoring the elusive nature of privacy. The exploration of unitary accounts reveals a lack of consensus on a singular definition, a consequence of privacy's inherently multifaceted character. Some definitions prove insufficient in covering the entire range of privacy issues, while others, in their broadness, risk blending with concepts like negative freedom. Typologies and pluralist conceptualizations emerge as valuable contributions to this discourse, endeavoring to offer a comprehensive view by delineating different forms of privacy. Notably, these frameworks often reference and build upon existing conceptualizations, demonstrating an ongoing dialogue within the scholarly community.

We have observed that despite the various theoretical approaches to privacy occasionally referencing each other, there is a lack of a shared fundamental understanding of the term's significance. This is problematic, as a minimum level of agreement on terms is considered a prerequisite for facilitating scientific progress through scholarly interaction (Hodgson 2019). Therefore, the aim of this work is to select a conceptualization of privacy whose understanding is fundamentally shared by as many researchers as possible, regardless of whether they consider it sufficient for comprehending privacy.

In the overview of the presented conceptualizations, the informational aspect of privacy emerges in all proposals, thus occupying a prominent position. Rössler (2005) and Allen (2021) explicitly refer to this aspect in contrast to other forms of privacy, defining it as "information, data, and facts about individuals" (Allen 2021), which is crucial for individual autonomy and the gradual differentiation of relationships. The latter point is reflected in Westin's (1967) privacy state of reserve, encompassing the selective disclosure or withholding of information. R. Clarke (1999; 2006) and Finn et al. (2013) further break down the information component into personal communication and personal data (and image, as in Finn et al. 2013). For Koops et al. (2017) and Solove (2006), the informational aspect is not only one of many, but even emphasized as the crucial component. Koops et al. (2017) argue that informational privacy is always "the other side of the coin" for all other forms of privacy. They state that it is a precondition for all other forms of privacy since a vested interest in privacy emerges from the desire to limit access to or regulate the utilization of information pertaining to every facet of human existence (Koops et al. 2017: 569). At the same time, informational privacy crucially combines aspects of positive freedom (informational self-determination) and negative freedom (excluding access to information) (see Berlin 2002). Solove (2006) also emphasizes this focus, and William A. Parent (1983b; 1983a) goes as far as asserting that *informational privacy*—understood as facts about a person—is the only legitimate use of the term "privacy."[7] At

[7] Not all authors share this perspective, arguing that with the physical aspect, there is another side of the coin (e.g., J.-L. Cohen 2004; Koops et al. 2017).

the same time, when privacy is primarily understood as informational privacy, it aligns with unified understandings such as the right to be left alone, limited access to the self, and control or claims to control access. Therefore, it can be assumed that the informational dimension is the common denominator among the various theoretical approaches. Consequently, empirical studies and results based on this understanding of privacy should be applicable to a vast number of other privacy researchers.

2.1.2 The *Objective* Value of Privacy

One of the most integral aspects of conceptualizing privacy is to discern the value of privacy. While this thesis deals with the *subjective* value of privacy—hinging on opinion or individual experience (see Sect. 4.2.1)—values can also be characterized as being grounded in evidence and demonstratable, making them less susceptible to easy debate or refutation. This is what is understood as *objective* in this thesis.[8] Many theorist emphasize an intrinsic and inherently beneficial nature of privacy (Inness 1996: 44–45).[9] Approaches to the value of privacy can be categorized into deontological and consequentialist (or functional) perspectives (Lindsay 2005: 144). Deontologists, focusing on dignity, autonomy, and personhood, argue that respecting privacy is a moral duty. In contrast, consequentialists, emphasizing utility, suggest that privacy's significance lies in promoting other goods, especially relevant in legal contexts (Hunt 2011). While deontologists emphasize the protection of fundamental rights, consequentialists seek to maximize social welfare (Lindsay 2005: 144).[10] Typically, the value of privacy is divided into three categories: the value of privacy to the individual, the value of

[8] The term "objective" is employed in this work in contrast to "subjective" value. The aim of this thesis is not to establish a definitive definitional boundary nor to engage in a debate about the meaning of "objectivity" or whether such a concept exists (in the context of values).

[9] While I acknowledge that privacy may also be an anti-social value and is sometimes viewed as divisive and detrimental to community, serving as a shield for wrongdoing like abuses within families behind closed doors, as for example argued by communitarians (Arndt 1949; Etzioni 2000), these issues are not further discussed since they do not directly relate to the issue of state privacy invasion related to security.

[10] As will be outlined later, this thesis builds upon the premise that privacy represents just one among several competing interests that individuals must weigh. Utilitarian-influenced consequentialist justifications are believed to be better-suited to approaching these processes (Lindsay 2005: 149) and will thus be emphasized. Nevertheless, the demarcation line between these two approaches is not always clear-cut, leading to recurring allusions to deontological justifications in the following discourse.

privacy to individuals in their relationship with others, and the value of privacy to society.

The value of privacy to the individual

Privacy yields two sets of benefits for individuals. Firstly, it provides a "sanctuary," free from social pressures (Benn 1971: 24). Secondly, it fosters human flourishing by offering spaces for emotional release, crucial for mental health and well-being. Privacy allows individuals spaces where they can be free from pressure to conform and from expectations of their role (Benn 1971; Jourard 1966). Erving Goffman (1956: 70) refers to this of "backstage" area. This aligns with the idea of personhood, asserting that individuals need separation for psychological and social development (Simmel 1971: 73). Privacy to the individual is further linked to creativity, concentration, and freedom (e.g., Gavison 1980: 435; H. Gross 1971: 176), safeguarding against the "chilling effect" on behavior when under observation (Fried 1984; Reiman 1995).[11]

Privacy, for Rössler (2005) and Jeffrey H. Reiman (1995), is a precondition of freedom, especially the freedom of choice, which is severely restricted without privacy. Essential rights like freedom of expression, association, conscience, and belief are intricately connected to the right to privacy (Goold 2010: 42–43). Furthermore, privacy prevents individuals from being categorized based on their perceived value—and is thus closely related to the concept of meritocracy—mitigating deepening inequalities and lost opportunities (Gandy 1993).[12]

The value of privacy to the individual's relations with others

Privacy extends beyond individual benefits, holding value in personal relationships (Gavison 1980; Rosen 2000: 410; Schoeman 1984). It allows individuals to maintain diverse social roles, fostering authenticity based on social conventions (Rachels 1975: 327). Additionally, privacy supports intimacy, love, and friendship since it allows for the exclusivity of certain information/behavior and thereby distinguishes intimate relationships from other human interactions (Bloustein 1964; Boling 1996; Fried 1984; Inness 1996).

[11] A "chilling effect" refers to the inhibition or suppression of the exercise of free speech or other rights due to the fear of negative consequences or repercussions (Horn 2005; Lyon 2001).

[12] For a more detailed overview on the value of privacy to the individual, see Magi (2011).

The value of privacy to society

While traditionally seen as an individualistic right, privacy has *social* value and value to society. Priscilla M. Regan's (1995) critique challenges the purely individual understanding of privacy, arguing that it is too easily sacrificed for societal interests such as medical research or security.[13] However, if understood as a social value, the significance of privacy is considerably higher, and trade-offs involving privacy must be weighed more carefully. Authors like Kirsty Hughes (2015) argue that privacy not only has societal value because of its socializing function (extending the value that privacy has for relationships to the greater society) but emphasize its value *to* society claiming that privacy is a common good, shared by many individuals and attainable only through collective efforts.

The *common good* of privacy does not only refer to the fact that privacy is shared by many individuals (*common* value), but also that it is only attainable when members work together in society (*collective* value). The loss of privacy is thereby seen as a societal problem (James Nehf (2003) draws a comparison to environmental damage) and it is argued that everyone needs a minimum of privacy in order for every individual to have privacy (Nissenbaum 2009: 87–88).[14] A third facet of the common good argument is privacy's *public* value: Privacy is considered essential to democracy, facilitating independent political judgments, contributing to citizens' political preferences, and supporting reasoned political discourse (Gavison 1980; Lever 2005: 15; Regan 1995: 225; Roberts 2015: 339; Simitis 1987: 734). Privacy is thus presented as a condition for citizens' political participation (Mokrosinska 2019: 112). Privacy acts as a counterbalance to the negative impact of surveillance on political participation, guarding against the "chilling effect" (Horn 2005; Lyon 2001).[15] Additionally, it safeguards against issues associated with totalitarianism, ensuring peaceful political decision-making (Nagel 1998) and maintaining the integrity of political associations (Schoeman 1992). Privacy also plays a role in enabling political participation for historically neglected groups (Lever 2005: 15; Roberts 2015: 339–40) and in voting, where secret ballots protect voters from social pressures (Nissenbaum 2009: 176–77). Respecting privacy may also be crucial when attracting persons to run for public office (Gavison 1980: 456).

---

[13] As outlined in Fn. 9, e.g., communitarians argue that (individual) privacy may promote antisocial ends (Arndt 1949; Etzioni 2000).

[14] This is particularly relevant against the background of machine learning technologies or artificial intelligence-based applications, such as facial recognition or behavior analysis. See also Fn. 6.

[15] For empirical evidence, see Cooper (2017), Hampton et al. (2014), Marthews/Tucker (2017), Penney (2016; 2017), Stoycheff (2016), and Stoycheff et al. (2018).

2.1.3 Privacy Invasions

In the preceding subchapter, I highlighted the intrinsic value of privacy, emphasizing its positive impact on individuals and society. Privacy serves as a sanctuary, shielding individuals from social pressures, fostering human flourishing, and contributing to the common good by upholding essential democratic principles. It also plays a crucial role in safeguarding rights, countering negative effects of surveillance, and facilitating political participation. Additionally, privacy enhances personal relationships by allowing diverse social roles and fostering intimacy. Despite its evident value, governments engage in privacy invasions, raising questions about the justifications for such actions and why individuals accept these invasions. This chapter explores various forms of privacy invasions (Sect. 2.1.3.1), governments' justifications for privacy invasions (Sect. 2.1.3.2), and individuals' reasons for accepting them (Sect. 2.1.3.3).

2.1.3.1 Defining Privacy Invasions

Privacy invasion occurs when an individual's privacy, regardless of its conceptualization, is diminished by someone else.[16] The acquisition of information or the individual's awareness of the invasion is not determinative. Privacy invasions are often synonymous with surveillance. Privacy and surveillance both revolve around the control of information—one for protection and the other for discovery. In popular and academic discourse, surveillance is often portrayed as the antithesis of privacy, with the former viewed as negative and the latter as positive in simplistic narratives. For instance, social psychologist Peter Kelvin (1973) highlights privacy as a nullification mechanism for surveillance. Though, debate persists on whether the two concepts are opposed or interchangeable (e.g., Marx 2015a). Some argue that privacy (or the invasion thereof) inadequately capture issues like social control and disciplinary practices and assert that the broader term "surveillance" better encompasses these concerns (C. J. Bennett 2001; Königs 2022). Others argue that the notion of (state) surveillance is to be preferred since it is broader than *privacy* highlighting that surveillance can be problematic even in cases in which citizens' privacy is not technically diminished (Macnish 2018; 2020; Menges 2020). At the same time and in a similar vein, some surveillance

[16] Privacy might not only be *invaded* but also be *eroded* (e.g., trough technological or social development). In this thesis, I explicitly use the term *invasion* to denote that there is a privacy invader (an agent). For a debate on what constitutes an agent, e.g., whether an algorithm should be considered an agent or not, see Macnish (2020). For a conceptualization of privacy invasions (differentiated into extraction, observation, and intrusion) and an analysis of its changing meanings, see Kasper (2005).

definitions do not exclude the existence of benign surveillance (P. T. Smith 2020; I. Taylor 2017)[17] and might thus not accurately capture the value of privacy. According to Marx (2015a), surveillance centers on the *agent* who *accesses* personal data, while privacy, in contrast, emphasizes the *subject* who *restricts access* to personal data using the same means. For the purposes of this study, the concept of privacy takes precedence, as it underscores the focus on the monitored individual. Simultaneously, for the sake of simplicity, I equate privacy invasions with surveillance, following Solove's (2007: 760) suggestion. I do not aim to delve into detailed conceptual debates but rather leverage the vocabulary of surveillance studies to address privacy invasions. This approach aligns with the literature's relative scarcity specifically dedicated to privacy invasions, allowing me to employ surveillance studies terminology.

Surveillance studies provide insights into potential forms of privacy invasions. Social structures of surveillance involve a *surveillance agent* (watcher/observer/seeker/inspector/auditor/tester) and a *surveillance subject*, about whom information is sought (Marx 2015b: 737). *Overt* surveillance, where the monitored individual is aware of the surveillance, contrasts with *covert* surveillance, where the subject is unaware, typically requiring legal authorization (Petersen 2012: 12–14). Nils Zurawski (2015: 33) distinguishes between *mass* and *targeted* surveillance based on the construction of suspicion: mass surveillance assumes uncertainty about the sought individual, relying on vague clues, while targeted surveillance starts with a suspicion and tests it.[18] Gary T. Marx (2002) introduces "*new* surveillance," characterized by technology as an extension of human physical and nervous systems to increase power and speed. While technology is not inherent in surveillance, it is considered central in contemporary surveillance, connected to knowledge production and management (Zurawski 2015: 39).

[17] Such as infectious disease control (Dandeker 2005: 225), the control of the health system (Zurawski 2007: 7) or surveillance as "guardianship" in parenting (Bogard 2006: 98–99).

[18] Lyon (2015b: 140) points out that the point at which mass surveillance becomes target surveillance is at best an "indeterminate threshold."

2.1.3.2 Justifying Privacy Invasions

In my exploration of privacy invasions, I concentrate on "the state"[19] as the primary surveillance agent (see Marx 2015b: 737).[20] Governments, to legitimize surveillance, highlight individual benefits (Gilliom 2001; Higgs 2001; Lyon 1994) and collective welfare (D. Glaser 2000; Manderson 1999; Sackett 1993). Citizens are cautioned about the dangers posed by crime (Gilliom 1996; Leman-Langlois 2002) and threats to national security, often tied discursively to national identity and constructions of "us" and "them" (Simone 2009: 2; see also Iacovetta 2000).

In public discourse, the primary directive governing surveillance is security (Bajc 2007: 1579), framed to counter terrorism, combat crime, and ensure encompassing sense of safety and well-being (Kroener & Neyland 2012: 142; see also Bali 2009; Wigan & Clarke 2006). The post-9/11 era is commonly linked to the significant expansion of state surveillance. However, Clive Norris (2007) demonstrates that the inclination to use surveillance as a criminal justice response predates the "war on terror." Some suggest that liberal states grant a privileged status to the "surveillance solution" (C. Norris 2007: 139). This section outlines the reasons behind governments' privileging of surveillance and how they justify it.

Preventive justice

Classic liberal perspectives on the state-citizen relationship emphasize citizens' duties and the state's commitment to ensuring security in exchange for citizens surrendering self-governance rights (Knowles 2009). While citizens' obligations are well-defined, the state's obligations regarding security are less clear (Ashworth & Zedner 2014: 7).

The state's role in providing security can be prospective or retrospective. Protection from becoming a crime victim represents prospective security, requiring the state to prevent harm and crimes. Meanwhile, the executive and judiciary prosecute crimes retrospectively. Preventive justice, emphasizing harm *prevention*, is not a

---

[19] It is hard to define who exactly is conducting surveillance, those who stand in for "the state" are many. At the same time, lines between public and private sector (Lyon 2015b: 145) and between law enforcement and intelligence (Bauman et al. 2014: 125) become blurred. Furthermore, due to extensive cooperation, one can no longer think in *national* dimensions (Bigo 2008). In the related literature, "state surveillance" (for example as opposed to "corporate surveillance") remains a popular term to define measures initiated and carried out by the executive branch of the state.

[20] Zuboff (2019) contends that states' surveillance is largely influenced by corporate logics, suggesting that these would need to be explored first. Since this is beyond the scope of the thesis, I will draw on existing knowledge regarding the logics of state surveillance.

new concept and has historical roots,[21] but its prominence has fluctuated over time. In the 20th century, preventive ideas resurged, influenced by intellectual and scientific factors. This resurgence intensified in response to a surge in terrorist acts in the early 21st century (Lyon 2003; Zedner 2007). Predictive justice aims to forecast crimes before they occur, justifying crime control practices on a *consequentialist* basis (Waldron 2003: 209; Zedner 2007: 261). This approach relies on the assumption that preemptive identification of security threats is possible, often involving data analysis to calculate the probability of future crimes.

The overarching goal of security is to be achieved through calculation, risk, and uncertainty, prudentialism and precaution (Ericson & Haggerty 1997; Johnston & Shearing 2002; Loader & Sparks 2007; O'Malley 2004). The rise of "pre-crime" societies,[22] characterized by a "ticking time bomb" mentality (Zedner 2008: 18), aligns with various social science theories; for example, with Ulrich Beck's idea of the "risk society" (1992), in which he sets out how the politics of knowledge determine the distribution of risk in a society. Scientific and technocratic discourses legitimize the position of powerful groups (such as the government) over marginalized social groups by preemptively labeling certain behavior as risky, criminal, or deviant (on risk management, see Ericson & Haggerty 1997). A similar finding is made by the concept of "actuarialism", which explains the extent to which data(sets) are increasingly used to predict criminal behavior and derive preventive measures from it (Feeley 2004; Feeley & Simon 1994; Harcourt 2003; O'Malley 2004).

Surveillance, being the dominant logic in law enforcement[23] and justified by its perceived precision and neutrality (McCulloch & Wilson 2015: 76), is criticized

---

[21] While it is often assumed that there has been a "preventive turn" (Edwards & Hughes 2009) and a "paradigm shift from punishment to prevention" (Ashworth & Zedner 2014: 26), O'Malley and Hutchinson (2007: 375) show that preventive justice is by no means a new logic, but that already the introduction of criminal justice institutions and the establishment of a formal police force is closely interwoven with the idea that the frequency or consequences of behavior that can lead to harm can be reduced or mitigated (see also McMullan 1998; Zedner 2006). In the writings of Blackwood (2001 [1753]), A. Smith (1978 [1763]), Bentham (2007 [1780]), and Colquhoun (2012 [1797]) already at the end of the 18th century, a variety of ideas can be found on how the state could preventively tackle problems of crime and social disorder through concrete interventions (see Ashworth & Zedner 2014).

[22] The term "pre-crime" as opposite of "post-crime" has been borrowed by criminologists from Philip Dick's science fiction short story "Minority Report" (1956) (Zedner 2007: 276).

[23] Various studies have shown that the preventive justice logic has become such a dominant ethos of criminal justice that other discourses are completely eclipsed (see, for example, David Bernard-Wills' (2012: 555) analysis of the introduction of the Anti-Terrorism, Crime and Security Act in the UK (2001), Greenberg/Hier's (2009: 472) newspaper analysis on CCTV discourses in Canada, or Suzor et al.'s (2017: 9–11) analysis of media reporting on Australia's metadata retention laws).

for its discriminatory consequences, such as social sorting (Lyon 2002; 2007a; Mau 2022), and for potentially exacerbating inequalities. Surveillance often relies on categorizations that mirror socio-economic disparities, contributing to profiling issues: Despite claims of risk assessment based on behavior, individuals are often profiled by categories such as homelessness or poverty (Sanders & Hannem 2012: 404). Similar trends are observed in monitoring welfare recipients (Dee 2013; Gilliom 2001: 13–14; Gustafson 2012: 643; Maréchal 2015: 57). Data mining, influencing criminal profiles, considers various characteristics, including country of origin, religious affiliation, ethnicity (Guzik 2009: 11; on the UK, see Patel 2012: 223–30).[24]

Through the consequentialist notion of pre-crime, this leads to the view that it is legitimate for law-abiding residents to also be subjected to surveillance if they are ascribed increased "risk" based on certain social characteristics of race, class, and gender. The arbitrary nature of this attribution and the resulting consequences is heightened by the questionable effectiveness of predictive behavioral science. It is difficult to estimate the success rate of surveillance and predictive crime technology (Miller 2014: 118). This is mainly due to the huge amount of data that is collected and analyzed every day. Attempts to identify very rare incidents or targets from a very large database are very likely to result in a very large number of "false positives". This is also scientifically referred to as "base-rate fallacy" (I. Brown & Korff 2009; Munk 2017; Schulan 2019). For example, crime mapping models based on demographic information and historical crime data can predict macro-level crime rates only with 70% accuracy (Belesiotis et al. 2018; Bogomolov et al. 2014).

It is not impossible that surveillance has a general deterrent effect and might therefore be ethically and empirically justified. Timothy D. Wilson et al. (2015), for example, were able to show in a randomized control trial study that some computer hackers were deterred by a warning that their behavior was being monitored by a surveillance program. Similarly, Hyeon Ho Park et al. (2012: 179) find that the crime prevention effect of the installation of close-circuit television[25] (CCTV) in Gwang Myeong City (South Korea) was significant. The number of robberies and thefts in the areas with CCTV installed reduced by 47.4%, while the areas without CCTV showed no change in the number of crimes. Most studies, however, find that surveillance reduces crime only to a small degree, that it is most effective in reducing vehicle crime in car parks or parking lots, and that it has little or no effect

[24] For the most part, however, it remains opaque to the public and even the software producers what information is used and how (I. Brown & Korff 2009: 125).

[25] Even though most camera surveillance systems are no longer "closed-circuit" due to technological development (Ferenbok & Clement 2013), the term and especially its abbreviation remain popular in the literature. I thus use it synonymously to "camera surveillance" (Goold 2002).

on crime in public transport and city center settings (Welsh & Farrington 2002; 2009). These conclusions are consistent with earlier research (D. T. Campbell & Ross 1968), which argued that anti-crime policy aiming at serious crimes such as terrorism had become, in practice, more often applied to less serious behavior and antisocial activities (like littering, traffic control, drunkenness, and public smoking). Other research indicates that, instead of deterring or preventing crime, surveillance merely displaces crime in various forms (M. Clarke 1994) and several studies find surveillance has no effect at all (Ditton & Short 1999; M. Gill et al. 2006; Phillips 1999). One problem in evaluating the effectiveness of surveillance is methodology: Surveillance is justified by the fact that evidence on the influence on crime rates is always found (Simmons 2016: 982). The central problem, it is argued, is that both, increases and decreases, in crime rates are interpreted as positive signs that surveillance programs must continue—either because there is an increased need for more security or the success of increased security is attributed to the effectiveness of surveillance (Haggerty 2009: 280–81).

The fact that the surveillance solution has a privileged position may also be related to the psychological biases surrounding technology. Marx (2002) defines the adulation of technology as a defining characteristic of modernity. The tendency for people to prefer technical solutions to social problems is referred to as "automation bias" (Miller 2014; see also Haggerty 2004: 494). This is partly because people per se trust automation (see e.g., Bogert et al. 2021) and partly because people are no longer able to take on tasks that computers perform for them in an automated way (Cummings 2004).

Privacy invasions as forms of control

In addition to the focus on crime and its investigation—justifications that states, though not always, communicate to their citizens—it is assumed that states inherently seek control over their population in general. While in Sect. 2.1.1.1, the concept of *control* was introduced in relation to the individual and their information, it is posited that surveillance is a political technology for population control (Ceyhan 2012), aiming to manage and "improve" the population for productive participation in the market and early detection and thwarting of potential threats to government stability. This implies that the population must be known both in terms of its actual behavior and in terms of the probabilities of its future behavior (Foucault 1991b). States' interest in monitoring and identifying individuals deemed "dangerous" is rooted in knowledge systems developed for population management. Surveillance becomes a primary means of concentrating authoritative resources, and it is believed that surveillance is deeply embedded in the historical formation of the nation-state (Giddens 1987: 181; Keiber 2015: 171). This perspective is rooted in the Durkheimian and Weberian schools of thought, wherein bureaucratic surveillance is understood as an administrative adaptation to the technical requirements of a structurally differentiated society (Dandeker 1994: 5).

2.1.3.3 Acceptance of Privacy Invasions

Recalling the multifaceted nature of the value of privacy, one might anticipate individuals to hold a strongly negative disposition towards invasions of it. Nonetheless, individuals regularly accept incursions into their privacy or generously share private information with others. Exploring the intricate dynamics of privacy, this section delves into the phenomenon of individuals willingly sharing private information, with a specific focus on state surveillance.

Privacy Calculus

The dominant theoretical lens (Dinev et al. 2015; H. J. Smith et al. 2011; Pavlou 2011), the "privacy calculus," draws on the concept of "homo oeconomicus," wherein individuals strategically weigh the benefits and costs of disclosing data(Laufer & Wolfe 1977).[26,27] This is in line with early contributions on the significance of citizens' perceptions of the output and outcomes of a policy which have emphasized the relevance of cost-benefit calculations for political support (Sears et al. 1980).

Rooted in social exchange theory (Homans 1961), this calculus posits that individuals engage in a transactional give-and-take (Kokolakis 2017: 125), sharing data when anticipating a positive net outcome, i.e., that expected benefits of disclosure

---

[26] Frequently, the privacy calculus is employed in conjunction with economic theories such as the theory of reasoned action, the expectancy-value theory, and utility maximization theory (Li 2012). The fundamental premise of the theory of reasoned action (Ajzen & Fishbein 1980) and its latter refinement, the theory of planned behavior (Ajzen 1985), is that individuals' beliefs and estimations regarding the potential consequence of a behavior are the primary factors influencing behavioral intentions. The expectancy-value theory posits that individuals gather information about various aspects of each choice option and assign a value to each of these aspects (Fishbein & Ajzen 1975). Utility maximization, on the other hand, describes how individuals weigh the different aspects against one another and then choose the option that maximizes their utility (Mas-Colell et al. 1995). In addition, insights from social psychological theories like social contract theory (G. R. Milne & Gordon 1993; Phelps et al. 2000) and social exchange theory (Andrade et al. 2002) have been integrated.

[27] While the concept was brought forward by Laufer and Wolfe (1977), Culnan and Amstrong (1999) were the first to call the concept the "privacy calculus." Dinev and Hart (2006) expanded on this paradigm and applied it to internet privacy behavior.

outweigh the costs (N. Lee & Kwon 2015). This dichotomy distinguishes between *privacy risks* or *costs* on one side and *privacy benefits* on the other.

Privacy costs arise from the perceived risks associated with sharing information and hinge on the lack of knowledge about how the personal data is utilized (Dinev & Hart 2006). These concerns about sharing personal information revolve around the *perceived* high risk of loss (H. J. Smith et al. 2011), reflecting the multidimensional nature of the objective value of privacy (see Sect. 2.1.2). Privacy concerns stem from a lack of knowledge about how surveillance agents, such as the state or corporations, may use one's personal information,[28] presenting a principal-agent problem due to information asymmetry (Li 2012). This asymmetry prevents individuals (the principal) from sufficiently monitoring the behavior of surveillance agents. Consequently, without knowledge of how surveillance agents use their information, individuals may hesitate to grant excessive control or withhold personal data (Yu et al. 2020). Despite privacy concerns, individuals may not always refrain from sharing personal information—a phenomenon known as the "privacy paradox" (Gerber et al. 2018; Kokolakis 2017).[29] This paradox arises when the *perceived* benefits of privacy disclosure can outweigh the perceived costs.

Perceived privacy benefits or gratifications can be understood as an individual's perception of the value derived from disclosing personal information. Previous research on technology adoption distinguishes between utilitarian benefits, captured by perceived usefulness, and hedonistic benefits, measured by perceived enjoyment (Fernandes & Pereira 2021). In the field of online consumer research, where the application of privacy calculus is most prevalent (Trepte et al. 2020), it is assumed that online consumers are interested in obtaining products or services timely and inexpensively, while the hedonistic value of a commercial exchange lies in its ability to meet needs for escapism, diversion, or emotional relief (Sun et al. 2015). Whereas most previous studies focus on utilitarian benefits, certain contexts emphasize the

[28] Concerns about undue use of personal information include data and identity theft, financial fraud, data gathering for advertising, cyber-bullying, or sexual harassment purposes (Stevic et al. 2022) as well as "function creep", which refers to the unintended expansion of the purpose or scope of a system, technology, or process beyond its original intent (Koops 2021).

[29] This paradox, i.e., the discrepancy between expressed concerns or attitudes and actual behavior, has long been one of the most prominent research topics related to privacy attitudes (Rosso et al. 2020). Interestingly, most systematic literature reviews show the absence of a privacy paradox on aggregate across most contexts except social network sites (Barth & de Jong 2017; Baruh et al. 2017; Kokolakis 2017; see also Penney 2017). Since it is rather older studies who find a privacy paradox while newer studies often fail to do so (Kokolakis 2017), Büchi et al. (2020: 4–5) propose an awareness change and learning effect over time. Based on these recent findings, I will not go into detail on the privacy paradox in this thesis.

significance of hedonistic benefits (Fernandes & Pereira 2021), such as online gaming, where individuals may willingly share personal information for hedonistic values (Pizzi & Scarpi 2020; Wakefield 2013). In the domain of state surveillance, research predominantly centers on utilitarian benefits (Fox et al. 2021), with individuals accepting surveillance for expected advantages like enhanced security (Dinev et al. 2008; Thompson et al. 2020). Recent findings indicate that individuals, in their considerations, extend beyond personal benefits to encompass potential advantages for others—a concept termed "other-focus" or "social calculus" (Buller & Burgoon 1996), discussed in scenarios like sharing location data during the COVID-19 pandemic (Nabity-Grover et al. 2020).[30]

Given the considerations of cost-benefit assessments, the privacy calculus in the literature is also referred to as a *deliberate* trade-off (Harborth & Pape 2023: 2). Despite some authors convincingly arguing that there is no inherent objective trade-off between security and freedom or privacy (see Sect. 2.3.2), subjective trade-offs are believed to be inherent in individual decision-making (Shaddy et al. 2021). However, the notion of self-disclosures as inherently deliberate is questioned, as they can be unconscious (Plangger & Montecchi 2020) or automatic (Bol et al. 2018) and may not be fully determined by rational calculation but by other independent factors (Adjerid et al. 2018).

Critique of the privacy calculus

Challenging the conventional narrative of a rational decision-making process, some empirical studies indicate that individual privacy behavior sometimes deviates from logical expectations. For instance, Matthew Kugler and Lior Strahilevitz (2015) demonstrate that the duration of surveillance does not significantly impact individuals' privacy expectations and has only limited effects on perceived surveillance intrusiveness, despite the anticipated increase in harm with prolonged surveillance. Similarly, Roger Tourangeau et al. (1989) note that individuals disclose more in online forms compared to pencil and paper questionnaires, despite the higher risk of tracking and dissemination in the online environment. Conversely, factors with seemingly little direct influence on disclosure risk and benefit consistently shape individuals' privacy decisions. Research indicates that respondents' disclosure behavior is significantly affected by the survey's appearance or subtle changes in the framing of disclosure decisions (Acquisti et al. 2012; John et al. 2011). Numerous studies underscore the malleability of privacy preferences and the impact of factors that do not align with objective trade-offs (Acquisti et al. 2015).

[30] Existing research has not yet explored the potential construction of hedonistic benefits in the context of state surveillance.

While traditional privacy research has predominantly portrayed privacy-related decisions as rational processes (Culnan & Armstrong 1999; Dinev & Hart 2006), recent decision-theoretic studies highlight instances where a rational calculus is not uniformly applied. Instead, individuals make irrational decisions in specific contexts characterized by uncertainty, asymmetrical information, or the application of heuristics (Acquisti et al. 2016). Emerging literature posits that psychological limitations, such as the inability to process all relevant information (Acquisti & Grossklags 2005; Acquisti 2009) or a bias toward immediate benefits over long-term consequences (Acquisti 2004; D. Wilson & Valacich 2012) may constrain rational considerations in the privacy calculus. Prior to disclosure, individuals may rely on cues from habits and non-conscious factors like emotions, which the rational trade-off view does not consider (Plangger & Montecchi 2020). Consequently, information disclosure can become a habit integrated into daily routines (Debatin et al. 2009; Zafeiropoulou et al. 2013), especially for frequently and regularly performed behaviors that become habitual and automatic over time (Limayem et al. 2007). In the post-adoption phase, this habitual behavior, particularly in the context of process gratification such as media or technology usage, can transform into a *rational* benefit (Quinn 2016).

Alternative/complementary approaches

Moving beyond an individual-centric view, societal processes assume significance especially in the context of state surveillance (Bauman et al. 2014). Notably, scholars emphasize the familiarity and normalization of surveillance, coupled with phenomena like fear and uncertainty. Surveillance has seamlessly woven itself into daily life, encompassing diverse monitoring forms from corporate listening technologies to public space video surveillance, thereby increasing its opacity (Rediger 2017). The normalization concept, originating with Jeremy Bentham (1791) and later expanded by Michel Foucault (1991a) through the panopticon metaphor, involves continuous individual supervision and control (Lyon 2007b; Whitaker 1999). This normalization process reconciles established norms with emerging technologies, as seen in the historical skepticism toward innovations like the Kodak camera (Warren & Brandeis 1890) or the telephone (Nissenbaum 2018: 846) that gradually became normalized over time. This social process, alternatively termed "familiarization" (Pavone et al. 2013) or "banalization" (Wright et al. 2010), is neutral (Selinger & Rhee 2021: 55), although frequently scrutinized in privacy invasions (Krueger 2005: 441).[31]

---

[31] This concern is often dismissed as a "technopanic" triggered by causal mechanisms like status quo bias (Thierer 2013).

Four types of normalization are identifiable: (1) transforming temporary emergency reactions into enduring practices, (2) selectively perceiving novel technologies, (3) unremarkable adaptation leading to privacy resignation or fatalism, and (4) the favorable embrace of normalization, particularly among students and young individuals (Selinger & Rhee 2021: 55). The rationalization approach aims to legitimize behavior amid privacy concerns, employing strategies such as emphasizing benefits over drawbacks, portraying privacy-eroding services as impersonal, fostering dependence on these services, and instilling the belief that privacy is no longer safeguarded, ultimately leading to surveillance acceptance.

An alternative perspective suggests that individuals may, under specific circumstances, forfeit privacy due to fear of the unknown, a concession unlikely under typical conditions, thus skewing an unbiased privacy calculus (Lewis 2005: 25). Governments, security entities, and the media skillfully exploit this fear, as examined through a sociological lens by Anthony Giddens (1990) and Beck (1992). Fear of the unknown becomes integral to risk management in contemporary society, where governance seeks to assuage anxieties and promise security by countering or mitigating specific threats. Institutions offering security balance trust and acceptable risk through guarantees, promises, and predictability, even though trust fundamentally relies on faith and intangibility. Risk management, dealing with probabilities and inherent unknowns, views security as an internal aspiration rather than an external certainty (Ericson & Haggerty 1997). Emphasizing risk and danger is central to the concept of a risk society (Beck 1992), where surveillance acts as a tool to minimize potential future risks, such as crime, and governmental disciplinary measures normalize the apprehension of these prospective perils (M. Lee 2001: 481).

Conclusion

The privacy calculus stands out as a widely acknowledged theory (Wirth 2018; Yun et al. 2019), a fact attributed in part to its adaptability with diverse variables and demonstrated resilience across various contexts (Fox et al. 2021; Miltgen & Smith 2019). In empirical literature, varying perspectives exist regarding the theory's efficacy in explaining behavior. Susanne Barth and Menno D.T. De Jong (2017) identify 35 empirical studies related to the privacy calculus, with only eight unequivocally finding that individuals base privacy decisions on rational risk-benefit calculations. In contrast, nine studies suggest little to no consideration of risk, and 18 studies imply biased risk assessment, leading the authors to propose that irrational processes may drive decision-making more than rational ones (Barth & de Jong 2017: 1055). Tobias Dienlin and Miriam J. Metzger (2016) caution that the trade-off of benefits and costs only partially explains behavior. In a US-representative study, they discovered that approximately 33% of self-disclosure is attributed to anticipated benefits, while 5% is influenced by perceived privacy concerns. Notably, this observation is primarily applicable to corporate surveillance, as research on state surveillance remains a minor fraction of the overall body of literature (Rosso et al. 2020). Only the COVID-19 pandemic has prompted an increasing use of the privacy calculus as an explanatory framework for government privacy invasions. Recent studies indicate that perceived benefits consistently predict public approval of state surveillance both before and during the crisis (Fernandes & Costa 2021; Fox et al. 2021; Thompson et al. 2020).

A pivotal factor to the privacy calculus is the role of promises or pursuit of security as a potential benefit of privacy relinquishment. The subsequent chapter delves into the concept of security, unraveling its significance for individuals.

2.2 Security

In the preceding section, the intricate interplay between security and the value of privacy was explored. Surveillance agents not only justify privacy invasions under the banner of security, but individuals are also significantly influenced by the pursuit of security. Despite the commonplace usage of "security" in everyday language, a universally accepted definition within academic discourse remains elusive. This chapter provides a succinct overview of diverse conceptualizations of security, acknowledging its evolving meaning over centuries.

The ancient Roman usage of the Latin term *securitas*, meaning "free from care" and denoting "a serene state of mind," initially associated security with internal tranquility (Arends 2008: 269). However, as circumstances arose that could compromise this serenity, security evolved to encompass the physical safety and political liberty of Roman citizens (Herington 2015: 24). This association of internal calm with freedom from fear prevailed during the pre-Enlightenment period.

From the era of Hobbes onward, the meaning of "security" shifted to align with the establishment of the authoritarian Leviathan to prevent civil unrest. Hobbes asserted that security could only be ensured by the state, compelling citizens to relinquish their natural right of self-defense (Sorell 2007). Throughout Enlightenment, security was seen as a state-given guarantee to the citizens to be protected from violence against their person and property (see works of Locke, Condorcet, Paine, Rousseau, Leibniz). The association between security and guarantee illustrates another important implication: security is seen as a *precondition* for the enjoyment of other rights and thus as "the most vital of all interests"

(Mill 1871: 190). In stark contrast to the inner calm of Roman *securitas*—to which the state is "at best irrelevant or, at worst, an impediment" (Herington 2015: 28)—political philosophers of that era regard the state as *necessary* for the maintenance of security.[32] The term "security" later became intertwined with "property, land, money, fortifications," and the means to secure these assets, such as armies and weapons (McSweeney 1999: 17–18). Despite this, explicit philosophical engagement with the concept of security remained relatively sparse, especially in comparison to other grand concepts like justice, liberty, and equality (Herington 2015: 28; Waldron 2006: 459). Patrick M. Morgan (1992: 466) contends that "security is a condition, like health or status, which defies easy definition and analysis," echoing Barry Buzan's (1991: 10) characterization of security as an "essentially contested concept."[33]

Like privacy, security draws meaning from diverse disciplines. For this thesis, philosophical, sociological, and psychological perspectives are particularly illuminating. To disentangle historical and contemporary understandings, scholars suggest viewing security not as a singular concept but as a reference to both a *state of being* and a set of *social and political practices* (Bubandt 2005: 279; Herington 2012: 11; McSweeney 1999: 13; Zedner 2003: 155).[34] This distinction will structure the subsequent chapter.

[32] Related is Weber's (1946) account on the state's monopoly over the legitimate use of force which is contested by scholars such as Garland (2002) who argue that the state's monopoly on security is an anomaly.

[33] Buzan leans on work of Gallie (1955). His claim of security being an "essentially contested concept" is coined a "widespread myth" by McSweeney (1999: 83–84) who claims that (a) serious contestation over the concept of security only began in the 1990 s (with Buzan being one of its opening debaters), not in the period before his book first appeared and (b) Buzan's implication that other concepts of the social order are different in that they are not contested is incorrect (see also Booth 2007: 97–100).

[34] Herington (2015) further differentiates a third concept, namely, security as *mode*. In this view, security does not have "value in and of itself" (G. M. Smith 2005: 488), but only denotes a relationship between a referent (e.g., an individual) and a particular good (e.g., access to water). Security is not more than "a mode of enjoying other goods, an underwriting of other values, a guarantor of other things we care about" (Waldron 2006: 471). In contrast to security as a *state of being*, security as a *mode* is perceived as a "thin" property (like e.g., hot or cold) that does not entail judgements about the goodness (Väyrynen 2021). This concept is not of particular relevance for this work and will thus not further be elaborated on.

2.2.1 Security as a State of Being

Security, as a *state of being*, represents a historically significant and valuable property of entities such as individuals, groups, and states (Herington 2015: 32). It encompasses what it means for a referent to *be* secure—a set of goods that the referent must enjoy. Three key questions guide the definition of security in this context: (1) Which entity can be secure or not (the referent object)? (2) What constitutes the security of this entity? (3) Is security achieved based on objective or subjective standards?

The referent objects

Traditionally limited to individual human beings, philosophical references to security have expanded to include entities such as houses or critical infrastructure—so that (theoretically) only syntactic validity limits the role of the referent object (Herington 2012: 16). Thus, a house or critical infrastructure can be as safe as a person or the state. Nevertheless, definitions of security mostly refer to individual human beings or groups, such as states, societies, or communities (Herington 2012: 15–16; Jore 2019). Entities are not mutually exclusive and security may apply simultaneously to an individual and a state. The choice of referent is both conceptual and normative, emphasizing the value of the secured object (Herington 2012: 16; 2015: 30–31). Thus, when talking about state security, it is essential to identify *why* the state is perceived as valuable (Booth 2007: 161). This results in a normative notion of who *should* be secured and an implicit appeal of the importance of this entity. The referent does not necessarily need to be the direct beneficiary of their own security. For instance, individuals may indirectly benefit from state security, even if they are not the primary referent of security (Herington 2012: 16).

What makes a referent object being secure?

When defining the conditions of security for an entity, scholars offer various perspectives. Buzan et al. (1997) emphasize the protection of existence, while Bill McSweeney (1999: 92) speaks of the provision of basic needs and John Locke (1967) defines security as freedom from threats of violence by other agents. Jonathan Herington (2015: 33–34) broadens the conceptualization, arguing that entities must enjoy a certain set of goods for being secure, encompassing everything the specific referent object has reasons to value: *Human* security aims to ensure that a person can enjoy certain goods (such as food and water) in order to function as a human being. *State* security sees territorial integrity and political independence as necessary conditions for sovereign states. Thereby, it is crucial to acknowledge that absolute security does not exist (Freedman 2016; Hendrickson 2002). Even if security were attainable today, the potential for *future* threats persists,[35] a topic I will explore in Sect. 2.2.2.

Subjective and objective security

Scholars distinguish between objective and subjective security,[36] where the former is defined as the "absence of threats to acquired values," and the latter as the "absence of fear that such values will be attacked" (Wolfers 1962: 150). While the two dimensions are interconnected—for example because the enjoyment of objective security depends on whether one feels secure[37] or because subjective security is influenced by the experience of objective security—the literature highlights mismatches between objective risk and subjective security, with entities over- or underestimating actual threats (Zedner 2003).

Objective security pertains to mathematical probability and countermeasure effectiveness (Schneier 2008), while *subjective* security involves beliefs about security that may not be rational or evidence-sensitive. An underlying premise is that *in*security is an undesirable psychological state (T. O'Brien & Tropp 2015: 137).[38] The focus on subjective security centers on individuals' or a group of individuals' *feelings* (Ainsworth 2010; Schneier 2008) or *emotions* (Cameron & McCormick

[35] Security always entails a future-perspective, such that whether "an entity enjoys a good securely in the present is determined by facts about the future" (Herington 2015: 30).

[36] Already in the earlier adoptions of the concept of security, namely the Greek notion of *ataraxia*, one can find the duality in terms of concrete circumstances (objective security), and the reference to the states of mind of individuals (subjective security). For an exemplary account of the latter see, e.g., Gidden's (1991) concept of "ontological security:" Giddens contends that while the "Western" world has witnessed advancements in material conditions and health in recent decades, these gains are counteracted by rising insecurity. This insecurity stems from economic instability, the breakdown of shared values, precarious living conditions, and environmental risks. As result, according to Giddens, individuals strive for ontological security, defined as the confidence people have in the continuity of their identity and the stability of their surrounding social and material environment. It encompasses maintaining a positive outlook on oneself, the world, and the future.

[37] Buzan (1991: 24) points out, for example, that government measures that objectively increase security can lead to a lower subjective sense of security only by initially increasing awareness of threats.

[38] Wonderly (2019: 167) argues that (subjective) security cannot simply be understood as the absence of another feeling (*in*security) and therefore proposes to understand security as confidence in one's agency (see also Giddens 1991).

1954: 557),[39] leading to research on why people feel insecure and the attitudes and behaviors they develop to restore a sense of security:

Based on a conceptualization of William B. Cameron and Thomas C. McCormick (1954), the literature identifies three broad, nonexclusive sources of *subjective* insecurity:

(1) Insecurity can be an emotional response to *sudden external threats.*
(2) Insecurity can stem from a relatively *constant threatening external situation* (the fear of losing the job or having a low income etc. (see e.g., Mau et al. 2012), or insecurity through competition or (actual or perceived) inferiority).
(3) Insecurity can be a *personality characteristic*, independent of present external conditions.

Since insecurity is perceived to be undesirable, individuals might be motivated to develop attitudes or engage in behaviors that seek to (re)establish a sense of security (Borel 1964). This security-seeking is believed to be a "basic human need"—in Maslow's (1943) hierarchy of need second only to physiological needs such as oxygen, food and water—or, as William I. Thomas (1923) puts it, one of the four whishes embraced as a common denominator to humanity. From the limited literature on risk research on individual action, two basic options for dealing with uncertainties emerge (Bonß 1995; Evers & Nowotny 1987; Stallen & Tomas 1988):

(1) Vigilant coping behaviors
    (a) by moving forward individually or through social learning processes to restore action competence, or
    (b) by searching for external protection through different forms of dependencies (see Blatz 1966), e.g., by forgoing personal freedom.
(2) Accepting coping behavior through pushing aside of uncertainty and continuation of previous actions.

The most relevant examples of formal definitions of security as a state of being for this thesis include *human security* and *national security.* The United Nations Development Programme (1994) defines *human security* as the ability to exercise choices "safely and freely—and [having reason to being] relatively confident that the opportunities they have today are not totally lost tomorrow." Other perspectives

[39] Emotions or feelings are affects—"nonconscious and unnamed experiences of bodily energy and intensity"—that become "actualized or concretized in the flow of living" through language, embodiment, custom, and technology (Gould 2010: 26).

posit that human security involves access to nutrition, shelter, and freedom from violence (King & Murray 2002) or being "free from fear" (Pavone & Degli Esposti 2012: 558). Similarly, *national security* implies territorial integrity, freedom from domination, and a basic level of welfare for citizens (Leffler 1990).

2.2.2 Security as Social and Political Practice

Security can also be understood as a *means* to an end, conceptualized as a *social* and *political practice* aimed at or promising a state of security. Even though the purported goals are either subjective or objective security, the pursuit thereof, i.e., security *practice*, may serve as an end in itself (Zedner 2003: 155). The emphasis on security pursuit arises from the challenge of determining its achievement, given the non-existence of absolute (objective or subjective) security (Freedman 2016; Hendrickson 2002). Even if attainable, the prospect of future threats perpetuates the ongoing pursuit, demanding constant vigilance. Notably, security actors, including governments (Zedner 2003: 157) and the private security industry (Percy 2007), find political and economic value in perpetuating the "war against crime" and "war against terror" narratives.

The concept of security as practice is particularly evident in critical domains of international relations, criminology, and geography (Herington 2015: 30) and aligns with postmodern thinkers like Mark Neocleous (2008), Michael Dillon (1996), or Anthony Burke (2006). Most prominently, it is, however, manifested in the theory of "securitization." Securitization involves designating an issue as a "security" matter, elevating it from regular politics to the realm of security, thus influencing policy-making as a form of "speech act" (Buzan & Wæver 2003: 491). In this view, security is not an objective or subjective condition but a result of the securitization processes (e.g., of control or exclusion) and practices (e.g., emergency measures). Once an issue is labeled a security problem, it bypasses political debate and is handled through specialized means that may defy normal legal and social norms (Buzan et al. 1997: 28).

Securitization's conceptual structure partly mirrors items we know from the surveillance literature, with the *securitizing actor*, typically a government or elite entity, "speaking security," and the *referent object* representing the threatened entity. The *referent object* can vary, expanding beyond the traditional focus on the state to encompass different sectors like environmental security. Securitization only occurs when the *audience* accepts the move as valid, conferring an intersubjective status to the threat (Buzan et al. 1997: 25).[40] While there is a broad literature on securitizing actors and the referent objects, audience's role is theoretically and empirically "radically underdeveloped" (M. C. Williams 2010: 212; see also Balzacq 2005: 179; Côté 2016; Floyd 2010: 50). It is not fully theorized when and why individuals agree to accept security claims, nor are there many empirical studies. This might also be the case because securitization's research agenda is said to rely on a limited range of research methods (Baele & Sterck 2015; Balzacq 2010b).

Securitization has been instrumental in early critical security approaches, contributing by broadening the concept of security beyond traditional domains and offering a constructivist operational method to analyze how issues transform into security concerns (Buzan et al. 1997: vii). It has gained popularity in studying various securitization processes, such as in the contexts of migration, climate change, global health, and religion (see Balzacq et al. 2016 for an overview). Two predominant "schools" of securitization exist: the Copenhagen School viewing security as negative, to be avoided (Wæver 1995), and the Welsh School defining security as emancipation, emphasizing its positive value (Booth 1991). Additionally, literature explores acts of de-securitization, redefining issues as non-security threats and removing them from the agenda (Buzan et al. 1997: 4). Despite its significance, securitization theory faces a wide range of critique (Sjöstedt 2019: 35–37), notably the assertion that one cannot evaluate securitizations' declarative claims without any reference to a state of being secure (Herington 2012: 13).

This chapter explored the evolving concept of security, tracing its historical roots from Roman times to the Enlightenment. It emphasized security as both a state of being and a set of social practices. Security, as a state of being, involves defining who or what can be secure, the conditions for security, and the distinction between objective and subjective aspects. The concept of security as social and political practice is most prominently debated in the literature on securitization, where issues are labeled as security matters, influencing policy-making. Despite its significance, securitization theory faces critique, notably is the lack of theorizing of when the *audience* accepts securitization claims.

---

[40] If the securitizing move has not garnered acceptance to the extent that emergency measures become feasible, it retains the status of a *securitizing move* but falls short of constituting a successful securitization.

2.3 Privacy Versus Security

The conceptualizations of privacy and security differ significantly. In most perspectives, these concepts are not explicitly interconnected,[41] rendering them neither mutually exclusive nor inherently overlapping. However, during crises, such as those involving terrorism, war, or pandemics, arguments often arise suggesting a competition between security—interpreted as human security (Chandler 2009)—and privacy or freedom, necessitating a delicate balance. This chapter dissects two fundamental explanations of this assumption and their respective criticisms. Some scholars propose a natural hierarchy among certain values, where the rational preference for security over liberty aligns with a needs pyramid. Others contend that values can compete, requiring individuals to make trade-offs. In line with the overarching research question, this chapter seeks to synthesize the findings from the preceding sub-chapters.

2.3.1 Security and Privacy in a Setting of Hierarchical Values

There is a widespread consensus among social scientists that a sense of security constitutes a fundamental human need (Fraley 2002; S. Goldberg 2014; Mikulincer & Shaver 2003).[42] Maslow's (1943) hierarchy of needs categorizes basic needs hierarchically, placing safety and security at the second level, following physiological needs (see also Thomas' (1923) basic wishes). Ronald Inglehart (1997) extends Maslow's work, introducing societal preconditions such as basic economic and security needs that must be met before individuals can focus on postmaterialist values like freedom and quality of life.

Individuals tend to prioritize lower-order needs when threatened, with security regarded as a "prime value" (Baldwin 1997). Unlike Hobbes, who posited a perpetual pursuit of security, Maslow suggests people exclusively focus on higher-order needs during periods of perceived security (Sætra 2022: 85). In this context,

[41] An exception is Gidden's (1991) concept of "ontological security," see Fn. 36, that is often related to privacy, as for example proposed by W. S. Brown (2000).

[42] See also Jost and Napier's (2011) *uncertainty-threat model* (see Huq 2013), *social identity and self-categorization theory* (based on Tajfel & Turner 1979; Turner et al. 1987; see O'Donnell et al. 2010a; 2010b), and Pyszczynski ' s (2004; et al. 2002) *terror management theory* that deals with typical reaction patterns that people develop in dealing with fear of death and awareness of their own mortality (see Huq 2013; Trüdinger 2018).

security and privacy are not in direct competition; rather, privacy presupposes a minimum level of security but not vice versa.

2.3.2 The Trade-off Between Privacy and Security

Alternatively, the trade-off-perspective posits security and privacy as opposing values engaged in a zero-sum game or equilibrium. Frank Bannister (2005), for example, argues that the greater the level of security, the more invasion of privacy exists for society, since all societies must balance both security and privacy. This paradigm assumes that gains in one inevitably lead to losses in the other, based on the idea that both can be measured in the same "currency." Post-9/11 and in line with the shift towards pre-emptive justice, the metaphor of balance gained prominence, with governments and societies envisioned as navigating a delicate equilibrium between effective security measures and civil liberties (Aquilina 2010; Bigo 2010; Bigo et al. 2008; Bronitt 2008; O. Gross 2009; Hardin 2004; Michaelson 2006; A. D. Moore 2011; Neocleous 2007; Solove 2011; Waldron 2003; 2006; Wolfendale 2007).[43] This perspective implies that sacrifices in privacy can be justified in exchange for increased security, assuming individuals are willing to make such trade-offs. This line of thinking has become pervasive since almost everyone—policy makers, citizens, and even scholars—approach the formulation of counterterrorism policies as a balancing act (Dragu 2011: 64; van Schoonhoven et al. 2014: 35).

The trade-off arguments find their initial grounding in considerations of a state of nature, a conceptual construct within major political philosophy figures. This construct, not a historical postulation, delineates the pre-government state of humans. Hobbes (1994: 76) characterizes the state of nature as a perpetual war, prompting individuals to seek security through the formation of governments, necessitating a relinquishment of some absolute freedom. Conversely, Locke contends that while individuals sacrifice some absolute liberty, they also seek protection against excessive government invasion, exemplifying a pursuit of negative liberty (Locke 1967). Although Locke rejects security as an absolute value (Sætra 2022), the origin of state power from a state of nature, involving a transfer of power from the people to a sovereign, serves as the foundational justification for the concept of "national security." This concept, however, conflicts

---

[43] Raab (1999) cites the 1981 Council of Europe Convention as one of the first privacy-related documents that introduces the metaphor of a balance.

with individual freedom (Neocleous 2007: 136–37). The metaphor of balance is pivotal in "Western" political discourse traditions (Beatty 2004).

This centrality extends to economic conceptions and legal frameworks in modern liberal democratic societies, with many legal documents emphasizing that rights are not absolute but must be carefully weighed against each other (Aleinikoff 1987). The concept of trade-offs, borrowed from economics (Simon 2020), posits that all resources, material and non-material, can be quantified in a common unit or "currency" (Sætra 2022: 4). Economists argue that resources and capacities are limited, leading to a zero-sum game where an increase in one good results in a reduction in another. Despite this reasoning being prevalent in politicians' statements, human decision-making often does not align with trade-off thinking (Friedewald et al. 2015). Nevertheless, policy decisions today heavily rely on impact assessments, akin to a "cost-benefit analysis," framing human behavior in economic terms. While early studies emphasized the relevance of individual cost-benefit calculations (see e.g., Sears et al. 1980), the modeling of such balances remains unclear (Waldron 2003).

While the metaphor has been used in context of the adaptation of data protection before (Raab 1999: 69–73), Eric A. Posner and Adrian Vermeule (2007) were pioneers in modeling the relationship between security and liberty as a trade-off, employing assumptions from welfare economics. Their model assumes that policy effects on security and liberty (such as privacy) can be depicted as an area on a two-axis diagram, forming a Pareto frontier where gains in one area lead to losses in the other. Two fundamental assumptions underpin this model: the measurability of security and liberty in comparable units and their sufficient distinctiveness for measurement on two perpendicular axes. The trade-off hypothesis has faced two main strands of critique. Internal critics do not dispute the balance metaphor but question the evaluation and judgment of trade-offs, while external critics challenge the metaphor itself (Mironenko Enerstvedt 2017: 176).

2.3.2.1 Internal Critics

Internal critics do not fundamentally challenge the idea of the balance metaphor but question the skewed nature of evaluations, asserting a systematic erosion of civil liberties in favor of security (Chandler 2009; O. Gross 2009). Jennifer Chandler posits six reasons underpinning the prioritization of security over privacy (see also O. Gross 2009; A. D. Moore 2011): First, security, defined as the preservation of physical well-being, is considered a foundational prerequisite for the enjoyment of other values, as discussed in Sect. 2.1.2. Second, human perception of risk is influenced by cognitive biases, leading to an overestimation of security risks (Tversky & Kahneman 1974: 1129; Sunstein 2007), often exacerbated by extensive media coverage (O. Gross 2009: 7–9). Simultaneously, people struggle to comprehend the consequences of diminished privacy, given the relatively abstract nature of civil liberties. Third, privacy is seen as having inherently limited value, while security is perceived as an unattainable absolute. While a conceptual maximum for privacy can be envisioned (Gavison 1980: 440), individuals consistently seek heightened security (Chandler 2009: 128–29). Fourth, restrictions on privacy predominantly affect a minority of the population, while (perceived) security enhancements benefit the majority. This prompts the argument that disadvantages for minorities should be disregarded if measures bring advantages for the majority (Waldron 2003; 2006).[44]

Fifth, faced with security threats or external attacks, social psychological reactions foster solidarity, leading individuals to temporarily set aside individual rights for perceived collective security benefits. Chandler (2009: 131) terms this a "rally effect," emphasizing the significance of the concept of *national* security, as people are averse to being labeled as unpatriotic (Aquilina 2010: 139). Lastly, Chandler (2009: 131) suggests that courts are increasingly inclined to grant governments fundamental rights restrictions. This is partly driven by a reluctance to be blamed for events that might have been prevented by a measure they overruled. Simultaneously, the executive branch enjoys procedural advantages over the judiciary, complicating oversight and regulation (R. A. Posner 2006; Solove 2011: 35–36).

2.3.2.2 External Critics

External critics challenge the notion of a precise security-privacy frontier, arguing that measures enhancing both security and privacy can be implemented. Examples include post-9/11 air traffic control measures such as the reinforcement of cockpit doors or the introduction of sky marshals (Schneier 2001), privacy-by-design approaches (van Schoonhoven et al. 2014: 100), or biometric encryption (Cavoukian et al. 2012).[45]

A significant criticism from external critics revolves around the imprecision of drawing a security-privacy frontier. The inherent challenge arises because privacy and security are not entirely mutually exclusive (Waldron 2003; 2006; Bigo 2010; Michaelson 2006). Moreover, questions arise regarding the consideration of rights

[44] Numerous studies show that, for example, the "war on terror" makes Muslims and those of Arab ethnicity more likely to be victims of false suspicion (Guzik 2009: 11; on the UK, see Patel 2012: 223–30).

[45] Trade-off proponents, however, insist that the trade-off thesis does not imply that there is no policy-making below the security-privacy frontier (E. A. Posner & Vermeule 2007: 26; Vermeule 2014: 35).

and the moral justification inherent in the trade-off model. E. A. Posner and Vermeule (2007) frame their model in terms of consequentialist and welfarist ethics, yet rights discourses, including fundamental civil liberties like privacy, are inherently anti-consequentialist (Waldron 2003: 194). This perspective contends that rights should not be subject to the calculus of social utility from a justice standpoint (Dworkin 1977), emphasizing the inviolability of a minimum set of rights.

Henrik Skaug Sætra (2022) adds that if privacy is entirely lost, security becomes unattainable. Nevertheless, there exists a debate, particularly explored by Jeremy Waldron (1989, 2006), regarding the appropriateness of the balancing metaphor when security is also regarded as a right (Ruddock 2004: 116–17). The suitability of the trade-off model as a framework hinges crucially on assumptions regarding the moral justification of fundamental rights. A notable challenge arises from the trade-off model's declaration of itself as an "empirical fact" (E. A. Posner & Vermeule 2007: 40). This pragmatic stance intentionally blurs the line between factual description and normative political and moral justification (Raab 1999).

In summary, while the trade-off and balance metaphors offer factual descriptions of many political processes (Swire 2006), they pose risks to individual liberties due to the inherent unequal valuation of security and privacy (Chandler 2009).[46] Nevertheless, understanding context-dependent decision-making processes and detecting trade-off processes in the attitudes and behavior of individuals can provide valuable insights, as for instance empirically shown by George Gaskell et al. (2004, see Sect. 3.2.2). Solove (2011: 35–36) suggests that one should not give in to the all-or-nothing fallacy, but instead weigh how much less security one can afford to uphold privacy. The following chapter will explore the extent to which trade-off processes can be detected in the attitudes and behavior of individuals

[46] As pointed out in Sect. 2.1.2, the loss of privacy of individuals (such as minorities) has indirect effects on the privacy of all.

3 The Subjective Valuation of Privacy

The field of privacy research and surveillance studies emerged in the 1980s, initially focusing on state and workplace surveillance. By the 1990s, the term "surveillance society" was coined, signifying the increasing invasion of privacy in everyday life. The 2000s were shaped by two pivotal events: 9/11 and the rise of social media. Edward Snowden's revelations on mass surveillance in the 2010s and the impact of state intervention during the COVID-19 pandemic in the 2020s further influenced research agendas (Lyon 2015b).[1] Despite over four decades of surveillance studies, scholars note a "clear lack of systematic understanding" of citizens' views on and responses to state surveillance (Reddick et al. 2015: 129).

This gap is surprising given the extensive surveys conducted by privacy research pioneer Westin from 1978 to 2004 (Kumaraguru & Cranor 2005) and Hayley Watson et al. (2017) having compiled a (non-exhaustive) list of more than 260 surveys on public attitudes towards surveillance, security, privacy, and trust administered between 1980 and 2011. However, these surveys often conceptualize privacy and security in unique terms, warranting a comprehensive analysis (H. Watson et al. 2017). This is the goal for this chapter. Here, my focus is a systematic analysis of the literature examining the interplay between attitudes towards privacy and security. I aim to comprehensively review existing works, delineate their findings, and identify gaps that this thesis aspires to fill.

The structure of this chapter unfolds as follows: In Sect. 3.1, I delve into an exploration of how the literature approaches the complex issue of attitudes towards surveillance by exploring the frameworks predominantly employed by scholars. Following this, I systematically examine the contents and findings of prior literature that has tackled the relationship between attitudes towards privacy

[1] For a more detailed analysis of the development of surveillance studies see Lyon (2007b) and Marx (2015b).

L. Antoine, *The Subjective Value of Privacy*, Wahlen und politische Einstellungen,
https://doi.org/10.1007/978-3-658-46462-2_3

and security. Section 3.2 focuses on studies that assume the trade-off between privacy and security as inherent, investigating individual preferences within this framework. Section 3.3 explores the literature that challenges the preconceived trade-off structure, probing whether individuals perceive the relationship between privacy and security as a trade-off. Section 3.4 broadens the scope to consider alternative values beyond privacy and security in the trade-off equation. The final sub-chapter consolidates the findings of existing literature.

3.1 Approaching Attitudes Towards Privacy

In Sect. 2.1.3.3, I discussed the privacy calculus as a major theoretical model, acknowledging its limitations due to theoretical critique and empirical evidence suggesting a broader array of factors influencing privacy decisions. Various frameworks, including H. Jeff Smith et al.'s (2011) Antecedents–Privacy Concerns–Outcomes (APCO) model, have emerged to reconcile these perspectives (see also Bélanger & Crossler 2011; Li 2011). The APCO model has proven to be particularly relevant (Benamati et al. 2017) since almost all positivist empirical assessments of privacy can be grasped through it. H. J. Smith et al. (2011) suggest that privacy concerns mediate the relationship between antecedents and outcomes such as (intended) behavioral reactions or attitudes towards regulation, arguing that, although different terms such as beliefs, attitudes, and perceptions are used, *concern* constitutes the central construct, specifically in the field of information systems research (see, e.g., Buck et al. 2022; Hong & Thong 2013; Li 2011).

Privacy concerns can be *broadly* defined as apprehensions related to the potential future loss of privacy resulting from the voluntary or involuntary disclosure of personal data (Dinev & Hart 2006) or more *narrowly* as the worry users have about how companies or organizations handle their personal information (H. J. Smith et al. 1996).[2] The concern-based approach posits that privacy is predominantly defined through non-disclosure or non-invasion. However, as outlined in Sects. 2.1.1 and 2.1.2, both the privacy construct itself and its value are multidimensional. Therefore, this study's central construct is not the (rather negative) privacy concern but the (positive) value of privacy (see Sect. 4.2.1). Various proposals have been put forth regarding antecedents to be considered within the

[2] In empirical research, two constructs are particularly utilized for privacy concern (Buck et al. 2022): the concern for information privacy (H. J. Smith et al. 1996; Stewart & Segars 2002) and Internet Users' Information Privacy Concerns (Malhotra et al. 2004).

model (Buck et al. 2022). However, it is worth noting that these antecedents and their relationships with privacy concerns have received relatively little attention (H. J. Smith et al. 2011).

The concept of the privacy calculus is thereby not discarded entirely in the APCO model but is closely intertwined with the concerns aspect. It is postulated that individuals' privacy concerns are either directly linked to behavioral outcomes or incorporated into a cost-benefit analysis. In this analysis, individuals perceive privacy concerns as drawbacks that they evaluate against the potential benefits of disclosing information. However, comparing various graphical and written representations and adaptations of the APCO model reveals that the positioning of the privacy calculus within the model is somewhat neglected, and authors refrain from specifying precisely when and to what extent the privacy calculus plays a role.

Especially concerning state surveillance, the literature emphasizes the role of trade-offs as in the privacy calculus. The prevailing frame for scholarly discourse is the alleged trade-off between privacy and security (Dragu 2011). The research designs employed often compel respondents to adopt the trade-off approach. The premise that achieving one desirable policy goal comes at the expense of another value is not new: from government spending and lower taxes to environmental protection and economic growth, desired outcomes are often accompanied by the loss of a second outcome (Citrin 1979; Hibbs 1979; Kuklinski et al. 2001). The (mostly unarticulated) underlying assumptions of public opinion on a privacy versus security trade-off include (a) the effectiveness of counterterrorism policies in reducing terrorism and (b) the belief that these policies curtail civil liberties (Krueger et al. 2020: 105). The assumptions that surveillance policies work and that they necessarily violate privacy are accepted throughout much of the public opinion literature, although doubts have been noted by some authors (Conti et al. 2014: 28–29). It is essential to recognize that ordinary citizens may not think in terms of trade-offs (Cas et al. 2017; Gaskell et al. 2004). While the critique has been acknowledged by some public opinion scholars, the trade-off frame continues to be frequently employed.

3.2 The Trade-off Between Privacy and Security: How do Citizens Decide?

Security versus privacy trade-off questions can manifest in various forms, as exemplified by survey questions like:

- "To curb terrorism in this country, do you think it will be necessary for the average citizen to give up some civil liberties, or not?" (Los Angeles Times 1995, cited in Lewis 2005),
- "Would you be willing to give up some of your personal freedom to reduce the threat of terrorism?" (Opinion Dynamics Corporation/Fox News 1995, cited in Best et al. 2006),
- "For each of the following measures, please tell me if you would support them as a means of reducing terrorist attacks or if you think they go too far. 1. increasing government surveillance of U.S. citizens [...]" (Gallup News Survey 1995, cited in Lewis 2005), or
- "Would you support new laws to strengthen security measures against terrorism, even if it meant limiting privacy protections such as restrictions on government searches and wiretaps?" (Hart and Teeter Research Companies/ NBC News/Wall Street Journal 1995, cited in Best et al. 2006).

These questions have been posed in surveys in the USA since the mid-1990s, and apart from a few months after 9/11, public opinion generally rejects the notion that sacrificing civil liberties is necessary to combat terrorism since citizens tend to prefer the civil liberties side. However, scholarly discussion on the privacy-security trade-off gained momentum after these events.

Studies employing trade-off scenarios have presented varying results. For instance, Darren W. Davis and Brian D. Silver (2004) found that US-American citizens (N = 1386), when presented with trade-off items, would often prefer freedom of communication over enhanced security through telephone and email monitoring. This is in line with Leonie Huddy et al.'s (2002) analysis of public opinion polls cited in news media. Sara Degli Esposti and Elvira Santiago-Gomez (2015)—as part of the SurPRISE project (see also Ball et al. 2019; Pavone et al. 2015)—discovered that the majority of Spanish respondents (N = 185) perceiving security and privacy as a trade-off were not willing to sacrifice privacy for more security. Hank C. Jenkins-Smith and Kerry G. Herron (2009) used a metaphorical query involving marbles to illustrate a zero-sum game between freedom and security, with respondents (N = 3006 US-American residents) slightly leaning toward security (on average 51 to 49 marbles). Lee Rainie and Maeve Duggan (2016) reported that in the context of workplace surveillance, a majority of respondents (N = 461 US-American adults) might be okay with employer surveillance if it reduces thefts in the office. Anna Gurinskaya (2020) found in a survey of Russian university students (N = 570) that they would be willing to sacrifice a significant share of their privacy for a feeling of security.

Not directly aligned with the trade-off approach, but associated with it, are Huddy et al.'s (2005) questions about whether respondents would be more concerned that the government might fail to enact strong antiterrorism laws or that new laws might excessively restrict civil liberties. This was part of a survey conducted in the USA (N = 1549 residents). Additionally, the Office of the Privacy Commissioner of Canada (2009) inquired whether respondents (N = 2028) were concerned that the current focus on security after the 9/11 terrorist attacks would unnecessarily restrict the privacy and civil liberties of Canadians. In both of these surveys, which differed from those previously mentioned by focusing on respondents' current states of concern or attitudes toward the government's actual performance, participants did not provide abstract opinions. Instead, they expressed fears about privacy infringement, leaning toward the privacy side in the zero-sum trade-off.

Overall, there is no clear consensus among respondents in trade-off situations, with some leaning toward privacy and others toward security. Public opinion appears to be divided on the issue, and none of the studies questions its measurement approach or suggests that the mixed results might be evidence for a rejection of the trade-off model.

3.3 Questioning the Trade-off: How do Individuals Perceive the Relationship Between Privacy and Security?

As discussed in previous theoretical chapters, the dichotomy between privacy and security may not be inherent. Numerous authors have stepped back to (a) evaluate the impact of security assurances on general privacy attitudes and (b) investigate attitudes toward the relationship between privacy and security without presuming an *a priori* trade-off but rather exploring to what extent individuals perceive one at all.

3.3.1 What is the Effect of Security Pledges on Privacy Attitudes?

In a framing experiment, Valentina Bali (2009) explored the extent to which the trade-off between privacy and security influences public opinion on the hypothetical implementation of standardized identification cards (referring to the USA's 'REAL ID' Act of 2005). Bali found that framing something as security-enhancing did not significantly alter the acceptance of respondents (N = 993 Michigan residents) compared to no frame or a frame highlighting both the benefits of increased security and the potential costs of decreased privacy. This aligns with Hans Vermeersch and Evelin de Pauw's (2017) findings, where exposure to a security frame did not significantly increase endorsement of new technologies by public authorities among Belgian university students (N = 438), except in the case of behavioral profiling. Conversely, Julia van Heek et al.'s (2017) results from a conjoint experiment indicate that an increase in security was a crucial factor in medical surveillance acceptance among German respondents (N = 130), suggesting a willingness to accept privacy invasions, especially when the promised security enhancement is significant. Lisa-Marie Wadle et al.'s (2019) framing experiment revealed a greater willingness to disclose data when security was promised (N = 561 German residents).[3]

Some studies focused on framing situations as *in*secure rather than explicitly referring to security as a benefit. Conrad Ziller and Marc Helbig (2021) found that individuals accepted surveillance more if primed with an insecure situation in a survey experiment conducted across Germany, Spain, France, and the UK (N = 6169). This finding is in line with Jennifer L. Merolla and Elizabeth J. Zechmeister's (2009) results from a survey experiment conducted in the USA and Mexico (five studies, total N = 1519). Similarly, Jaspreet Bhatia and Travis D. Breaux (2018) demonstrated, through a vignette experiment (N = 80 US-Americans), that participants were more willing to share information when the purpose of surveillance was disclosed and related to human security, such as investigating threats of harm or terrorism.

[3] It remains unclear, however, to what extent the authors' results are significant. In addition, they did not include a comparison group not receiving any frame.

3.3.2 Is there a Trade-off?

Merolla and Zechmeister (2009) employed a straightforward approach, asking respondents whether the government should prioritize preventing terrorism even if it means violating civil liberties. Even in the aftermath of 9/11 (January 2002), the majority of respondents (N = 522 US-Americans) favored taking steps to prevent terrorism without violating basic civil liberties. Several authors, including Gaskell et al. (2004) have explored the acceptance of new technologies using a risk and usability framework. Gaskell et al. (2004: 187) argue that individuals consider technologies as trade-offs only when they perceive them as both risky *and* useful at the same time (see Table 3.1). Only then they see them as exchangeable goods that can be traded. Otherwise people are either concerned, trusting, or not interested in the issue (for a similar conceptualization, see Friedewald, van Lieshout, & Rung 2016).

Table 3.1 Perceptions of Riskiness and Usefulness

		riskiness	
		high	low
usefulness	**high**	Trade-off model	Trusting attitude ('relaxed')
	low	Concerned attitude ('skeptical')	Uninterested

Source: Gaskell et al. (2004: 187)

This conceptualization was extended to surveillance technology by Vincenzo Pavone and Degli Esposti (2012) who found that people predominantly viewed surveillance technologies as either useless and harmful or useful and harmless based on results from focus group discussions in Austria, Germany, Denmark, Spain, Hungary, and Norway (N = 156), challenging the trade-off model. Michelle Cayford et al. (2019) further supported this by indicating that individuals (N = 359 Dutch university students and their parents) tend to be either concerned or trusting but do not consistently engage in a privacy-security trade-off. Brian S. Krueger et al. (2020) used European study results to examine Gaskell's thesis in the USA. Among 1036 surveyed residents, the majority expressed concerns about government actions like reading emails or wiretapping, while trusting national ID cards or pre-flight x-rays. Notably, one in four respondents showed a trade-off stance on reading emails and wiretapping, and one in six on wiretapping and pre-flight x-rays (Krueger et al. 2020: 109).

Similarly to Gaskell et al., Heng Xu and Tamara Dinev (2012) conceptualized a trade-off based on "government intrusion concern" and "perceived need for government surveillance." However, their survey data on US-American residents (N = 422) revealed, similar to the findings of Pavone and Degli Esposti (2012), that respondents were either concerned about government intrusion or perceived a need for government surveillance, challenging the existence of a trade-off. Sun Sun Lim et al. (2009), in a cross-cultural study with residents from New York, Bangalore, Seoul, Singapore, and Sydney (total N = 1261), found a negative correlation between government intrusion concerns and perceived need for government surveillance, further undermining the trade-off hypothesis.

Degli Esposti et al. (2017) identified a positive relationship between attitudes toward privacy and security when analyzing results from SurPRISE's citizen summits across various European countries (six countries, N = 113–244). They argued that individuals might perceive privacy and security as part of a broader concept of human security, suggesting compatibility rather than antagonism. Michael Friedewald et al. (2015) investigated perceptions of a trade-off using survey data from all EU countries (excluding Croatia, N = 27,195) and likewise found a positive relationship between attitudes toward privacy and security. While not entirely discarding the trade-off hypothesis, they argued that the absence of a significant negative relationship, indicating that those valuing security do not disregard privacy, provides convincing evidence against the trade-off mindset in EU citizens. Tijs van den Broek et al. (2017), using the same data as Friedewald et al. (2015), explored privacy and security concerns' effects on surveillance acceptance across different settings. Their findings suggested that citizens do not intrinsically link privacy and security; instead, they "simply want both" and consider privacy and security relevant for their well-being (van den Broek et al. 2017: 15–16).

In addition to standard survey questions and analytical methods, researchers have employed survey experiments to assess the privacy-security trade-off. Bali (2009) found that a balanced frame, presenting both the reduction of terrorism threats and the loss of civil liberties, did not significantly alter respondents' attitudes toward surveillance measures compared to the control group that was not exposed to any frame, suggesting that individuals have inherited the idea of a trade-off. Eric Andrew Finkelstein et al. (2017) used a discrete choice experiment, revealing an overall willingness of US-Americans (N = 652) to make trade-offs between civil liberties and security. However, this effect varied among political affiliations, with liberals adhering to the trade-off logic more than conservatives.

In summary, the intricate relationship between privacy and security challenges the conventional trade-off paradigm. The literature explores various factors, including the framing of security measures and perceptions of risk and usefulness, revealing inconsistent patterns in individuals' attitudes. While some studies suggest that framing situations as insecure can boost surveillance acceptance, others indicate variable effects of security-enhancing frames. The research questions the existence of a clear trade-off, as individuals express concerns about specific government actions while trusting other security measures simultaneously. Additionally, findings challenge the trade-off hypothesis by suggesting a positive relationship between attitudes toward privacy and security. Overall, these findings highlight the need for a more nuanced understanding of the complex interplay between privacy and security, surpassing oversimplified dichotomies.

3.4 Related Trade-offs in the Privacy-security Nexus

The privacy calculus theory posits that individuals consistently navigate calculations between perceived costs/risks and benefits when disclosing personal information. Beyond the traditional dichotomy of privacy versus security, additional factors come into play. In a study by W. Kip Viscusi and Richard J. Zeckhauser (2003), using airport checks as an illustrative scenario, US-American law students (N = 94) demonstrated a willingness to trade civil rights for convenience. Their findings revealed that as waiting times increased, respondents became more amenable to additional profiling measures for others, such as racial profiling (79% acceptance). However, when individuals themselves faced scrutiny, nearly half preferred longer waiting times (44% willing to wait up to 60 minutes), indicating a reluctance to compromise their own civil rights. Extending this analysis to public transport, Emma Carter et al. (2015) demonstrated that people are willing to trade privacy (via increased CCTV) for more convenient and quicker travel. Interestingly, their list experiment (N = 489 US-American adults) suggested a willingness to sacrifice some security for greater convenience. Research on privacy-intrusive social networking sites (SNS) by Hanna Krasnova et al. (2010) and Sushma Mishra et al. (2012) revealed a conscious awareness among users of potential privacy risks. Despite this awareness, individuals willingly disclosed personal information on SNS for the sake of convenience, enhanced relationships, and enjoyment (N = 259 StudiVZ and Facebook users in Germany and N = 129 undergraduate students at a US-American university). Similarly, studies on apps, such as Mark J. Keith et al.'s (2013) and Verena M. Wottrich et al.'s (2018), demonstrated that individuals might compromise privacy concerns for perceived higher app value (N_1 = 1025 US-American college students,N_{2a} =

183 students of a "Western European university", $N_{2b} = 687$ Dutch online panel members).

Efforts to quantify these trade-offs often involve survey experiments where respondents indicate the amount they would pay to incur certain costs or receive specific benefits. Neil Robinson et al. (2010) estimated that British internet users (N = 2058) would accept data sharing across the private sector for an average reduction of £30 for a passport. Similarly, Sunil Patil et al. (2015: 24) found that EU citizens (N = 27,000) were willing to pay 7.50 Euro more for their internet provider if no information on them was stored. Simultaneously, individuals express a willingness to pay for enhanced security. Robinson et al. (2010) discovered that respondents would pay £3.10 more on ticket prices for increased privacy-intrusive CCTV cameras at train stations. Sunil Patil et al. (2014) estimated the willingness to pay for standard and advanced CCTV in Denmark, Italy, and Romania (N = 770) (see also Potoglou et al. 2010).[4]

A stated preference experiment by Sunil Patil et al. (2015: 32) on health data indicates that individuals valued private information and money on the same scale. They found that while individuals were willing to pay for healthcare professionals to access their health data, financial compensation was sought if additional entities, such as fire fighters and rescue teams, were granted access (see also Sunil Patil et al. 2016). Rainie and Duggan's (2016) results suggest that, when offered monetary rewards, individuals were willing to allow companies to monitor their shopping habits but showed reluctance regarding their driving habits, social media activities, and habits at home, emphasizing the nuanced nature of privacy preferences influenced by the type of information shared and the value of offered rewards.

In conclusion, the dynamic relationship between perceived risks and benefits seems to extend beyond the dichotomy of privacy versus security. Whether observed in travel scenarios, SNS, or app usage, individuals demonstrate a willingness to trade privacy for convenience, relationships, and monetary reward. Quantifying these trade-offs through survey experiments reveals the economic dimensions of privacy preferences. Notably, individuals express a dual willingness to pay for both enhanced security measures and the preservation of their own privacy.

---

4 While not quantifying the average price that individuals would be willing to pay, Sunil Patil et al. (2015) find the same relationship surveying individuals in all EU member states (N = 27,000).

Conceptual Framework and Research Strategy 4

This work aims to contribute to the existing research on the subjective value of privacy in several ways. The following chapter will, on the one hand, identify the current gaps in research based on the extensive literature review presented in the previous chapters. On the other hand, it will discuss to what extent the present study intends to address and fill these existing research gaps. This discussion will be accompanied by an explanation of the methodological approach in the subsequent chapters, including associated assumptions. This chapter serves as a bridge between theory and empirical research. Its structure is as follows: I will first outline the identified blind spots in the existing literature. Thereafter, I will set forth some basic theoretical assumptions that guide this work, especially focusing on the understanding of *subjective value* and *privacy* within this thesis. In Sect. 4.3, I explain my empirical approach that seeks to address the identified blind spots. And finally, in Sect. 4.4, I explain some methodological assumptions, addressing the issue of researching attitudes towards privacy and the analytical approach.

Supplementary Information The online version contains supplementary material available at https://doi.org/10.1007/978-3-658-46462-2_4.

L. Antoine, *The Subjective Value of Privacy*, Wahlen und politische Einstellungen,
https://doi.org/10.1007/978-3-658-46462-2_4

4.1 Identification of Blind Spots in the Existing Literature

In the previous two chapters, I discussed both theoretical and empirical research concerning the connection between privacy and security: *Chap. 2* introduced the theoretical underpinnings of the privacy-security nexus, delving into the ongoing debate within privacy research regarding its definition. This debate primarily centers on the distinction between unified definitions and pluralist conceptualizations. Unified definitions, such as the right to be alone or control over information, face challenges of being either too narrow or excessively broad, prompting the development of pluralist typologies to capture the multifaceted nature of privacy. Notably, informational privacy, encompassing aspects of negative and positive freedom, emerges as a key element in these typologies.

The chapter then explored the primarily beneficial nature of privacy, examining deontological (emphasizing dignity and autonomy) and consequentialist (highlighting utility) perspectives. Privacy was elucidated as benefiting individuals and society, crucial for freedom, personal relationships, and democracy. Subsequently, I examined privacy invasions, including diverse forms, governmental justifications, and societal acceptance. Privacy invasion, defined as diminishing an individual's privacy through surveillance, encompasses targeted and mass surveillance. Government justifications focus on security, preventive justice, and the rise of "pre-crime" societies, with debates on the efficacy of surveillance in crime prevention and concerns about discrimination. Privacy invasions are also seen as tools for political control, aligning with historical notions of state authority. Acceptance of privacy invasions is explored through the privacy calculus theory, which suggests individuals weigh costs and benefits. Despite its popularity, empirical studies challenge the theory, revealing deviations from rational decision-making. Alternative perspectives, like the normalization of surveillance and the role of fear, set the stage for further exploration of security concepts.

Moving forward, the concept of security was defined as a historically significant state, prompting discussions on objective versus subjective security, securitization as a social and political practice, and critiques of securitization theory. The subsequent subchapter investigated the interplay between privacy and security, presenting two perspectives: a hierarchical arrangement where security is foundational and a trade-off between privacy and security. Historical roots and critiques of these perspectives were discussed, acknowledging the complexities of context-dependent decision-making processes.

Chapter 3 addressed the clear lack of systematic understanding of citizens' perspectives on state surveillance. It systematically analyzed existing literature on the interplay between attitudes toward privacy and security, examining frameworks such as the APCO model. The prevailing trade-off frame between privacy and security was scrutinized, with a focus on how citizens decide when faced with conflicting values. Contrary to the assumed trade-off, findings suggested a nuanced relationship, challenging the notion of an inherent trade-off and revealing individuals' willingness to trade privacy and security for convenience, relationships, and monetary rewards. This nuanced nature of privacy preferences emphasized the dynamic interplay between perceived risks and benefits beyond the traditional privacy versus security dichotomy.

Despite the abundance of literature on the topic, there are some gaps in the existing body of work. This thesis aims to address six of these blind spots, which will be outlined in the following sections.

4.1.1 Lack of Empirical Knowledge about Attitudes Towards State Surveillance in General

Illuminating citizens' orientations, e.g., via survey research, fulfills two primary functions: firstly, it allows society to learn about itself, involving both citizens and the scientific community. The knowledge gained can influence social or political behavior. Secondly, survey research permits the observation of citizens by political elites. For their responsiveness and decision legitimization, political elites can continuously assess societal problem perceptions as well as individual needs and interests, particularly between elections (Luhmann 2000).[1]

In the realm of politics, policies serve as the foundational function of the political system, aiming to address societal issues by making authoritative decisions on substantive matters (Almond & Powell 1978: 394). The issue of legitimacy (and thus public approval) is of paramount importance in policies involving the infringement of individual civil rights, such as state surveillance (Trüdinger & Steckermeier 2017: 421). Since the late 1970s, literature has exhibited a growing interest in individuals' privacy choices and their consequences (R. A. Posner 1978; Stigler 1980). It explores various aspects, including people's anticipation and evaluation of costs, benefits, and other consequences related to safeguarding their privacy. However, most studies in this area focus on privacy decisions in a commercial context (Pomfret et al. 2020). Despite extensive consumer research and a rather good understanding of when consumers are willing to disclose private

[1] For a debate on the extent to which survey research findings can be considered a surrogate for public opinion, see, among others, Herbst (1992) as well as Glasser and Salmon (1995).

data, the research on state surveillance is less cohesive. While insights from consumer research are considered informative for the research on state surveillance (Dinev et al. 2008), not all contexts can be readily adapted—especially given the structurally different government/citizen and business/customer relationship. A significant challenge in the research on state surveillance is the lack of a clear systematic understanding of the phenomena of interest. Three main reasons are identified in the literature:

(1) Existing research exhibits limited cross-referencing due to varying conceptual definitions (H. Watson et al. 2017). As elucidated in Chap. 2, divergent interpretations of privacy significantly contribute to authors holding diverse and occasionally conflicting perspectives on specific phenomena. This challenge is further compounded by the necessity for a reduction or simplification in the operationalization of concepts during the collection of attitudes.
(2) Authors, often potentially guided by scientific systemic considerations, tend to overly generalize their findings, initially derived from specific—and often even completely artificial—contexts, to a broader level (Kokolakis 2017). This practice contributes to a fragmented depiction of relationships, as expounded in Chap. 3.
(3) Simultaneously, divergent interpretations of meta-concepts, like the trade-off, complicate the literature, making it difficult to establish a unified understanding. The trade-off rhetoric gained momentum particularly post-9/11. However, the ubiquitous use of the term gradually displaced its original economic sense, wherein privacy and security could exist in equilibrium, and an enhancement in one inevitably led to a reduction in the other (Chandler 2009; Vermeule 2014). In the surveillance/privacy literature, some authors perceive the increasing trade-off rhetoric as a danger, sparking a debate on the actual existence of trade-offs, lacking a unified understanding (van Lieshout et al. 2013). Influenced, perhaps, by the critical stance of many authors, there is almost unanimous consensus that no inherent trade-off exists between privacy and security (Zedner 2009: 135–36), while concurrently, a substantial portion of authors find evidence supporting individuals' active weighing of costs and benefits.

In summary, the insufficient amount of research on state surveillance in comparison to other policy domains indicates a notable absence of systematic inquiry in existing studies. Section 2.1.3.3 elucidated that individuals may accept surveillance, including state surveillance, due to its familiarity and normalization. However, the intriguing turn of events in the case of the long-debated "privacy paradox" (Gerber et al. 2018; Kokolakis 2017), whose empirical existence is suddenly elusive (Büchi et al. 2020), underscores the necessity for regular and comprehensive research on state surveillance. This need arises not only for the scientific community to better comprehend individual decision-making processes but also potentially to transparently reflect to citizens what other members of society consider "normal."

At the same time, the field of empirical surveillance studies navigates challenging terrain: Considering surveys themselves can be construed as a form of surveillance, with some individuals perceiving them as an invasion of privacy (Haggerty & Gazso 2005; Marx 2007), the scientific community potentially contributes to the normalization of surveillance. Simultaneously, scholars must exercise caution in interpreting and communicating their results, particularly regarding representativity, acknowledging a degree of important non-randomness structured into response rates (Haggerty & Gazso 2005: 175)—detailed further in Sect. 4.4.1.

Concurrently to the increasing scope of state surveillance (Kampmark 2020), there is a call from the judiciary for the executive to set boundaries on state invasions of privacy (Vagle 2017). For example, in the case of Germany, the Federal Constitutional Court urged the government to compile a comprehensive "overall surveillance calculus" (*Überwachungsgesamtrechnung*) (Stahl 2020). According to the concept, it is necessary to not only assess the proportionality of individual surveillance instruments, but it is also necessary to determine whether the overall burden on the citizen is reasonable within the context of an overall assessment of all state surveillance measures (Bieker et al. 2018; Roßnagel 2010). The current federal government, according to the coalition agreement, aims to heed this call (Roßnagel et al. 2022). While the assessment is supposed to be objective, it has been noted that subjective perceptions of individuals might be considered in the political discourse, too (Büscher et al. 2022).

In summary, the first major blind spot is the general lack of comprehensive research on state surveillance, despite the need for a better understanding of subjective privacy appreciation.

4.1.2 Lack of Cross-National Studies in Specific

Within the literature, it is consistently acknowledged that attitudes toward surveillance and privacy are contingent on the context (Nissenbaum 2009; Tsapogas 2017), e.g., understood as the circumstances shaping the setting (Porcedda 2017: 191). Various factors, such as a country's surveillance level (Budak et al. 2013:

105) or its democratic status (Brettschneider, 2010) but also historical legacies (T. H. Bennett & Gelsthorpe 1996: 73), experience with previous terror attacks, and its political past, either communist (Svenonius & Björklund 2018: 126) or colonial (McCulloch & Pickering 2009: 636), have been posited to influence attitudes toward surveillance. Despite this recognition, Chap. 3 highlights a predominant reliance on single-country samples in the existing studies, an observation noted by Elia Zureik and L. Lynda Harling Stalker (2010) over a decade ago.

Zureik and Harling Stalker (2010) outline two crucial reasons for advocating cross-cultural studies in the field of privacy research. Firstly, based on the fact that globalization has detached concepts of privacy and surveillance from the nation-state (Bigo 2008), the inequitable distribution in the currently available survey data is striking, with only a few attempts to investigate the same phenomenon across diverse countries using standardized research instruments. Secondly, cross-national studies are deemed indispensable for testing and evolving general theories of society, requiring aggregated survey data from numerous societies to analyze the impact of mass beliefs and values on societal-level phenomena (Inglehart & Welzel 2004). This aligns with the interdisciplinary nature of surveillance studies, enhancing methodological approaches (Zureik & Harling Stalker 2010: 16).

Despite progress, particularly through EU-funded projects like PRISMS (Friedewald et al. 2017), PACT (Sunil Patil et al. 2015), and SurPRISE (Pavone et al. 2015), which assessed European citizens' cross-national perspectives on surveillance and privacy (under the EU's Seventh Framework Programme for Research and Innovation, FP7), the focus still primarily centers on specific regions. While including Europe broadens the scope beyond the USA, it does not provide a truly global perspective. We know, however, from previous research that information privacy concerns differ between cultural regions (e.g., Capurro 2005; Chiou 2009; Dinev et al. 2006; Farrall 2008; Lowry et al. 2011; Luther & Radovic 2012; Ur & Wang 2013), and most notably and potentially fundamentally between the Global North and Global South (Ahmed et al. 2017). A cross-national context, as global as possible, is essential not only for testing the influence of macro-variables but also for examining country heterogeneity of individual-level findings, which is for example known for other attitudes like trust in government (Jamal & Nooruddin 2010) or populist stances (Wuttke et al. 2020).

In summary, the second major blind spot involves the prevalent reliance on single-country samples in existing studies in combination with a restricted regional focus on the USA and Europe, hindering a comprehensive understanding of the global nuances and contextual factors influencing attitudes toward surveillance and privacy.

4.1.3 Limited Methodological Approaches

The third blind spot scrutinizes the survey methods outlined in Chap. 3. The most classical form appears to be single-country studies, a point I have already addressed, based on survey data. Surveys, particularly population-based surveys, are considered the standard method for gathering information about larger populations and for the ability to generalize across broader processes. The issue with classical surveys is that they typically cannot establish causal relationships, even though many scholars imply this in their analyses. The fact that only the strength of the correlation between variables can be determined does not allow one to make statements about the direction of the effect. Moreover, it may even be the case that the correlation arises only due to the inclusion of additional variables, so that in reality, there is no significant relationship between the variables. As a result, statistical analyses of cross-sectional survey data are notoriously subject to misleading findings (Gaines et al. 2007).

In the context of the privacy-security nexus, especially in literature focusing on state surveillance, we observe that attitudes expressed by respondents are typically linked together, and causal evidence is sought from the correlation. Alternatively, abstract questions weighing privacy versus security are posed within one item, as exemplified at the beginning of Sect. 3.1. The ex-post interpretation of results largely depends on how the respective *authors* postulate the relationship between certain concepts, rather than how the *respondents* perceive them. This has significant negative implications for validity, as results may not be easily replicable, especially since the assumptions made are not always transparently presented. Similarly, this poses challenges for communicating the correct results to the public, as the findings tend to be overly generalized (Preibusch 2013). Especially concerning the privacy calculus, this leads to the aforementioned debate about the (non-)existence of a trade-off. Within the securitization literature as well, it is noted that the methodological approach is mostly confined to classical quantitative surveys (Baele & Thomson 2017).[2] At the same time, many studies are based on convenience samples such as student samples or other small-N samples, which further restricts generalizability (Cornesse et al. 2020).

Correlational survey research falls short of establishing causality, merely quantifying associations between variables by exploring the predictive links among multiple predictors and a criterion variable. Acknowledging this limitation in

[2] In the field of securitization, I am only aware of Baele et al.'s (2018) survey experiment assessing the impact of numerical arguments in security communication conducted in the United Kingdom.

correlational attitude surveys, the third major blind spot is a lack in studies unraveling causal interactions using more sophisticated analyses in the research aiming at understanding the value of privacy.

4.1.4 The Role of the Privacy Calculus within APCO

In addition to the three overarching blind spots, three specific areas will be explored below, revealing distinct needs for attitude research towards the privacy-security nexus. The privacy calculus has been accorded a prominent position within the literature. For many years, it was the prevailing model for explaining attitudes toward privacy and, in particular, privacy-related behavior (Wirth 2018; Yun et al. 2019). The fundamental idea was that before individuals act in relation to privacy (such as disclosing or withholding certain data), they weigh the potential costs and benefits of their actions against each other, sharing data when anticipating a positive net outcome, i.e., that expected benefits of disclosure outweigh the costs (N. Lee & Kwon 2015). However, in recent years, the model has fallen into disrepute, especially as many scholars questioned the basic assumptions of the homo economicus. In particular, the idea that individuals can or do completely rationally weigh costs and benefits was deemed unrealistic (Acquisti et al. 2016). Instead of the privacy calculus, the literature shifted focus to other models to explain privacy behavior. The APCO model (H. J. Smith et al. 2011) stood out, under which a majority of established models could be subsumed. The structure is kept simple: there are antecedents, such as individual factors or contexts, that influence the degree to which individuals are concerned about privacy. This concern may (but does not have to) manifest in certain behaviors.

Interestingly, the idea of the privacy calculus is not entirely discarded; rather, it is acknowledged that a certain extent of cost-benefit analysis is indispensable for the formation of specific privacy attitudes/concrete actions. It is postulated that individuals' privacy concerns are either directly linked to behavioral outcomes or incorporated into a cost-benefit analysis. However, the exact role and timing of the privacy calculus within the APCO model remain somewhat neglected, as authors refrain from specifying precisely when and to what extent the privacy calculus plays a role.

Some authors place it within the concerns facet (e.g., Dinev et al. 2015), implying that the development of concerns is already dependent on the imaginary weighing of costs and benefits that the subsequent action could have. Others view it more closely related to the outcome (e.g., H. J. Smith et al. 2011), suggesting that privacy concerns flow into the privacy calculus as potential concerns and are then weighed against potential benefits. Still, others position the privacy calculus outside the APCO model (e.g., Jia et al. 2015; Potoglou et al. 2015), suggesting that it is perceived as an alternative, albeit relevant, path. None of the authors provides clear justifications for their choices (see also Buck et al. 2022: 49).

The lack of theorization regarding the positioning of the privacy calculus within the APCO model leads to a diminished understanding of the privacy calculus, especially regarding what goods are specifically weighed against each other. In the context of state surveillance, it is primarily security gains that are discussed as possible benefits (Dragu 2011). In contrast to literature on private-sector privacy decisions, there are few discussions about alternative benefits that respondents could consider in their decision about the acceptance of privacy invasions. This is surprising, as social psychology literature on decision-making suggests that a variety of monetary and non-monetary incentives influence individuals' decision-making (e.g., Lefebvre & Stenger 2020). At the same time, the focus on costs seems to be only on privacy concerns, while analogously, monetary and non-monetary costs could also influence the calculus.

The relatively narrow focus on the goods of privacy and security aligns with the conceptualization of the privacy calculus as a deliberate trade-off (Harborth & Pape 2023: 2). This concept is based on the economic assumption that *two* goods are weighed against each other. Thus, no statements can be made about the calculus when more than two goods are involved, although it is assumed that multiple factors are being weighed against each other—or at least, to anticipate the potential critique of limited cognitive capacity which might argue that individuals can only assess a restricted number of costs and benefits at the same time (Acquisti & Grossklags 2005; Acquisti 2009), different individuals may consider different goods.

This brings up another point: in the APCO model, the consideration of a variety of antecedents presupposes the idea that different individual characteristics and different contexts have different influences on privacy decision-making (Buck et al. 2022: 45–46). However, how the antecedents relate to the concerns facet is rather undertheorized. It is conceivable, for example, that the privacy calculus may work differently for different groups of people. Not only might certain groups weigh different costs and benefits against each other, but this could also mean that certain individuals may be more likely than others to enter into a privacy calculus. This aspect has not been addressed in the literature so far.

In summary, the fourth identified blind spot revolves around the insufficient theorization of the privacy calculus within the APCO model, leading to an incomplete understanding of when and to what extent the privacy calculus influences privacy decision-making. The narrow focus on privacy and security goods in the privacy calculus as a deliberate trade-off neglects the consideration of multiple goods and fails to explore how different individuals or groups may engage differently in the privacy calculus. This leads me to the following sub-question: *To what extent do individuals consider cost and benefits when forming their privacy attitude?*

4.1.5 Securitization Theory's Omission of the Role of the Audience

My fifth identified blind spot focusses on securitization theory's weakness in addressing the role of the audience. Securitization theory posits that security threats are constructed through intersubjective processes involving *securitizing actors*, authorized by society to "speak society," and *audiences* whose agreement is necessary to confer an intersubjective status to the threat (Buzan et al. 1997: 31). This conceptualization places security within the realm of subjective definition among individuals. In general, intersubjective beliefs, shaped through social interactions, have been shown to contribute to the construction of shared meanings, norms, values, and identities. These shared beliefs not only influence our interpretation of objective reality but also shape our interests and behavior (Guzzini 2000).

In the securitization framework, the audience, termed the "addressee of the speech act" (Floyd 2019: 54), plays a pivotal role. The audience is distinct from other components such as aggressors, referent objects, or functional actors (Floyd 2016; Buzan et al. 1997). The success of a securitizing move hinges on audience acceptance, highlighting its fundamental role in creating shared security meanings and justifying security policies (Buzan et al. 1997; Balzacq 2005; Stritzel 2007). Even though securitization research is said to turn increasingly towards sociological or practice-based approaches (Balzacq 2010a), philosophical, language-focused considerations still play a significant role.[3] This emphasizes the distinctiveness of the theory since this discursive legitimization separates securitization form other security theory. However, understanding the audience within securitization processes remains underdeveloped, with criticism directed at the inconsistent treatment and lack of clarity surrounding its identity and purpose (Balzacq 2005; Côté 2016; Floyd 2010; Salter 2008; M. C. Williams

[3] In short, the *linguistic* approaches center on the speech acts of securitizing actors, emphasizing the existential nature of threats whereas *sociological* approaches emphasize the contextual characteristics of practices and the non-discursive actions of actors within those contexts.

2010). Some authors have noted that securitization theory is conceptually inconsistent when integrating "illocutionary" speech acts (as originally formulated by Wæver 1995) and the construction of intersubjective values through recognition and authorization (as highlighted by Buzan et al. 1997: 32). It is argued that defining securitization as an speech act that realizes the speaker's intention, where the audience appears to be a passive body, conflicts with its characterization as an intersubjective process, reaffirming the agency of the audience to actively determine the success or failure of the securitizing move, creating a logical tension (Côté 2016). While theory tends to marginalize the agency of the audience, detracting from its intersubjective nature (Balzacq 2005: 179), empirical literature underscores its active role in the securitization process.

Empirical studies are increasingly turning towards the role of the audience, primarily revealing the dynamic nature of the securitization process. First, securitizing moves do not seem to happen in isolation but are connected to other contextual moves, indicating an iterative process where previous actor-audience interactions influence future securitizing moves (Wilkinson, 2007; Salter, 2008). Second, audiences seem to actively contribute to the intersubjective construction of security meaning in various contexts, dispelling the notion of passive agents in securitization theory (Bourbeau 2011; Lupovici 2016).

Simultaneously, a debate has arisen in the literature about the problematic nature of speaking about a singular audience given the multiplicity of audiences. Various securitizing acts occur through the mutual constitution of different securitizing actors and audiences (Murphy 2020; Salter 2008). Drawing on E. Goffman's (1956) research, which posits that each situation is a new scene, and individuals perform different roles depending on who is present, this debate challenges the notion of a singular audience (Salter 2008). At the same time, it has been shown that the identity of the audience varies depending on the context, highlighting the contextual dependence of securitization audiences in authorizing security speech and legitimizing actions sought by securitizing actors (Côté 2016). Divergent interpretations of similar securitization moves appear to result in significant variations in security outcomes (Hansen 2011; Stritzel 2014).

We know from the framing theory, which shares many similarities with the securitization theory (Baele et al. 2018),[4] that how framing works differs between

---

[4] According to Baele et al. (2018) securitization processes' components (securitizing actor, the audience, the context and the securitizing move itself) strongly mirror Entman's (1993) locations of the framing process: communicator, receiver, culture and text. There is a debate, however, to what extent securitization should distinguish itself from the concept of framing (e.g., S. D. Watson 2012).

different social groups and contexts. Specifically, it is suggested that the susceptibility of frames might be contingent upon individual characteristics and contexts. Alongside different personality types, socio-demographic characteristics, or political attitudes are used as explanatory factors (Wyszynski & Diederich 2023). Interestingly, this point has not yet been raised in empirical research on the susceptibility to securitization. This may also be due to the limited range of research methods applied in securitization research thus far (Baele & Sterck 2015; Balzacq 2010b). From research on the acceptance of privacy invasions, we know that a multitude of individual and contextual factors has been considered to explain privacy attitudes in general (Buck et al. 2022: 45–46). This suggests that there are concrete antecedents for the susceptibility to security frames as well.

Addressing the influence of individual characteristics on the acceptance of securitizing moves could mitigate two shortcomings of securitization research: firstly, it contributes to a more precise understanding of the determinants of success or failure of securitizing moves by examining how audience characteristics impact the outcome of the securitizing move and subsequently potentially also the securitizing actors' formulation of the move. Secondly, this improved understanding would produce generalizable conclusions that transcend particularistic results of specific scenarios.

To sum up, the fifth blind spot revolves around the understudied role of the audience in securitization theory. In that sense, it complements the urge for more research on the value of privacy. Exploring who is more likely to be susceptible to a securitizing move might enhances our understanding of securitization processes in general. This leads me to the following sub-question: *To what extent does the susceptibility to accepting security frames differ between individuals and contexts?*

4.1.6 Privacy as a Personality Trait

I have outlined above that it is relatively common in research on privacy attitudes and behavior for authors to extrapolate general conclusions about privacy from their situation-specific findings (Kokolakis 2017). This is considered one of the reasons for the research yielding partially contradictory results, particularly regarding the extent to which security considerations influence privacy decisions. This partially inexplicable inconsistency in results, in turn, leads to a lack of cohesion in empirical research. The underlying issue of the alleged inconsistencies, however, lies more in the question of whether findings are really inconsistent (implying that privacy can be regarded as a latent personality trait leading individuals to perceive different surveillance scenarios in a similar manner) or whether privacy is perceived so differently that one cannot compare results across spheres of life at all.

In the theoretical literature, two distinct research strands emerge: cognate-based and value-based definitions (H. J. Smith et al. 2011). The first approach suggests that privacy can be conceptualized as a personality trait, aligning with established concepts in personality psychology. This perspective, rooted in empirical literature, is exemplified by Westin's (1967) taxonomy of privacy concerns, classifying individuals as privacy fundamentalists, privacy pragmatists, and privacy unconcerned. Empirical studies demonstrate that these individuals exhibit similar privacy behaviors across various domains, indicating stable personal dispositions (e.g., Malhotra et al. 2004; Sameer Patil & Kobsa 2005; Schaub & Cranor 2020; H. J. Smith et al. 1996; Taddicken 2014). Conversely, the second approach challenges the notion of privacy as a personality trait. Scholars argue against classifying privacy as a stable disposition, citing weak predictive abilities of privacy measures and the existence of a "privacy paradox" (Awad & Krishnan 2006; Bandara et al. 2018; Mosteller & Poddar 2017). Influenced by Helen Nissenbaum, this perspective suggests that privacy concerns are context-dependent and vary across different life aspects. Nissenbaum (2004; 2015) introduces the concept of "spheres of life" or "social domains," where norms dictate suitable information disclosure within specific contexts, proposing that the value of privacy is contingent upon the sphere of life.

While empirical evidence for both approaches is found, particularly in the realm of research on surveillance or the relinquishment of privacy in commercial contexts, there is limited research on state surveillance. Little investigation exists into whether individuals perceive and evaluate state surveillance measures as such, compare across different state surveillance scenarios, and use this evaluation as a basis for specific decision-making. Alternatively, individuals may not consider state surveillance as a general phenomenon but instead evaluate each state privacy invasion independently. Both variants would contribute to the debate on reconciling diverse research findings. A better understanding would emerge of how spheres of life, potentially due to divergent logics, influence individuals' perceptions and whether the focus should be on distinguishing these spheres or rather on the nature and form of privacy invasion, the extent of information collected, or the justification for the measure.

In Sect. 4.1.1, I have elucidated that certain courts compel the executive to conduct an "overall surveillance calculus." This directive is based on the understanding that various governmental measures may accumulate (into a single overall calculus of state surveillance), reaching a potential maximum threshold of surveillance that is acceptable for citizens (Friedewald et al. 2022). To further inform the political discourse surrounding this comprehensive assessment of surveillance, it would be intriguing to explore to what extent the individuals' appreciation of privacy can be conceptualized as a single personality trait. This would shed light on whether the courts' mandate aligns with individual perspectives on governmental privacy invasions or deviates from them.

Thus, the sixth and final blind spot revolves around the question of whether privacy is a latent personality trait or context-dependent, with two contrasting approaches—cognate-based and value-based definitions—shaping the debate. Limited research on state surveillance accentuates this blind spot, hindering a comprehensive understanding of how individuals perceive and evaluate such measures, potentially influencing the broader discourse on privacy in both academic and political arenas. This leads to the following research question: *Is privacy a stable personality trait or a context-dependent variable?*

4.2 Theoretical Assumptions

Before elucidating how this work addresses the identified gaps in the existing literature, it is crucial to articulate the conceptual framework underpinning this study, specifically outlining the understandings of *subjective value* and of *privacy* that guide my investigation into the nature of the subjective value of privacy.

4.2.1 Defining what is Meant with *Value*

In Sect. 2.1.2, I have previously expounded upon the notion that privacy holds an objective value, both for individuals and society as a whole. In order to explore the extent to which individuals also attribute a *subjective* value to privacy, this section aims to succinctly elucidate my understanding of subjective value. The term "value" carries diverse connotations across various academic disciplines (Brosch et al. 2016). Within the realm of economics, an objective value typically refers to a monetary amount or any other tangible commodity; the subjective value of an outcome for an individual is often referred to as utility. In the domain of social sciences, values are conceptualized as fundamental orientations that aid individuals in selecting from a potentially boundless array of actions and conceivable attitudes. They are regarded as abstract notions of desirability (Kluckhohn

1951). A widely accepted concept is that of a hierarchically organized human system of convictions, in which values hold a pivotal position (Peffley & Hurwitz 1985). They structure an individual's (political) attitudes and serve as justifications for behavior (Converse 1964: 211). In contrast to superficial opinions and (political) attitudes, values are believed to be relatively stable constructs deeply embedded within a person's identity (Rokeach 1973). Since not all values can typically be simultaneously realized, conflicts emerge among them. Thus, the idea of countervalues is widespread (e.g., freedom versus equality, freedom versus security, or privacy versus security). Such hierarchies of values differ between persons, social groups, and societies, often engendering tension-laden clashes of values. As conflicts of values unravel deep-seated, identity-forming convictions, they frequently manifest in highly contentious and unyielding debates (Scherer & Roßteutscher 2019).

Within this study, the term "value" is intended to be employed in a dual sense: firstly, to convey its (positive) valence, and secondly, to encompass the sociological understanding as a relatively stable orientation that fundamentally structures attitudes and shapes behavior. While this study does not address the question of whether privacy inherently embodies a value—given the presumption that values can only fulfill their guiding and meaningful function when their number is limited (Scherer & Roßteutscher 2019: 215)—the focus is rather on probing the nature of the value of privacy. In the ensuing theoretical framework, I will delineate how the value of privacy can be approached.

4.2.2 Defining what is Meant with *Privacy*

In contemporary societies, a multitude of actors, encompassing both governmental and private sector entities, invade privacy, primarily involving the acquisition, retention, and examination of personal data. While lines become increasingly blurred, state-initiated and private sector privacy invasions exhibit disparities in terms of their extent, jurisdiction, objectives, and underlying incentives (Connor & Doan 2021). It thus seems appropriate to differentiate between them. A comprehensive analysis of all facets of privacy, however, would exceed the scope of this thesis. Therefore, I limit my analysis to state privacy invasions since its implicit and explicit citizen–state relationship is of high interest for political science. As outlined in Sect. 2.1.3, the identification of those conducting surveillance is challenging, given the numerous entities that represent 'the state'. In this thesis, state surveillance is broadly defined as the initiation and execution of privacy invasion by the executive branch of the state, contrasting with private or corporate surveillance. Historically, extensive state surveillance was emblematic of authoritarianism (Königs 2022). Authoritarian states renowned for their extensive surveillance systems include, e.g., the Soviet Union, the German Democratic Republic, China, and North Korea (for an overview, see, e.g., Dunnage 2016). However, over the past decades, established liberal democracies have also become increasingly willing to extensively monitor their citizens (Cate & Dempsey 2017). Traditionally, state surveillance has been associated with the state's monopoly on the use of physical force within society (Sætra 2019) and its inevitability (Lyon 1994; 2003): While companies (at least de jure) require (at minimum implicit) consent to gather data from their users or customers, state surveillance, at most, can be characterized by acceptance or support (Nam 2019). Therefore, individuals (in theory) can cease using certain private services if they find the privacy practices of the providers unsatisfactory, but typically face limited options for avoiding state surveillance. This phenomenon impacts the understanding of privacy.

As explicated in Sect. 2.1.1, this thesis adheres to a conceptualization of privacy primarily of an informational nature. According to Koops et al. (2017), informational privacy can be understood as an overarching aspect encompassing various other forms of privacy. They posit that informational privacy manifests itself in every other dimension of privacy, representing an individual's vested interest in restricting access to and control over the use of information pertaining to their own life. Within the context of state surveillance, one can simplify this by envisioning the state's interest in acquiring specific information about its citizens, who in turn presumably have an interest in safeguarding this information. The extent and nature of this interest form the overarching subject of inquiry in this thesis. By restricting the focus on the value of privacy concerning state surveillance, the issue of security inevitably comes to the forefront as the predominant guiding principle directing state surveillance activities (Bajc 2007: 1579), as expounded upon in Sect. 2.3. Drawing upon the prevailing literature within this domain, this thesis specifically examines the influence of security interests on the value of privacy within the privacy calculus and their moderation by antecedents. The following sections introduce the three empirical sub-studies, their underlying research questions, and the respective methodologies employed to address these inquiries.

4.3 Addressing the Identified Gaps and Structure of the Work

The empirical investigation of the identified blind spots, outlined in the upcoming chapters, is structured into three studies, which will be detailed further below. The division into three studies is driven, on the one hand, by idiosyncratic reasons stemming from the availability of existing data collections and the limited extent to which new survey instruments could be incorporated into survey projects that met certain quality criteria—such as the decision to forgo data collection from convenience panels. On the other hand, this division allows for a certain degree of multistage research, enabling the construction of the questionnaire instruments for the second and third studies to be informed by the results of the first study.

The blind spots outlined in the previous chapters can be divided into two groups. Sections 4.1.1–4.1.3 deal with overarching points in the research field, while Sects. 4.1.4–4.1.6 raise specific substantive gaps.

The first point, the lack of empirical knowledge about attitudes towards state surveillance in general, is somewhat of a meta-point, addressed partly through the extensive analysis of the literature in Chapters 2 and 3. Furthermore, by specifically focusing on *informational* privacy, I hope to enhance the applicability of my findings for a broad range of researchers—since everyone seems to agree that there is an informational notion to privacy—allowing my empirical results to be relevant for various theoretical research paradigms within the field.

The lack of cross-national studies is addressed by utilizing data from two cross-national surveys. For the first study, I use data from the *International Social Survey Program* (ISSP) and its 2016 *Role of Government module* (Edlund & Lindh 2019; ISSP Research Group 2018), involving more than 20,000 survey participants across 30 countries. The third study is based on data from the *Public Attitudes towards the Liberal Script* (PALS) survey (Giebler et al. 2023a; 2023b), with over 50,000 respondents across 26 countries. Figure 4.1 illustrates the countries from which individuals were surveyed for this thesis. We observe that individuals were surveyed from not only 41 different countries but also that the combination of both surveys allows me to explore very heterogeneous country contexts, covering all regions of the globe and diverse political and cultural settings. The study of cross-comparative contexts comes with its challenges, both in general and specifically related to privacy and security, which will be revisited later (see Sect. 4.3.2).

Additionally, I address the issue that a large share of the existing research is based on student samples. In the two cross-national studies, mixed sampling strategies were employed: In some countries, data are derived from probability

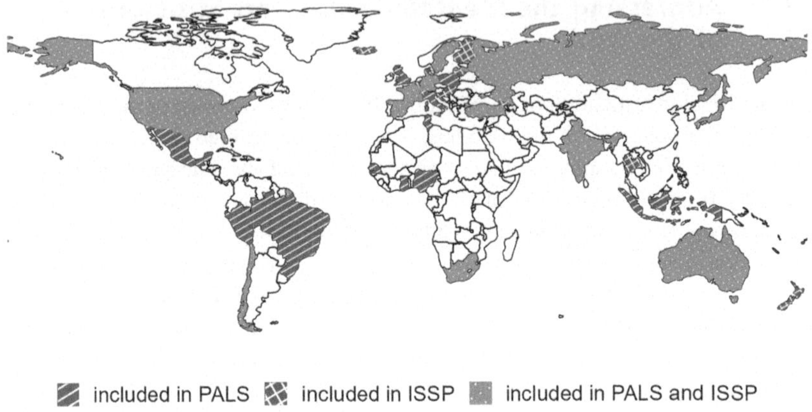

Fig. 4.1 Countries included in the analyses

samples, where respondents were selected through random-walk or random digit dialing procedures. In other countries, quota-sampled online nonprobability panels were used. The latter is also the case for the second study, which is based on data collected as part of the *Conflict of Values in Germany survey* (Giebler et al. forthcoming) with around 5000 respondents in Germany. Thus, all three studies are based on samples that aspire to represent selected characteristics within the population as accurately as possible, allowing me to draw conclusions about the real population from the results. Implications of the (diverging) sampling approaches are addressed in Sect. 4.4.1.

For the third point, it has been highlighted that the majority of studies on state surveillance rely on correlational survey data. I address this by having conducted survey experiments, particularly in studies two and three. The analysis of standard cross-sectional survey data follows the logic that scientists attempt to identify relationships between variables by ex post facto controlling for spurious relationships using multivariate analysis techniques (Auspurg & Hinz 2014: 9). Survey experiments, on the other hand, manipulate a stimulus and randomly assign respondents to different experimental groups. By varying question wording and order, survey experiments can provide crucial insights into the factors influencing how individuals answer survey questions (Gaines et al. 2007).

Using an experiment to measure attitudes has several advantages compared to standard survey data and observational research designs. Survey experiments are explicitly designed to elucidate how humans make multidimensional choices and evaluations (Hainmueller et al. 2015: 2395). Especially for valence issues, like in this case, researchers are interested in the multidimensionality of preferences underlying an individual's single assessment of a policy whose goal is rather undisputed. At the same time, experiments are believed to be particularly suited for measuring delicate and sensitive topics, such as surveillance and privacy and allow researchers to make causal claims (Dietrich & Crabtree 2019: 347). In addition to the significant advantage of enabling causal statements, survey experiments can offer additional distinct methodological benefits. They allow for the comparison and testing of case-specific findings. Thereby the method can help to overcome two interrelated weaknesses: (a) general causal claims based on case-specific findings (Guzzini 2011: 329), and (b) biases resulting from case selection (i.e., when cases are chosen given particular values of the dependent variable) (Geddes 1990) and analysis (when researchers' normative views permeate the analysis) (Baele & Sterck 2015: 1122; Floyd 2010).

While survey experiments have been very popular in market research since the 1950s, including the studying of consumers' privacy attitudes, they have only gained the attention of scholars interested in attitudes towards surveillance in the last decade. Applications include factorial survey experiments on attitudes towards state surveillance (e.g., Garcia & Geva 2016; Ziller & Helbling 2021); discrete choice experiments, e.g., on attitudes towards security measures in public transport (Sunil Patil et al. 2014); framing experiments on the acceptance of new security-oriented technologies (e.g., Bali 2009; Vermeersch & de Pauw 2017) and on state internet surveillance (Siegel 2013); stated preference experiments, e.g., on electronic health data storage, access, and usage (Sunil Patil et al. 2016); and list experiments, e.g., on support for the application of facial recognition technologies by the police (Bromberg et al. 2020).

In the following, I provide a more detailed description of the three studies and discuss how each one addresses the three additional identified gaps in the literature.

Study 1: The moderation of the value of privacy by security promises (Chap. 5)
In the first study, I aim to contribute to addressing two of the identified blind spots. Firstly, it has been observed that the role of the privacy calculus within the APCO model is rather ambiguous. I thus seek to explore the extent to which the value of privacy is moderated by the privacy calculus. Specifically, I focus on the (alleged) benefit of security which governments often promise to justify surveillance measures and gain them public support. It is usually claimed that individuals are more willing to have freedom and privacy restricted than waiving a promise of increased security (Trüdinger 2020: 319). However, empirical

evidence to support this claim has been scarce—especially from a comparative perspective. Simultaneously, in this study, I tackle the question of the role of the audience in securitization processes, a dimension we have learned has been neglected in empirical literature. Thus, I address the question by asking:

First, *do security promises have an effect on the subjective value of privacy?*
Framing effects are not universal but shaped through individual characteristics by serving as "critical intervening variable[s] between opinion and information" (Haider-Markel & Joslyn 2001: 522). It is thus likely that there are variables, both on the individual and the macro level, that moderate the postulated relationship, namely influencing its direction and/or strength.

Second, *which micro and macro factors moderate the effect of the security-based justification on the subjective value of privacy?*
In order to address these questions, I utilize data form the ISSP. In doing so, advantage is taken of the fact that specific questions reference national security, while others do not, allowing me to compare responses within respondents. In the analysis, the unjustified statement provides "the baseline preference against which to judge the impact of framed conditions" (Dennis Chong & Druckman 2007: 106). The additional individual-level information contained within the dataset enables me to differentiate between various demographic characteristics. Of particular significance is the variable related to voting decisions, which, when combined with additional data, allows me to not only assess support for the government but also to determine left-right political party preference through the use of data from the Manifesto Project (Volkens et al. 2020). Furthermore, the number and diversity of countries included in the dataset permit an examination of macro-level features, which are also integrated into the analysis, e.g., the Liberal Democracy Index from the "Varieties of Democracy Project" (V-Dem) (Coppedge et al. 2021).

Study 2: The influence of benefits other than security on the value of privacy (Chap. 6)
While the first study focusses primarily on the influence of security promises, the second study tries to disentangle the privacy calculus even further and investigates which other costs and benefits individuals might consider. Support of policies in general, and of privacy-related policies in specific (Friedewald, van Lieshout, Rung, et al. 2016), potentially also depends on financial and non-financial costs and benefits, the design of the policies as well as the context in which they are implemented. The second study thus seeks to analyze:

First, *which benefits other than security and which costs influence the value of privacy and to what extent?*
The effects of the policies' characteristics might differ between different populations. I am interested in the extent to which individual characteristics moderate the effects. This leads to the question:

Second, *which micro factors moderate the effect of these costs and benefits on the subjective value of privacy?*
An underexplored aspect in the APCO framework is the role of contexts (Buck et al. 2022). While it is acknowledged that cultural differences can influence privacy concerns, the framework does not adequately focus on comparing subjective and objective costs. It is well-documented in the literature that, for instance, in the realm of security, the differentiation between objective states and subjective perceptions can diverge significantly, yet simultaneously play a crucial role in shaping attitudes (Zedner 2003). I thus try to answer the question:

Third, *how do subjective and objective risks and costs influence the value of privacy?*
To answer these research questions, I conducted a pre-registered factorial survey experiment in Germany in November 2021 as part of the *Conflict of Values in Germany survey*. I do not restrict the analysis to the experimental variables but also include respondents' characteristics and other stated attitudes. The collection of postal codes allows me to merge the survey data with Police Crime Statistics of the Federal Republic of Germany (Bundeskriminalamt 2021a; 2021b) to assess the objective risk of crime the respondents are facing.

Study 3: The value of privacy in different spheres of life (Chap. 7)
In the first two studies, I consider the privacy-security nexus and the approach to the subjective value of privacy particularly in relation to surveillance for the prevention, detection, or clearance of crime and terrorist attacks. This strong focus is also reflected in the existing literature, which (at least prior to the COVID-19 pandemic) concentrates almost exclusively on just that sphere of life with respect to state surveillance. Yet crime and terrorism are far from the only objective and subjective threats that people face. In the third study, I want to discuss the question:

To what extent does the value of privacy differ between spheres of life?
For this purpose, I compare individual privacy attitudes across the spheres of terrorism, health concern, and financial fraud. These three areas are not only regularly found in surveys on the greatest subjective threats to the public (e.g., Bader et al. 2020; R + V 2022), but realistic security promises can be formulated

for the government side in each case. Finally, the validity of the combination of the stated attitudes is tested by assessing its ability to predict privacy-related survey behavior of the respondents.

The study is based on data from a pre-registered factorial survey experiment which was part of PALS. Therein, I investigate how people rate a possible increase in security—in this case introduced as experts' expected effectiveness—compared with privacy invasions for different scenarios. In the joint analysis of the three scenarios, I seek to answer the question of whether privacy is perceived rather sphere-dependent, meaning that individuals make a separate privacy decision for each sphere of life, or whether privacy can rather be understood as personality trait that is relatively stable across spheres of life. In this context, I also aim to ascertain to what extent privacy behavior can be predicted based on the value attributed to it by the respondents.

Applying the APCO Model

The research endeavors of the three studies can be illustrated with the APCO model. Earlier, it has been emphasized that the APCO model is the most prominent macro model in assessing privacy attitudes. In this thesis, I apply the APCO model as follows (see Fig. 4.2): From existing research various antecedents are derived that are have shown to influence an individual's attitude toward privacy in previous studies, as in the original model. As elucidated in the preceding section, the utilization of the term "value of privacy" for the current study appears more appropriate for several reasons than the emphasis on "privacy concerns" employed in the original APCO model. The value of privacy either directly influences the outcome or is moderated by the privacy calculus, a subjective weighing of risks/costs against benefits. However, it is pertinent to contemplate that antecedents may not only forecast the value of privacy but also the extent to which it is integrated into the privacy calculus—one focus of Study 1—and influence what is happening within the privacy calculus—as addressed in Study 2. Thus, the original APCO model is supplemented with two additional interrelations, depicted by the dashed connecting lines in Fig. 4.2. The outcome in this thesis is the (stated) acceptance of privacy invasion, i.e., its reflection in individual behavior—which is one of the issues dealt with in Study 3. Furthermore, Study 3 addresses the comprehensive examination of the APCO model in various contexts. For the purpose of this study, the APCO model thus assumes an organizing function and is not exhaustively examined in detail.[5]

[5] The APCO model is said to not take into account the influence of behavioral economic and psychological factors in detail. This has prompted scholars to propose the *enhanced* APCO model that focusses on privacy *behavior* and considers amongst others, biases, bounded

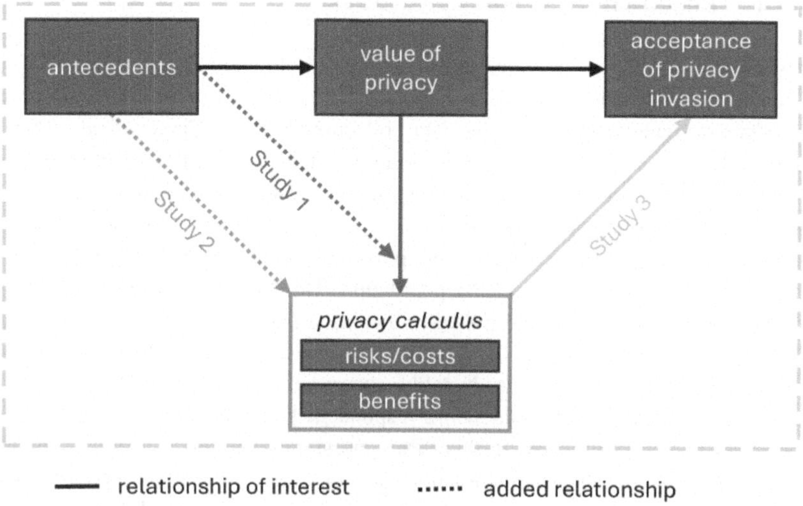

Fig. 4.2 Theoretical framework. (*Note:* The solid lines are adopted from the original model, while the dashed lines represent relationships that have been added to illustrate connections that are newly tested in this study. *Study 1:* The moderation of the value of privacy by security promises; *Study 2:* The influence of benefits other than security on the value of privacy; *Study 3:* The value of privacy in different spheres of life)

Given the substantial situational and context-dependent nature of privacy decisions, the following studies incorporate additional social-psychological, sociological, and economic approaches. This approach aligns with common practice, as demonstrated by Christoph Buck et al. (2022).

4.4 Methodological Assumptions

As outlined in the preceding section, all three studies in this research employ quantitative survey data. This entails several implications.

---

rationality as well as the individual effort (Dinev et al. 2015). In this thesis, I will only touch upon those issues peripherally since my focus primarily lies on stated attitudes and less on the behavioral component of the model.

4.4.1 Researching Privacy Attitudes

Despite the prevalence of quantitative surveys in studying privacy attitudes, it is acknowledged that participation reluctance, driven by privacy concerns, may introduce systematic bias into the data collection process (Singer et al. 2003). Studies suggest that individuals harboring skepticism toward surveillance are less likely to be represented in central phone registers or commercially compiled lists of internet addresses (Wall 2005). As a result, there exists a likelihood of systematic bias in the collected data, potentially underestimating the extent of privacy concerns within the broader population. This bias, evidenced by a historical decline in survey response linked to increased public anxieties about privacy (Couper et al. 1998; Goyder & Leiper 1985; Singer et al. 2003) necessitates careful interpretation of results. Notably, surveys themselves may be perceived as a form of surveillance, influencing respondent behavior (Haggerty & Gazso 2005; Marx 2007). However, in this thesis, no significant correlation was found between (proxy measures of) national surveillance levels and non-response rates in the cross-national surveys conducted (see Appendices D.7 and F.10).

For cross-national surveys (Studies 1 and 3), methodological considerations extend beyond general survey challenges to encompass the quality and comparability of individual national surveys. Two key sources of error are highlighted: the uniform functioning of measurement instruments across translations and the representativeness of samples drawn in different countries (measurement error) as well as the representativeness of the respective country samples (coverage/sampling/non-response error). Within PALS, these challenges were addressed through rigorous processes such as cognitive interviews, pilot studies, and standardized translations (Giebler et al. 2023b). For a detailed discussion concerning translation in the ISSP context, see Dorothée Behr and Evi Scholz (2011). Cultural variations in privacy perceptions further underscore the complexity of studying attitudes toward surveillance, including differing societal perceptions regarding privacy and surveillance, as well as variations in attitudes towards broader concepts like public/private or family, ethnicity, and class identity (Wood et al. 2007).

Regarding the issue of coverage/sampling/non-response error, both ISSP and PALS employ diverse survey modes and, consequently, different sampling methods in various countries. Different survey techniques are believed to have distinct implications, potentially influencing the participation and response behavior of respondents. Robustness checks demonstrate that no significant mode differences emerge, as detailed in Appendices D.1 and F.3.

All three studies utilize data from surveys where privacy is just one aspect among several investigated issues. H. Watson et al. (2017) argue that surveys lacking a specific focus on people's attitudes toward surveillance or privacy-related topics may be insufficient for gaining additional insights into the nature or privacy attitudes, since, amongst others, space constraints lead to a systematic neglect of specific term definitions and the interconnectedness of surveillance, security, and privacy. As highlighted earlier, there are limited cross-national surveys exclusively dedicated to this complex set of issues. Consequently, researchers often resort to individual items within general cross-national survey projects (see Edlund and Lindh (2018; 2019) for a debate on the inclusion of surveillance items in the ISSP). Adhering to H. Watson et al.'s recommendations, I aim to address the interplay between privacy and security more specifically in Studies 2 and 3, where I actively contributed to the survey design.

Alternatives to large-scale surveys used to study attitudes towards privacy and security include qualitative interviews (e.g., Dixon et al. 2003; Elueze & Quan-Haase 2018; Menichelli 2017), focus group discussions (e.g., Degli Esposti et al. 2017; Degli Esposti & Santiago-Gomez 2015; Luther & Radovic 2012; Pavone et al. 2015; Tsapogas 2017), and analyzing people's online behavior, such as search engine queries or social media use (e.g., Kosinski et al. 2014; Stoycheff 2016; Stoycheff, Liu, et al. 2018). As with other areas of attitude research, there is an ongoing debate about the most suitable methods for exploring individual attitudes. The choice of methodology hinges on research interests: While large-scale population surveys usually aim to draw samples as representative as possible to make statements about the entire population, more qualitative approaches focus on presenting the range of possible attitudes (Pavone et al. 2015) or gaining a deeper understanding of the relationships between various constructs.

A substantial portion of the data, particularly in Studies 2 and 3, is derived from online panels, namely computer-assisted web interviews (CAWI). From a total survey quality perspective (Biemer 2010: 818), online surveys offer many advantages over other modes: they are relatively cost-effective (Olson et al. 2021: 14) and can provide fast and timely data (De Leeuw et al. 2019: 151). Thanks to advanced technology, dynamic questionnaires can be designed, allowing for complex questions and experiments, as well as skip patterns and filtering. Measurement can be enhanced through graphical presentation (Olson et al. 2021: 13), and due to the absence of an interviewer, responses may be less influenced by social desirability (De Leeuw et al. 2019: 151)—which is particularly important for questions about sensitive topics such as privacy and surveillance. Furthermore, metadata (e.g., response times) can routinely be collected (Conrad et al. 2006:

246). However, a disadvantage specific to online surveys is the unequal availability, quality, and reliability of technology infrastructure, as well as potential technological illiteracy in some regions. Even though internet penetration is high in most countries, especially in those of the Global North, it is lower in others. As a result, the online and offline populations differ significantly in important characteristics such as gender, age, and education—even in countries with relatively high internet coverage (Sterrett et al. 2017). In the case of PALS, national internet penetration was taken into account when selecting the survey mode, and in countries with low internet coverage, computer-assisted personal interviews (CAPI) were conducted (see Giebler et al. 2023b).

A pervasive discourse surrounds the issue of representativeness in research methodologies. Probability samples, obtained through random sampling, are widely regarded as the benchmark in research methodologies (Kohler 2019). Nevertheless, the escalating rates of non-response and persistent challenges in reaching hard-to-access populations have introduced representativeness concerns even within probability samples.[6] Moreover, the burgeoning costs associated with face-to-face interviews have spurred interest in survey methods that are both time-efficient and cost-effective. The emergence of online sampling techniques and the prevalence of online panels have sparked a reevaluation of the applicability of nonprobability samples in the realm of social sciences (Baker et al. 2013).

A defining characteristic of nonprobability samples lies in the unknown or unquantifiable selection probability of respondents, stemming from the absence of a sampling frame from which respondents are drawn. Respondents voluntarily include themselves in the sample from an indeterminate universe, such as responding to a survey invitation link or joining an online panel. This self-selection process can introduce selection bias, leading to a sample that diverges from the broader population from which the researcher seeks to make inferences. Any variable influencing the selection of respondents into the sample, such as internet access, and subsequently, socio-demographic characteristics like class or age, introduces bias into the sample (Kohler et al. 2019; Mercer et al. 2017). In contrast, random sampling in theory circumvents such biases, as the random selection of respondents should, theoretically, eliminate any differences

[6] The literature engages in a debate on the continued significance of distinguishing between probability and nonprobability panels. Predominantly, a considerable number of internet panels integrate methodologies that include a certain degree of randomization. Additionally, scholars have observed that scarcely any survey exclusively relies on a pure probability sample. This is attributed to factors such as incomplete or outdated address registers and the prevalence of high non-response rates, both of which contribute to the introduction of biases (Ansolabehere & Schaffner 2016: 77).

between the sample and the population. Another challenge associated with nonprobability sampling is the inability to estimate the magnitude of bias or the precision of outcomes. This is due to the fact that methods for estimating inferential statistics, such as confidence intervals, necessitate random samples. While the data for Studies 2 and 3 partly originate from nonprobability panels, the stratification based on selected sociodemographic characteristics, coupled with post-stratification weighting, which aims to align the sample distributions with known characteristics of the target population within the country, contributes significantly to enhancing the precision of nonprobability panels (Cornesse et al. 2020).

In addition, there are specific research contexts where the utilization of nonprobability samples is deemed appropriate (Kohler 2019). For instance, nonprobability samples can be conducive to drawing causal inferences, especially when the homogeneity of the treatment effect across respondents can be reasonably assumed. This assumption may be plausible when the sample is derived from a distinct, homogeneous population or when the causal effect is universally applicable. Even in cases where assuming homogeneity of the treatment effect is not tenable, nonprobability samples can serve as a valuable tool for discerning interactions of the treatment effect across subpopulations within the sample. Nonprobability samples find utility in conducting survey experiments, particularly those employing multidimensional factorial designs (Auspurg & Hinz 2014). Inferences drawn from survey experiments based on nonprobability samples have been demonstrated to align relatively closely with those derived from probability samples (Coppock 2019; Mullinix et al. 2015). Given that studies 2 and 3 leverage data from survey experiments, the fact that these partly originate "only" from quota-based nonprobability panels should still yield meaningful and applicable results and implications as well as make them comparable to data from probability sample.

4.4.2 Analytical Approach

In the two cross-national studies, I assume that respondents are nested within countries. Additionally, Studies 2 and 3 are survey experiments, and Study 1 is assumed to have a survey-experimental nature, in which outcome variables are nested within respondents (Auspurg & Hinz 2014: 85–104).

For this reason, I employ multilevel analysis. The theoretical underpinning of multilevel analysis recognizes that individual attitudes and behaviors are influenced not only by individual characteristics but also by contextual conditions

(Huckfeldt 1986: 1). The notion of the contextual dependence of individual attitudes and behaviors is widely accepted in the social sciences (Barton 1968; Books & Prysby 1991; Coleman 1986; Dalton & Anderson 2011). Various theoretical approaches have been developed to explain context effects (e.g., Burbank 1997; Huckfeldt & Sprague 1995; Putnam 1966).

In a multilevel analysis, the presumed effects of individual and contextual characteristics on a dependent variable are integrated into one model. Such a model is expected to better capture reality compared to individual and aggregate data analyses. For the implementation of multilevel analysis, a stepwise approach is recommended (Hox et al. 2017: 42–46; Snijders & Bosker 2011: 102–8). While the decision to pursue a multilevel analysis should primarily stem from theoretical considerations (Tausendpfund 2020: 130), one can mathematically compute the proportion of variance in the dependent variable attributed to the contextual level, via the intraclass correlation coefficient (ICC). A larger ICC underscores the significance of accounting for contextual factors. However, the literature presents diverse recommendations for a minimum ICC threshold (Jäckle & Schärdel 2017: 154), contingent on the research question and group size. Existing "guidelines" propose an minimum ICC range of 0.05 to 0.3 (Tausendpfund 2020: 130).

Multilevel analysis has been shown to be less reliable when the number of contextual-level units is too small (Hox 2010: 233; Raudenbush & Bryk 2002: 283). Therefore, there is an ongoing debate about the minimum number of countries required for reliable estimates.[7] For analyses with too few cluster-level units, the literature (e.g., Elff et al. 2021; Stegmueller 2013) recommends using restricted maximum likelihood estimation (REML) instead of maximum likelihood estimation (ML). Consequently, I conducted robustness checks using REML in Studies 1 and 3 (see Appendices D.1 and F.3).

In the two cross-national studies, I consider all countries equally. In contrast to a proposed "population-scaled weight," which makes an adjustment to ensure that each country is represented in proportion to its population size (Kaminska & Lynn 2017: 127) and thus for example allows for statements on a specific region, I opted to calculate a weight that takes each country into account equally as proposed by Christian Welzel (2013: 143).[8] In addition, post-stratification weights

[7] While Austin (2010) and Stegmueller (2013) suggest that five contextual-level units might be sufficient, Paccagnella (2011) argues for a minimum of ten, Moineddin et al. (2007) propose at least 30, and Maas and Hox (2005) find that 50 higher-level units are necessary.

[8] There is a conceptual distinction between equally weighted and population-weighted estimates of attitudes; they measure different phenomena. Equal consideration assesses attitudes between countries as a whole, whereas population-weighted estimates gauge attitudes among all citizens of each country of the world. Given that country samples are not representative

are used to align the data with the distributions of certain variables in the population of the respective national population. There is disagreement in the literature about the use of weights in the analysis of survey experiments (Miratrix et al. 2018). I chose to use weights throughout to make the results of treatment-only effects comparable to those in which they are interacted with nonexperimental variables. When interactions are included, the respective results are normally presented as marginal effects to illustrate the relationship (R. Williams 2012).

of the world population—although PALS employs a structured country selection approach (Giebler et al. 2023b: 12–14)—my results should not be construed as indicative of representativeness for all global residents.

5 The Promise of Security

In the preceding chapters, I have explored the nuanced discourse surrounding the presumed trade-off between privacy and security, acknowledging the ongoing theoretical and attitudinal debates.[1] The juxtaposition of these concepts becomes palpable in individuals' daily lives, particularly amid privacy invasions, where states justify surveillance by underscoring individual benefits, collective welfare, and the imperative of countering crime and terrorism. Within public discourse, the predominant legitimizing principle for surveillance is the assurance of security, a narrative that governments employ to rationalize potential encroachments on civil liberties (Bajc 2007: 1579). The strategic framing of issues as matters of security imbues them with urgency, granting authorities broader latitude to enact comprehensive measures (Bajc 2007: 1579).[2] In this context, security is construed

Supplementary Information The online version contains supplementary material available at https://doi.org/10.1007/978-3-658-46462-2_5.

[1] Some of the findings of this study have been published in Antoine (2022).

[2] The evidence of the positive (and even causal) relationship between surveillance and security, however, is inconclusive and fairly contradictory. Systematic reviews of related research for example find that CCTV reduces crime only to a small degree. CCTV is most effective in reducing vehicle crime in car parks or parking lots; and it has little to no effect on crime in public transport and city center settings (Welsh & Farrington 2002). Other research indicates that, instead of deterring or preventing crime, surveillance merely displaces crime in various forms (M. Clarke 1994) and several studies conclude that surveillance has no effect at all (Ditton & Short 1999; M. Gill et al. 2006; Phillips 1999). For other forms of surveillance like internet surveillance, it is difficult or even impossible to quantify effectiveness of surveillance. Cayford and Pieter's (2018) study supposes that there is no evidence of information technologies' surveillance being effective in improving security.

L. Antoine, *The Subjective Value of Privacy*, Wahlen und politische Einstellungen, https://doi.org/10.1007/978-3-658-46462-2_5

in terms of citizens' safety, synonymous with "freedom from fear" or "human security" (Pavone & Degli Esposti 2012: 558). Despite individuals recognizing that privacy and security need not be antagonistic, a persistent narrative reinforces the notion that concessions in privacy are a prerequisite for the enjoyment of security.

Remarkably, the literature predominantly focuses on the debatable nature of trade-offs, equilibrium, or balance, neglecting a thorough examination of how security *promises* might shape privacy attitudes. Promissory politics, particularly the pledge of security, is acknowledged as a significant influence on individuals' preferences (Aradau 2014). People might take security promises into account when forming their opinions on policies since they (a) permanently want to diminish the threat of possible future damages (e.g., Beck 1992) and (b) are exposed to the state whose legitimacy is based on promising security to its citizens (Campbell, 1992: 56; see also Hobbes). Governments, leveraging the increasing demand for security, increasingly justify policies by emphasizing the need to safeguard security (Königs 2022).

Designating an issue as a security matter lies at the core of securitization theory, wherein securitization actors—in this case the government—aim to persuade an audience of the necessity of certain measures in the name of security. Securitization only occurs when the audience accepts the move as valid (Buzan et al. 1997: 25). However, the role of the audience in the securitization process remains inadequately explored (Balzacq 2005: 179; Côté 2016; Floyd 2010: 50; M. C. Williams 2010: 212). While some authors acknowledge the potential cultural, social, and geographic influences on attitudes towards privacy and security (e.g., Budak et al. 2017; Menichelli 2017), a comprehensive investigation into the degree of variation and associated factors regarding the susceptibility towards the acceptance of securitization moves is lacking. This chapter seeks not to polarize privacy against security but rather to unravel the role of security *promises* in evaluating government privacy interventions, forming part of the broader privacy calculus (H. J. Smith et al. 2011). My central research questions are: (1) Do privacy attitudes differ when surveillance is framed with the promise of security? (2) How can differences in attitudes towards security-justified and non-justified surveillance be explained?

Drawing on data from the *International Social Survey Programme* (ISSP) and additional country-level data at the country level, I conduct a cross-national multilevel analysis encompassing 30 countries and over 20,000 respondents. The literature suggests that justifying privacy invasion measures in the name of security tends to increase individuals' willingness to sacrifice freedoms. However, empirical evidence supporting this hypothesis on a cross-national scale is lacking. My findings reveal a significant positive effect of a security frame on the acceptance of privacy invasion measures. Notably, this effect varies substantially based on individual predispositions at the micro level and contextual factors at the macro level, specifically the liberal democratic nature of the respondent's country. The framing effect strongly correlates with the level of liberal democracy, with no significant correlation found with support for the government or political orientation. These results are particularly intriguing in light of the apparent divergence between the presumed demand for increased security and growing skepticism about privacy invasion measures. This implies that justifying privacy restrictions for security reasons encounters greater resistance in less liberal-democratic societies.

5.1 Security Promises as Mode of Government

Governments are inherently driven by the imperative to secure positive evaluations of their policies, either to facilitate smoother implementation or to enhance their chances of re-election. Extensive research on public opinion consistently highlights the impact of framing—a process encompassing the selective presentation, emphasis, and exclusion of information that shapes a coherent interpretation and evaluation of events (P. Norris et al. 2004: 4). Coined by E. Goffmann (1974) framing is a rhetorical tool employed to set and influence the public agenda, particularly by politicians seeking support for their policies. Frames, whether centered on national security or the promise of enhancing citizens' safety, subtly emphasize certain values and core beliefs (Daniel Chong 1996).

As discussed in Chap. 3, the prevalent approach in surveillance and privacy research often involves contrasting security with liberty (see contributions in Friedewald et al. 2017). This approach is frequently applied in the form of discrete-choice models (e.g., Sunil Patil et al. 2014) or as a conflict of values. Based on the assumption that competing values and demands in a society can only be realized at the expense of each other, privacy and security are conceptualized as a virtual zero-sum game. The legitimacy of this model is contentious, with scholars expressing skepticism about its validity. Despite political framing, individuals generally do not appear to starkly contrast privacy and security (e.g., van den Broek et al. 2017: 15). Public responses to surveillance vary across individuals and countries (e.g., Dencik & Cable 2017: 764). The question, however, to what extent individuals react differently to security promises, i.e., frames, and the factors underlying these differences has been overlooked in current literature.

Government policies—like surveillance measures (Nakhaie & de Lint 2013)—are assumed to garner support from citizens who perceive potential benefits from these policies (Trüdinger 2020: 319). Given the fundamental status of security as a human need, aligned with framing and securitization literature, I posit the following hypothesis:

H1: *Compared to no justification given, a security frame enhances acceptance of state privacy invasion.*[3]

5.2 Whom do Promises Convince?

Framing effects, serving as "critical intervening variable[s] between opinion and information" (Haider-Markel & Joslyn 2001: 522), are not universally experienced but are shaped by individual characteristics. To understand the nuanced dynamics of framing, I explore variables that moderate the hypothesized relationship's direction and strength. While securitization literature has not extensively delved into *who* is (more likely to be) securitized,[4] recent interest has grown in understanding how framing moderates and mediates attitudes (Borah 2011: 252).

Considering the limited human capacity to process information (S. T. Fiske & Taylor 1984), scholars draw varying conclusions about framing effects. Some suggest a mitigating effect: the introduction of a frame in attitude formation supersedes other relevant considerations, leading to a shift in focus, termed "hydraulic patterns" by Nam-Jin Lee et al. (2008). This shift was empirically supported for example in a study on attitudes toward the framing of counterterrorism policies by Mary E. Brinson and Michael Stohl (2012). Others propose that framing intensifies preexisting attitudes. Ziva Kunda's (1990) theory of "motivated reasoning" contends that individuals align new policy-related information

[3] This is not to say that endorsing reasoned surveillance measures cannot be a rational decision. In his essay on the security-liberty debate, Solove (2008a) suggests that an individual's or executive's preference for one or the other should depend heavily on external factors, such as how likely a threat to liberty is or how effective a countermeasure would be. While the latter will not be varied across respondents, I seek to control for the former, namely the country's terror attack legacy. In addition, security is not the only justification that makes individuals possibly giving up their privacy. Market research literature has shown that individuals are willing to give up privacy if they receive other barter objects like monetary discounts (e.g., Acquisti et al. 2013: 253) or non-monetary equivalents such as convenience (e.g., Viscusi & Zeckhauser 2003: 116) in exchange.

[4] See e.g., Côté's (2016) criticism of the omission and the lack of common understanding of the role of the audience from the research agenda. See also Chap. 4.

with existing preconceptions, fostering belief polarization (Cook & Lewandowsky 2016). Individuals with different preconceptions may become even more distant from each other by the same new information. This polarization effect is particularly pronounced on politically contentious issues (e.g., Dharshing et al. 2017).

In addressing the second research question, this study examines how respondents' attitudes toward state surveillance differ when a security justification is introduced. Two micro-level predictors—government support and political orientation—are derived from the literature. Cross-national research consistently demonstrates that contextual factors influence individuals' attitudes. Consequently, a macro-level predictor, a country's level of liberal democracy, is included to account for inter-country variations.

Existing literature extensively explores the effects of government support on individuals' attitudes toward proposed policies. Trust in the government positively correlates with citizens' willingness to acquiesce to its demands and regulations (Levi & Stoker 2000). This finding extends to the acceptance of surveillance measures, where state surveillance approval aligns with perceived governmental trustworthiness (van den Broek et al. 2017: 27; Friedewald et al. 2015: 19; Nakhaie & de Lint 2013: 160; Davis & Silver 2004): State surveillance garners approval when individuals trust the government to handle assessed data with care. Simultaneously, there is an implicit assumption that individuals trust the government not to exploit the urgency of a security need. In the securitization literature, the effectiveness of securitization moves hinges on the securitizing agents, typically the government, emphasizing the existential nature of a threat to justify emergency actions (Buzan et al. 1997: 6). Success in securitization requires the establishment of a necessary intersubjective relationship, wherein the agent convinces the audience of the exceptionality of the action; without this relationship, securitization is deemed unsuccessful (see e.g., Vultee 2010b: 88). Consequently, I hypothesize that highlighting national security as a justification for surveillance measures should be particularly persuasive to those who tend to be supportive of the government:

H2: Government support is positively correlated with the susceptibility to the security frame.[5]

[5] On the other hand, it could also be argued that security justifications have little impact on the acceptance from those who already support the government but rather, by shifting the issue into the non-normal, primarily influence those who (in non-exceptional times) would rather oppose the government. Due to the lack of empirical evidence of this direction of relationship, I test hypothesis H2 in its above form.

Policy researchers have demonstrated that the potency of framing effects is intricately tied to political orientation (Dennis Chong & Druckman 2013; Dharshing et al. 2017). Left-right ideology is seen as a "product of motivated social cognition" (Jost & Hunyady 2005: 264). Supporters from both ideological camps typically exhibit disagreement across various issues, lacking a shared foundational understanding concerning aspects such as taxes, migration, or sexuality. This everyday distinction between the political left and right is believed to reflect ubiquitous ideological distinctions in the approach to threat and uncertainty (Jost & Napier 2011: 91). John T. Jost and Jaime L. Napier (2011) provide evidence that conservatism is associated with uncertainty avoidance and heightened attention to threats, while liberalism exhibits the opposite tendencies.

Empirical evidence overwhelmingly suggests that individuals identifying with a rightist political orientation tend to be more supportive of surveillance measures (e.g., Friedewald et al. 2015: 21). Van den Broek et al. (2017: 29) rationalize these findings by noting that, in general, left-wing oriented respondents are more critical of public actors' activities, while issues related to "law and order" form a core aspect of rightist policies. Drawing from Jost and Napier's (2011) insights, it is posited that rightist attitudes are closely linked to uncertainty avoidance and heightened threat perception, making individuals more susceptible to security frames. Conversely, leftist individuals are hypothesized to be less inclined to endorse government emphases on national security.

H3: Rightist political attitudes are positively correlated with the susceptibility to the security frame.

According to Corey Brettschneider (2010: 77), a nation ' s commitment to democratic governance implies an obligation to safeguard individual privacy. The concept of collective self-determination, exemplified through political participation opportunities, presupposes a foundational level of individual self-determination. In democratic settings, citizens must be endowed with the right to autonomously manage their private affairs. Notably, robust state surveillance is commonly associated with autocratic regimes within public discourse. Historical instances of autocratic surveillance states, such as Nazi Germany and the Soviet Union, persist alongside contemporary examples like China. Nonetheless, a clear correlation between the degree of democracy and the intensity of surveillance is not evident. Empirical evidence indicates instances where countries scoring high in democracy indices implement substantial surveillance measures, as observed in the case of Denmark (Pavone et al. 2015: 70). The prevailing argument maintains that governments employ surveillance primarily to uphold order and control (Weller

2012: 58), often justified broadly under the pretext of countering *enemies of the state* (Bigo 2012: 280). The differentiating factor between democracies and autocracies lies in the determination of who constitutes the "enemy of the state," or the source of insecurity. In democracies, a minimal consensus on defining this source is imperative, whereas non-democratic countries may lack such a requirement. Given the lower accountability of non-democratic governments for their surveillance measures compared to democratic counterparts (Dandeker 2005: 40–42), security concerns are more frequently invoked as justifications for surveillance serving alternative purposes (Wirth et al. 2019: 1340). Consequently, security rationales should find greater acceptance when articulated by governments in liberal democracies than in autocratic regimes.

H4: The susceptibility to the security frame is positively correlated with a country's level of liberal democracy.

5.3 Data and Methodology

In contrast to traditional framing experiments, this study does not derive data by comparing framing effects among different experimental groups with a reference group. Instead, the data are obtained by comparing responses to two questions from the same respondents. The data source is the ISSP's 2016 Role of Government module (ISSP Research Group 2018). Question (a) inquires, "Do you think that your government should or should not have the right to monitor e-mails and any other information exchanged on the Internet?" Question (b) asks, "Some people think that governments should have the right to take certain measures in the name of national security. Others disagree. Do you think that your government should or should not have the right to collect information about anyone living in your country without their knowledge?" Each question employs a four-point Likert scale.

This study leverages the assumption that these questions represent "alternative descriptions of what is essentially the same decision problem" (LeBoeuf & Shafir 2003: 77). Question (b) introduces the phrase "in the name of national security" while question (a) does not. Looking at the speech act itself, the utterance of security can be understood as a *promise* implying that audience acceptance is vital for successful securitization (Wæver 1995: 55). Simultaneously, it can be interpreted as a *justification* understood as the government explaining itself to the public (Waldron 1987: 149). According to Tabitha Bonilla (2022: 15), promises as justifications have become increasingly critical to political strategy. Given the focus on assessing the success of this promise, question (a) is considered *unjustified*, and question (b) is deemed *security-justified*. In my analysis, the unjustified statement provides "the baseline preference against which to judge the impact of framed conditions" (Dennis Chong & Druckman 2007: 106). While this design does not strictly enable me to draw causal relationship, it is well suited for analyzing the relationship between response patterns due to the size of the dataset.

While acknowledging the distinction between the security frame in the two questions, it is important to note variations in the forms of surveillance they address. Question (a) is more specific, addressing the monitoring of e-mails and online information, while question (b) involves the more general concept of collecting information. Recognizing that respondents may hold stronger opinions on specific questions (Kaplan et al. 2013), the study assumes that the effect of the security-justification might be underestimated rather than overestimated.

Moreover, I can only assume that individuals associate the second sentence of question (b) ("Do you think your government should...") with the initial statement regarding the provision of security. If they do not, the impact of the justification will be reduced, potentially leading to an additional underestimation of the effect of the security-justification. At the same time, one could argue that any justification, whether related to security, or, e.g., money or convenience, might bolster the acceptance of a measure. Also, it remains opaque whether respondents see a salient difference between "monitoring" and "collecting information"—the former being more passive and the latter being rather acquisitive—and their equivalents in the translated versions of the questionnaire. In addition, given that items and modules are not randomized in the ISSP, there is the potential for anchoring effects. However, since question (a) is consistently posed before question (b), the security frame, at the very least, cannot influence attitudes toward the unjustified item. While recognizing the differences between the two questions and their order within the survey, the cumulative effect of the assumptions implies that the impact of the security-justification is likely to be underestimated, affirming the conservative nature of my assumptions rather than an excessively liberal stance.

To analyze individual response behavior, the study employs stacked data, duplicating responses for each respondent and creating a dummy variable to distinguish originals (0) from copies (1). A new variable, "attitude towards surveillance," is then formed, assigning the answer to the unjustified item (a) to originals (0) and the answer to the security-justified question (b) to copies (1). A three-level model is employed to examine differences within respondents, between respondents, and between countries. The first hypothesis is tested based on the association between "attitudes towards surveillance" (dv) and dummy (iv), while hypotheses H2–H4 are tested based on the association between "attitudes towards surveillance" (dv) and the interaction of the corresponding variable with dummy (iv).

Trust in government is not directly addressed in the ISSP module. Therefore, government support is gauged using voting behavior and whether respondents voted for the party of the head of the incumbent government. Despite limitations, this approach aligns with Christopher J. Anderson and Yuliya V. Tverdova (2003: 103) who assert that elections create a lens through which people evaluate their political context (see also Houston et al.'s (2016) empirical validation). Equating incumbent government vote with trust in government is certainly not optimal but seems to be the best of the available options for including an explanatory variable that is so central to the model given the existing literature. Data on government parties are obtained from the *Database of Political Institutions* (Cruz et al. 2016). The utilization of the voting variable presents two notable drawbacks. Firstly, the question is not posed in certain countries within the sample (see Fn. 68). Secondly, in specific countries within my sample, such as Australia, Belgium, and Turkey, voting is compulsory, potentially impacting government support, as suggested by Krister Lundell (2012). However, in my sample, there is no discernible relationship between mandatory voting and government support. Furthermore, participation rates are not significantly higher in these countries compared to others in the ISSP dataset. Consequently, I posit that the mandatory nature of voting should not exert undue influence on the study's results.

Political orientation is ascertained through respondents' voting behavior, too, underpinned by the assumption of ideological congruence between voters' preferences and their elected representatives—an association observed in various empirical studies (e.g., Golder & Stramski 2010; Klingemann et al. 2006). To operationalize political orientation, the ISSP individual data is linked with data from the Manifesto Project (Volkens et al. 2020) using the left-right variable derived from the respective elected parties. This variable, based on the work of Michael Laver and Ian Budge (1992), measures political orientation on a scale ranging from far left (-100) to far right (100).

As a metric for *liberal democracy*, the Liberal Democracy Index from the "Varieties of Democracy Project" (V-Dem) (Coppedge et al. 2021) is employed. According to V-Dem's conceptualization, liberal democracy embodies "the intrinsic value of protecting individual and minority rights against a potential 'tyranny of the majority' and state repression more generally" (Coppedge et al. 2016: 582). The index incorporates expert evaluations of a country's electoral democracy, along with three additional components: the rule of law ensuring respect for civil liberties, judicial constraints on the executive branch, and legislative checks and oversight of the executive (Coppedge et al. 2016: 582).[6] While acknowledging the impact of the currently prevailing political climate on respondents' attitudes, the literature suggests that *experiences* with authoritarian regimes continue to exert cultural effects on attitudes toward surveillance. Although this chapter does not delve into this aspect extensively, an additional model is calculated to account for the post-communist legacy (including it as a dummy variable). Extensive research on surveillance in post-communist societies supports the contention that historical experiences continue to shape contemporary perspectives (see e.g., Los 2003; 2005; Svenonius & Björklund 2018).[7]

I control for demographic factors, including age, gender, and education, utilizing data from the ISSP. Additionally, the country's terror legacy is considered, drawing on information from the *University of Maryland's Global Terrorist Database* (2019).[8] An additional model is computed, incorporating "migration

[6] While some authors generally question validity of the use of democracy indices, Boese (2019) shows that compared to other indices (Polity IV and Freedom House Index), V-Dem stands out with respect to the underlying definition and measurement scale, as well as the theoretical justification of the aggregation procedure.

[7] Theoretical and empirical research suggest that people in former communist states are more positive about internet and digital surveillance (Friedewald et al. 2015: 55) and there is a structural lack of understanding of human rights protection and privacy (Nagy 2017: 447–48). Surveillance is framed as a measure to protect national culture and national political independence (Nagy 2017: 447–48). A society's experience with surveillance is not limited to post-communist states, Tsapogas (2017: 226) finds that the rule of the Greek military and its surveillance still influences citizens' attitudes towards state surveillance. Other studies find an effect of Germans and Italians still bearing a legacy from their dictatorships in the 1930 s and 40 s (Fonio 2011; S. Gill 1995; Luebcke & Milton 1994). However, due to operationalization and space restraints, this will not be addressed.

[8] As surveillance is often framed as an "anti-terror measure," actual terrorism is likely to affect people's acceptance of these measures. I use the University of Maryland's Global Terrorist Database's country-specific score between zero and ten for the relative impact of incidents.

background" as an extra control variable.[9] A detailed variable overview and distributions are available in Appendices D.4 and D.5.

The full dataset comprises more than 48,000 respondents from 35 countries (including countries from all regions of the world—see Appendix A.6 in the electronic supplementary material), surveyed between 2015 and 2018 (dataset version 2.0.0). In the analysis, the sample size is much smaller (21,164).[10] To test the hypotheses, I conduct a three-level analysis with the two answers nested within respondents, nested within countries. The dependent variable has four scale points. Since it leads to the same results as an ordered logit model (see Appendix A.1 in the electronic supplementary material), I calculate a three-level linear model[11]. In following Andrew Gelman's (2008) approach, all numeric variables are standardized by dividing them by two standard deviations. As proposed by Jan P. Heisig and Merlin Schaeffer (2019), I include the justification variable as random slope when including cross-level interactions, since it is situated on the lower level.

[9] Especially in studies focusing on surveillance in the USA, immigration background or ethnic group membership are often-tested variables. Researchers include these categories in order to explain behavioral variance in people on a group statistical level, differentiating between an autochthonous population and culturally or racially others. Several authors find that domestic surveillance is closely correlated with racial surveillance (Ryan 2018: 43) leading to a "hyper-surveillance" of certain ethnic groups (A. Goffman 2009; Remster & Kramer 2018). When tested, studies almost unanimously find that ethnic group membership has an effect on the attitude towards surveillance. Preponderantly, researchers chose to use the dichotomy White/non-White and find a negative effect on the attitude towards surveillance for the latter (Bali 2009: 247; Davis & Silver 2004: 31; Spriggs et al. 2005: 42; Viscusi & Zeckhauser 2003: 107). As proposed by the *Conference of European Statisticians'* 'Recommendations for the 2020 Censuses of Population and Housing' (UNECE 2015: 136), I define persons with a "migration background" as persons whose both parents were born abroad.

[10] This is mainly due to missing data in the ISSP's vote choice variable (Great Britain, the Philippines, Suriname, and Thailand) as well as Taiwan and Venezuela not being included in the Manifesto Project dataset. Additional analyses (see Appendix A.3 in the electronic supplementary material) show that the exclusion of any variable related to individuals' vote choice (and thus significant increase of N) does not significantly alter the results.

[11] Based on graphical analyses, I find that level 1-residuals are normally distributed. However, heteroscedasticity cannot be ruled out. Thus, I decided to apply robust standards errors. There must be a sufficient number of upper-level cases to properly determine estimates with standard maximum likelihood estimate—especially if there are explanatory variables at the upper level. Although my 30 countries might be enough, I calculated an additional model based on REML estimates, as proposed by Elff et al. (2021), see Model 5 in Appendix A.1.

5.4 Analysis and Discussion of Results

The analysis begins by examining the mean acceptance of privacy invasions across the 30 countries included in the sample. Figure 5.1 illustrates that, on a global scale, the average respondent tends to disagree with government privacy invasion. Moreover, in most countries, the average citizen expresses disagreement with governments having the authority to invade their privacy. Notably, India, Belgium, Australia, Norway, Sweden, and France are exceptions, where the average citizen tends to agree with governments invading privacy. The figure presents mean acceptance for claims with and without security justifications; average approval decreases when only considering privacy invasion without justification. As discussed earlier, I will revisit these country differences while exploring levels of liberal democracy as a potential explanatory factor.

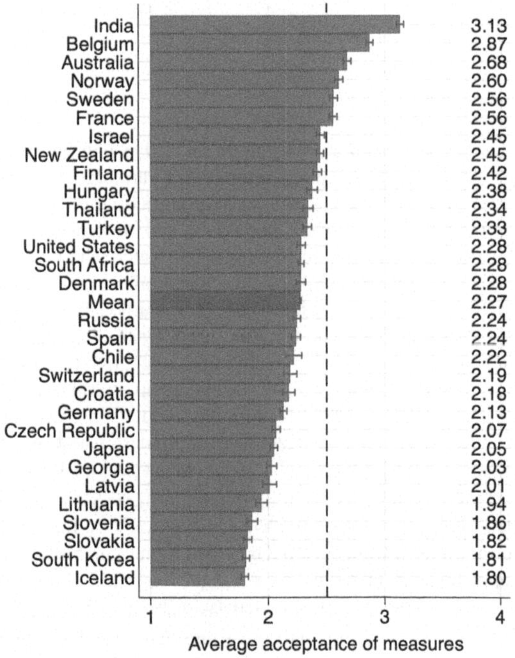

Fig. 5.1 Mean acceptance of privacy invasions by country. (*Note:* The capped spikes indicate the respective 83%-confidence intervals of the average country acceptance to assess the difference of means (see Austin & Hux 2002). N = 21,164. Average acceptance of surveillance measures is calculated as the mean response to the two items. Within each country, post-stratification weights are considered, for the overall mean, I additionally include a weight to adjusting for the different country sample sizes)

Turning to the examination of the impact of security promises, a multilevel approach is adopted to account for assumed variations at both the micro and macro levels. Following the recommendation of Joop Hox et al. (2017: 42–46), this assumption is tested by initially calculating an intercept-only model, where the intercept is modeled as random, and no explanatory variables are included (see Appendix A.1 in the electronic supplementary material for all models). In this null model, approximately 42% of the variability in respondents' attitudes towards surveillance is attributed to differences at the third level. Although no universally agreed threshold exists, any variation above five percent in between-group variation would warrant the adoption of a multilevel approach.

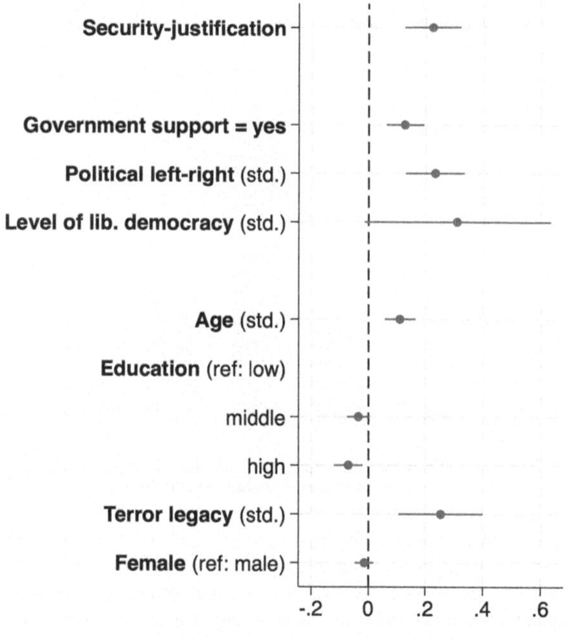

Fig. 5.2 Individual-level and country-level effects on acceptance of state surveillance. (*Note:* 95% confidence intervals, N = 21,164. Results stem from a three-level linear regression model including post-stratification weights on the individual level as well as country weights adjusting for the different sample sizes. For the underlying model, see Model 2 in Appendix A.1 in the electronic supplementary material)

The significantly positive correlation observed in 5.2 between the security justification dummy variable and attitudes towards surveillance indicates that the acceptance of security-justified surveillance is markedly higher than that of unjustified surveillance. This finding is substantiated by a Wilcoxon matched-pairs signed-rank test (Wilcoxon 1945). Consequently, I cannot reject hypothesis H1 and posit that, compared to no frame, a security frame enhances attitudes towards state surveillance.

However, this difference in attitudes does not uniformly apply to all respondents. While 33% of respondents are more supportive of surveillance measures when presented with a security frame, 47% of respondents do not alter their attitudes, and 20% of respondents express more negative attitudes (see Fig. 5.3). In the subsequent analysis, I aim to elucidate the factors contributing to the variations between unjustified and security-justified statements.

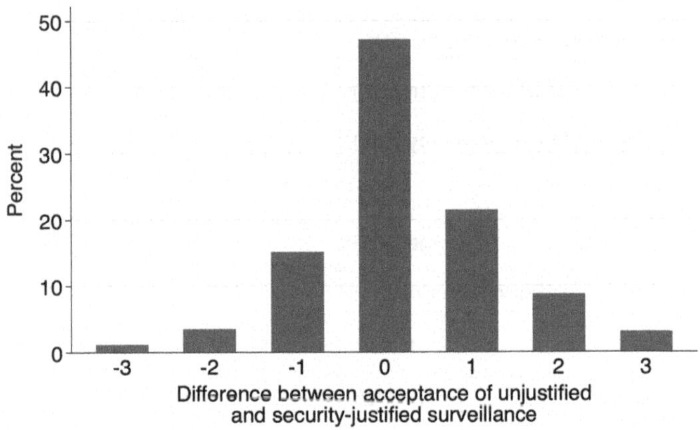

Fig. 5.3 Attitudinal differences depending on presence of justification. (*Note:* N = 21,164. The difference is calculated as acceptance of justified surveillance measures *minus* acceptance of non-justified surveillance measures. Positive values thus indicate higher acceptance for the former than for the latter and vice versa for negative values. The figure is based on the distribution considering post-stratification weights on the individual level as well as country weights adjusting for the different sample sizes)

As indicated above, the hypotheses H2–H4 are evaluated by examining the coefficients for the interactions between the justification variable and the explanatory variables. I find that, while the interaction coefficient for liberal democracy is highly significant, the same cannot be said for trust in government and political orientation (see Appendix A.1, Model 3 in the electronic supplementary material).

To facilitate a more nuanced interpretation of these coefficients, an examination of the predictive margins is warranted (see Fig. 5.4).

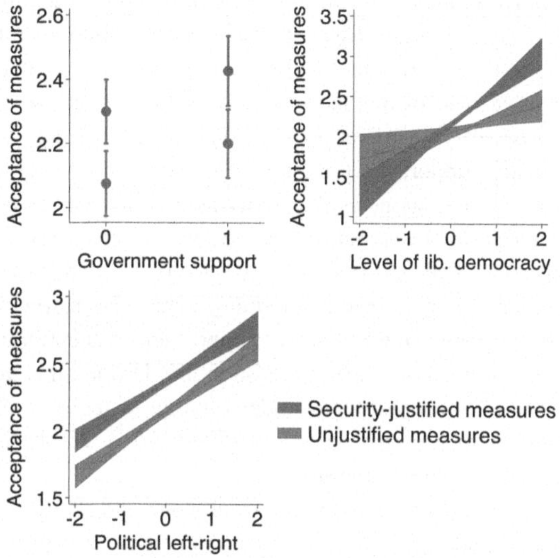

Fig. 5.4 Predictive margins of interactions of justification dummy and explaining variables. (*Note:* 95% confidence intervals, N = 21,164. Marginal effects after a single three-level linear regression model including respective two-way interactions between justification dummy and government support, political orientation, and level of liberal democracy as well as control variables as outlined above. Model includes post-stratification weights on the individual level as well as country weights adjusting for the different sample sizes. For the underlying model, see Model 3 in Appendix A.1 in the electronic supplementary material)

Figure 5.4 illustrates that for both individual-level variables, namely government support and political orientation, the security-justified measure exhibits a higher average acceptance than the unjustified measure across respondents at each level. Specifically, the two parallel graphs for political orientation demonstrate that the acceptance gap between the two almost measures remains roughly consistent across all levels of the x-axis.[12] This pattern holds true for government support as well, although it may be somewhat less visually discernible. Contrary to the hypothesized positive relationship, my results do not show a significant

[12] Even though it seems that, for individuals with very right-wing political attitudes, the difference between security-justified and unjustified measures becomes insignificant.

correlation between government support and the susceptibility to the security frame. Additionally, no significantly negative relationship is observed, which was mentioned as a possible alternative based on the assumption that securitization might be particularly persuasive to otherwise government-critical individuals (see Fn. 63). Therefore, my findings suggest that the trust relationship between the security agent (i.e., the government) and the audience (i.e., the population) does not play a substantial role in the success of a securitization move. Support for the government's security justification does not appear to depend on whether individuals personally support the government or not.

Public opinion research suggests that individuals differentiate between different state actors and prefer some actors' surveillance over others (Hallinan et al. 2012: 267). While the ISSP questions do not specify the entities included in the term "the government," leaving room for interpretation by respondents, the lack of a clear relationship between government support and susceptibility to the security frame prompts the need for further investigation. Despite this uncertainty, the results contribute to the underexplored understanding of the role of the audience and its relationship with securitizing actors (Côté 2016), emphasizing the need for additional research in this domain.

Similarly, for political orientation, no significant correlation with the security justification is found. On average, leftists and rightists appear to be equally influenced by a security justification, notwithstanding their differing levels of acceptance. Consequently, hypotheses H2 and H3 must be rejected.

On the other hand, concerning the level of liberal democracy, the results indicate a notable difference. The security-justified measures' graph exhibits a significantly larger slope than the unjustified measures' graph, suggesting that in more liberal countries, the impact of the security justification is more pronounced. Hypothesis 4 is therefore accepted. An intriguing observation is that in less liberal countries, the security frame appears to have a negative effect. In countries classified as rather illiberal, such as Hungary, India, and Turkey, respondents tend to express stronger support for non-justified surveillance measures compared to those with security justification. In contrast, in more liberal countries like Sweden and Norway, respondents demonstrate more positive attitudes towards security-justified measures. One possible explanation for this finding draws on Didier Bigo's (2012) concept of the "enemy of the state" and the potentially distinct connotations of the concept of national security in different political contexts. It is believed that in democracies, the term emphasizes preserving the territorial integrity of the state from external threats, while in autocracies, it focuses more on internal threats to the political integrity of the nation (Peceny et al. 2002: 19). The security justification may trigger different connotations depending on the level of liberal democracy in a given country. In any case, the results underscore the need for more in-depth research to better understand these nuances; especially because the correlation between (standardized) coefficients is comparably strong.

The inclusion of control variables does not alter the observed effects. Older individuals and residents of countries with a terror legacy tend to display higher levels of acceptance, while higher levels of education are associated with lower levels of acceptance. Gender differences do not reach significance. Neither having a migration background nor residing in a country with a communist past exhibits a significant relationship with the acceptance of surveillance measures in general, nor are their relationships with susceptibility to the security frame significant.

In the literature on the acceptance of surveillance measures, it has been acknowledged that cultural, social, and geographic contexts matter (e.g., Budak et al. 2017; Menichelli 2017). The results not only contribute to this literature but also suggest that the macro level may be more crucial than previously thought, as the country-level variable is the only variable of interest that demonstrates a significant relationship with the security justification. To comprehend the role of context more thoroughly, further cross-national research is necessary. In addition to a more detailed analysis of a country's legacy such as terrorism, past regimes, or colonialism (see McCulloch & Pickering 2009: 636), potential macro-level explanatory variables could include a country's level of surveillance (Budak et al. 2013: 105), more nuanced measures of liberal democracy, related concepts such as press freedom (Bakir 2015), and cultural indicators (Gellman & Dixon 2011) like Geert Hofstede's (1980) cultural values, commonly used to predict privacy attitudes (see e.g., Budak et al. 2017; Dinev et al. 2006).

Regarding the two strands of literature postulating the effects of framing in relation to predisposition, an investigation was conducted to determine if the attitudinal differences between the respondents regarding the unjustified claim on state surveillance could account for individuals' attitudinal differences. Testing the polarization assumption, the results indicate a highly significant and negative relationship between attitudes towards unjustified surveillance measures and the attitudinal difference. This implies that the lower the baseline attitude towards surveillance, the higher the susceptibility to security framing, contradicting assumptions about polarization effects, which would have led to higher baseline attitudes being positively correlated with the susceptibility.

For the hydraulic patterns assumption, which posits that the strength of predictors decreases when individuals are exposed to a frame, a comparison of predictors for attitudes towards unjustified and security-justified surveillance was conducted (see Appendix A.2 in the electronic supplementary material). The direction of coefficients remained consistent between the models (except for gender). Regarding the strength of the relationships, an increase in the magnitude of most correlation coefficients was observed, such as government support, political orientation, liberal democracy, and education. However, there were decreases for age and gender. Therefore, the hydraulic patterns hypothesis cannot be unequivocally supported: while it holds true for sociodemographic variables, framing leads to an increase in the influence of certain predictors.

5.5 Conclusion

The chapter pursued a dual objective: firstly, to examine the presence of a framing effect related to security within the ISSP dataset, and secondly, to investigate the factors contributing to the aforementioned effect. While the results concerning the first inquiry, indicating that surveillance measures are generally viewed more positively when framed in the context of security, align with the established body of literature on securitization, the insights into the second aspect illuminate a relatively underexplored research area.

The multilevel regression analysis unveiled a noteworthy correlation between a country's level of liberal democracy and susceptibility to the security frame. Individuals in liberal democracies exhibited a higher likelihood of responding to a security frame compared to those in less liberal-democratic societies. Intriguingly, in the latter, the absence of justification for surveillance measures resulted in even greater acceptance than instances where security justifications were provided. However, government support and political orientation did not exhibit the hypothesized effects. No significant interaction between the two and the susceptibility towards the security frame could be identified.

This study makes a significant contribution by challenging the notion of a monolithic "public," revealing distinct audience reactions to securitization moves. Leveraging the unique ISSP data, the research provides empirical evidence transcending national or regional boundaries, drawing conclusions from diverse global perspectives. Nonetheless, acknowledging certain limitations is crucial.

A point of contention raised in the study is its reliance on the ISSP, a survey not explicitly designed for analyzing attitudes toward surveillance or privacy issues. While there is disagreement with assertions that such surveys are inherently useless for this research—H. Watson et al. (2017)—the study recognizes potential limitations, such as the absence of detailed information on the reasons behind individuals' attitudes toward surveillance, questions about individuals' threat perception as well as more questions related to liberal values on an individual level. In addition, the study of attitudes towards surveillance is potentially always limited due to a biased non-response rate: since surveys are themselves essentially a form of surveillance, some individuals might interpret them as a privacy invasion (Haggerty & Gazso 2005; Marx 2007). However, no significant correlation is found between the countries' (proxy measures of the) national level of surveillance[13] and the respective non-response or refusal rates (see Appendix A.7 in the electronic supplementary material).

Another criticism involves the study design. Unlike experimental designs, this research can only make limited statements about treatment effects and causal relationships. The potential for respondent priming and the possibility that questions may introduce bias due to not only varying with regard to the (non-)presence of the justification are acknowledged. Additionally, the study recognizes the challenge of estimating framing or securitization effects for highly contentious issues, like state surveillance, where historical context and pre-existing securitization may influence responses as emphasized by Stéphane J. Baele et al. (2018: 465). If issues have a long history on the political agenda in real-life, securitization might already have taken place and researchers are no longer able to formulate *neutral* statements. There is thus the risk of underestimating framing or securitization effects. Since statistically significant differences can still be found, this point can be neglected.

At the same time, the operationalization of independent variables at the individual level also comes with weaknesses, as indicated in Sect. 5.3. Operationalizing political orientation through the left-right stance of elected parties may be a common practice; nevertheless, there is a need to question the extent to which (a) respondents actually perceive a party as a whole when they vote for it, as opposed to selecting specific policy areas as decisive for their choice (see, for example, literature by Herbert Kitschelt (1994), Hanspeter Kriesi et al. (2008; 2012), or Daniel Oesch and Line Rennwald (2018) suggesting that a one-dimensional categorization of parties may be insufficient, given that party placements on economic and cultural issues can vary significantly). Simultaneously, (b) against the backdrop of increasing fantasies of upheaval by right-wing groups in recent years (such as around the 2023 storming of federal buildings in

---

13 Stoycheff et al. (2018: 6) propose to measure the degree of state surveillance with *Freedom House's Freedom on the Net Index*' 'violations of user rights' dimension that assesses government monitoring of individuals' internet activity as well as negative "repercussions for online speech and activities, such as imprisonment, extralegal harassment, or cyberattacks" on a 0–40 scale, with higher scores indicative of greater surveillance (Freedom House 2016).

Brasília by supporters of Brazil's former president Jair Bolsonaro echoing the January 6, 2021 attack on the US Congress or within the "Reichsbürger" movement in Germany), it may be worth considering whether there is not a linear relationship, but rather whether far-right attitudes could also lead to lower acceptance of surveillance (Bjørgo 2023).

The operationalization of government support through the choice of one of the ruling parties is necessarily a construct, too. Not only does a vote not necessarily imply congruence with political content—as outlined above—but also, in coalition governments, the government's agenda (for example regarding security policy) may diverge significantly from the (pre-election) particular interests of an individual party—particularly in fragmented party systems where the party that appoints the head of government does not necessarily have significantly more votes than other coalition partners.

Despite these limitations, the findings offer important implications for understanding how frames influence attitudes toward surveillance, contributing an international perspective to existing literature. The study, one of the first to empirically explore individuals' persuadability by security promises, particularly highlights the significant correlation between the level of liberal democracy and response to the security frame. Future research is warranted to delve deeper into individual attitudes toward state surveillance, shedding light on the willingness to trade privacy for security. In particular, the finding that the effect of the frame differs significantly depending on the democracy level of the respondent's country invites future research—for example, with regard to who is thought of when speaking about "the government."

Determinants of Public Support for Privacy Invasions

6

Building on insights from the previous chapter, which revealed that individuals respond to security promises, this chapter delves deeper into the privacy calculus.[1] It aims to assess how different factors, such as risks, costs, benefits, and various forms of (in)security, influence the acceptance of privacy invasions. Specifically, I address the question: What benefits do individuals consider in their privacy calculus?

While people generally prefer to live in a secure environment, I argue that the decision to support security policies is not solely based on the trade-off between security concerns and protecting one's privacy and freedom. I contend that support for such policies also depends on financial costs, impacts on individual convenience, policy design, and the contextual factors surrounding their implementation. This study contributes to the existing literature by enhancing our understanding of the factors that drive public agreement with proposed security measures.

To measure the causal effects on the approval of security measures, I conducted a pre-registered factorial survey experiment involving 4955 respondents in Germany as part of the *Conflict of Values in Germany survey* (Giebler et al. 2024). Survey experiments are gaining popularity in policy attitudes research because they enable researchers to draw causal conclusions from their findings, in contrast to traditional survey questions (Auspurg & Hinz 2014). My results

[1] Some of the findings of this study have been published in Antoine (2023).

Supplementary Information The online version contains supplementary material available at https://doi.org/10.1007/978-3-658-46462-2_6.

L. Antoine, *The Subjective Value of Privacy*, Wahlen und politische Einstellungen,
https://doi.org/10.1007/978-3-658-46462-2_6

reveal that, in general, German citizens are willing to accept far-reaching surveillance measures, but financial costs and negative effects on individual convenience significantly decrease this support. Surprisingly, the salience of a security threat has no significant impact on individual support. I also find that individuals value privacy primarily due to self-interest; when they are not the ones under surveillance, factors other than the extensiveness of privacy interventions determine support. Moreover, subjective insecurity is a strong predictor of support for privacy invasions.

The chapter's structure is as follows: First, I review existing literature on support for surveillance policies and derive hypotheses from the works. Then, the German context is briefly introduced and data, research design, and methods are outlined. Next, I present the empirical results, followed by a discussion, a brief section on limitations and future research, and a summary.

6.1 Support for Surveillance Policies

Public support for surveillance measures is considered to be dependent on their scope (Friedewald, van Lieshout, Rung, et al. 2016). Therefore, it is essential to consider both the context of implementation and the design of such policies to determine who supports which measures.

Public acceptance of government policies is influenced by individual contexts and environments (Tversky & Simonson 1993). Psychological reactions to threats play a significant role in understanding public support for surveillance measures, as being threatened is directly related to the perceived necessity of countermeasures such as surveillance. Research has shown that individuals perceiving greater threats are less likely to support civil liberties (Davis & Silver 2004; Dietrich & Crabtree 2019) and more likely to endorse counterterrorism measures (Huddy et al. 2005; Ziller & Helbling 2021). Studies on the German population have shown that being threatened by crime has a positive effect on acceptance of surveillance technologies (Trüdinger 2019; Van Heek et al. 2016), leading me to assume that:

H1: Higher security threat results in greater policy support.

Surveillance measures differ in terms of (a) the type of data collected and (b) their target audience, with technological advancements enabling the collection of an increasing range of information. Information sensitivity, which relates to individuals' willingness to self-disclose different types of information, is a concept used in online services research. It is assumed that individuals attribute different levels of intimacy to various types of information, with more intimate information posing greater risks upon disclosure. Potential losses due to information disclosure can be material (e.g., loss of financial or other assets), physical (e.g., loss of life or health), or psychological (e.g., loss of social status or relationships) (Mothersbaugh et al. 2012: 77). Furthermore, surveillance can either be targeted, and thus directed towards specific persons or groups of interest, or *un*targeted (referred to as "mass surveillance," "bulk interception," or "dragnet surveillance"). Targeted surveillance (such as wiretapping) depends upon the existence of prior suspicion of the targeted and is thus closely tied to addressing (perceived or actual) insecurity (Ziller & Helbling 2021: 996). In contrast, untargeted surveillance (such as CCTV surveillance, number plate recognition systems, or biometrical passports), collects information without specific targets and thus from (potentially) all members of the society. People are assumed reluctant to support policies that constrict privacy rights. This resistance may be driven by an appreciation of privacy as a value for itself (Rössler 2005: 69–70), the fear of potential losses (Mothersbaugh et al. 2012: 77), the appreciation of autonomy over security, moral concerns, and self-interest (Stigler 1980), implying that:

H2: Higher extensiveness of the privacy invasion results in lower policy support.

Individuals tend to support policies they perceive as personally beneficial (A. Campbell et al. 1960: 208; Margalit 2013: 81), favoring policies that promise savings rather than additional costs, both in terms of money and time. The relationship between financial costs and the design of privacy invasion policies is debated. Existing literature, influenced by consumer research,[2] often assumes that individuals are rational actors with stable privacy preferences, valuing privacy not per se but for its economic benefits (Acquisti et al. 2013: 253). However, this literature consistently finds low privacy valuations. For example, Spiekerman et al. (2001) find that almost all customers are willing to give personal data in order to receive purchase recommendations and discounts—even those who expressed high levels of concern about privacy. Rose (2005) and Beresford et al. (2012) find that most people are not willing to pay any additional amount to ensure the

[2] Due to the scarce literature on policy-specific factors influencing individual attitudes towards state surveillance and the fact that individuals' attitudes towards state surveillance are assumed to often correspond to their decisions and behavior in light of commercial surveillance (see e.g., Dinev et al. 2008; Frik & Gaudeul 2020), I believe that it is legitimate to draw conclusions from this literature, even though I acknowledge that the government/citizen relation is not equal to the business/customer relationship.

privacy of their information. While most research focuses on consumerism, the question of a monetary price for privacy has also been included in surveys on acceptance of state surveillance. In Noellie Brockdorff, Sandra Appleby-Arnold, Christian Hawellek, et al.'s (2015: 22) survey on Germans' views on surveillance, the majority of respondents indicated that they would not be "willing to pay more taxes so that more money is allocated for carrying out surveillance"—independent of the content of the surveillance measure.[3] This suggests that:

H3: *Financial costs have a stronger effect on support for a policy than the extensiveness of the privacy intervention.*

In terms of convenience, consumer research suggests that individuals are willing to pay certain prices for increased convenience in their lives, known as *the* "price of convenience" (Ng-Kruelle et al. 2002) or "tyranny of convenience" (Andrejevic 2007: 139). The desire to save time and eliminate drudgery often takes precedence over abstract concepts like privacy, democracy, or equality. This is exemplified in airport security research, where respondents were more willing to compromise civil liberties when it resulted in reduced waiting times (Viscusi & Zeckhauser 2003: 116). I assume that:

H4: *Inconvenience has a stronger effect on policy support than the extensiveness of the privacy intervention.*

Returning to the issue of security, the literature distinguishes between *objective* and *subjective* security. *Objective* security represents the mathematical probability of risk and effectiveness of countermeasures (Schneier 2008) or the absence of threats to acquired values, while *subjective* security refers to the absence of fear that such values will be attacked (Wolfers 1952: 484). Beliefs about (in)security can be irrational or non-evidence-based (Wolfers 1962: 150). Although the dimensions are related, individuals may overestimate or underestimate actual threats (Zedner 2003). In the social psychological literature, the misperception of risks is typically attributed to cognitive biases, such as the availability bias (Tversky & Kahneman 1974), vividness bias (Nisbett & Ross 1980), or social amplification bias (Sunstein 2005).[4]

[3] In contrast, V. K. Smith et al. (2009) find that US-American citizens are willing to pay higher taxes for antiterror measures.

[4] *Availability bias:* Individuals tend to answer the relatively challenging question of how likely it is to become a victim of a specific crime by relying on the simpler question of how easily they can imagine becoming a victim of a crime (Jackson 2011). *Vividness bias:*

It has been consistently assumed in the literature that being threatened by crime has a positive effect on the acceptance of surveillance technologies. This holds true for studies addressing the objective dimension of threat—as I have outlined for hypothesis H1—and those focusing on the subjective component. However, a direct comparison of these two factors as potential predictors for attitudes or behavior regarding state surveillance has not yet been undertaken in the literature. From the psychological literature on predicting intolerance, we know that anxiety and the perception of threat serve as better indicators for the development of intolerant attitudes than objective risk (S. Milne et al. 2019). Similarly, research has found that perceived threat is a better indicator than objective health risk for the frequency of preventive actions in the context of the COVID-19 pandemic (Kłosowska et al. 2022). This aligns with decision-making theories such as prospect theory, which is based on the understanding that individual behavior varies depending on the *perceived* certainty of an occurring event (Kahneman & Tversky 1979).

Given the assumption that individuals' subjective insecurity might not align with the objective risk and the literature's consensus that subjective perceptions appear to be more effective predictors of behavior than objective terms, I propose that:

H5: *Subjective insecurity correlates more strongly with policy support than objective insecurity.*

6.2 The German Case

To test the hypotheses, I conducted a pre-registered factorial survey experiment in Germany in November 2021. Germany has seen an increasing focus on public attitudes toward surveillance in recent years. For instance, based on data from a quota-sampled online survey, Brockdorff, Appleby-Arnold, Hawellek, et al. (2015) reported that a majority of Germans oppose surveillance measures such as CCTV, geo-location tracking, and internet monitoring, perceiving them as ineffective in reducing crime and subjective insecurity. Sabine Trepte and Philipp K. Masur's (2017) survey indicated that Germans, in general, place a high value on

Individuals are more likely to rely on information that has been vividly and emotionally presented, such as through media or the government, rather than abstract probable information (Agerberg & Sohlberg 2021). *Social amplification bias* operates similarly, where, considering information collection costs, public opinion is viewed as a proxy for the most informed opinion (Kasperson et al. 2022).

privacy and do not believe that its importance has diminished in society. Their findings also showed that a substantial portion of the German population holds strong objections to government data surveillance. In the previous chapter, we could also see that in global comparison, Germans tended to reject government privacy invasions. A research project on surveillance in Germany by Eva-Maria Trüdinger and Leonie C. Steckermeier (2017) found that political trust plays a pivotal role in shaping public acceptance of surveillance, while policy-specific information has a less significant impact. Germany has a unique historical context due to its experiences with the Nazi regime and the German Democratic Republic, which has led to a distinct relationship with security and surveillance (Frohman 2020). Moreover, Germany has comparatively strict regulations regarding privacy and data protection (Ziller & Helbling 2021: 997), and the population is generally more critical of state surveillance than in many other countries, prioritizing the protection of privacy.

Considering these factors—and despite acknowledging the importance of country-specific historical path dependencies—I regard Germany as a "least-likely case" and assume that, given the population's general reluctance toward surveillance measures, specific characteristics of proposed policies should have little impact on their support. Any significant effects observed in Germany would be indicative of their potential occurrence elsewhere.

6.3 Data and Methodology

In this section, I provide details about the data collection, the methodology and the statistical models employed in the study.

Data collection

The pre-registered[5] experiment was conducted as part of a larger online public opinion survey[6] with respondents recruited from an online access panel administered managed by a collaborating survey company conducted in November 2021.

[5] The pre-registration (Miguel et al. 2014) for the survey experiment called "Privacy and Security Trade-offs in Germany" can be found on Open Science Framework (Foster & Deardorff 2017): https://osf.io/r568f/?view_only=9b8c84c93d2a4fc0aae6c4b48fdcbfd6.

[6] The project called "Wertekonflikt in Deutschland"(*Conflict of Values in Germany*) was carried out in collaboration with colleagues of the Junior Research Group "Comparative Survey" of the Cluster of Excellence "Contestation of the Liberal Script" (Giebler et al. 2024). It received a positive vote of the Central Ethics Committee of the Presidency of Freie Universität Berlin (ZEA-Nr. 2021–024, 03.11.2021) prior to the data collection.

The sample of 4955 respondents was stratified by gender, age, education, and place of residence (federal state), ensuring it closely matched offline population distribution in Germany among individuals aged 18 to 75.

Methodology

For this study, I employed a survey experiment, which offers several advantages over standard survey data and observational research designs (see Sect. 4.3). In factorial survey experiments like mine, respondents are presented (fictional) descriptions of a situation that systematically differ in discrete attributes. They are then asked to evaluate each scenario according to criteria such as support, agreement, or perceived usefulness. The systematic variation of the situational factors presented allows me to isolate the effects of individual situational factors, thus enabling me to determine the causal influence of these factors (Auspurg & Hinz 2014). The experiment utilized a fractional factorial design, which runs only a subset of the factor combinations present in a complete experimental design.[7]

Each respondent was presented with six fictitious scenarios, with each scenario comprising five dimensions, each with three levels. These dimensions included information about criminal offenses in Germany, possible measures to reduce these offenses through a government-established database, the nature of data stored in the database, the target population for surveillance, and associated financial costs and convenience factors. The levels of crime figures are based on actual crime statistics in Germany: In 2020, there were about two million cases of robbery, theft, and assault (Bundeskriminalamt 2021a). This figure is used in the second level, while the figures are half and twice as large in the first and third level respectively. As we have learned in Sect. 2.2, it is important to distinguish between subjectively perceived threats and objectively threatening situations since these two do not necessarily have to correspond with each other (Trüdinger 2019: 33). In addition to distinguishing between subjective and objective components, the construction of (in)security is also closely intertwined with the reporting of security threats or victimization figures. It is believed that security threats are

[7] By not having to use all combinations, there are more respondents per combination. Using SAS for determining the experimental design, the saturated design allowing for three-way interactions needed 131 vignettes. As six vignettes per person seemed reasonable in terms of survey fatigue and intra-individual estimation power (Auspurg & Hinz 2014: 47–49), the smallest possible fractional design that could be identified is based on 144 vignettes. D-efficiency, a measure of the goodness of an experimental design (see Auspurg & Hinz 2014: 27–33), for this design with 144 vignettes was 79.78. I instead used 198 vignettes which increased the D-efficiency to 93.04. Each respondent received six vignettes successively and, thus, there were 33 vignette blocks.

necessarily socially constructed and numerous studies have demonstrated that individuals' perception and acceptance of measures can be influenced by discourses that define the threat, such as information about the level of victimization (Lipschutz 1995). Using the number of victims as proxies for the manipulation of the level of threat is common practice, especially in survey experimental research on topics such as attitudes towards anti-terror policies (e.g., Garcia & Geva 2016) or choices of public transportation (Berryessa & Caplan 2020). In my case, the variation of crime numbers comes closer to manipulating the objectively threatening situation. However, framing experiments inevitably incorporate a subjective component (E. Goffman 1974). This aspect will be addressed in the discussion of the results.[8]

The second dimension varied *data collection*, moving from (1) registered addresses (lowest privacy intrusion since it should be known to the state anyways[9]), to (2) images and videos of public surveillance cameras, and (3) data on private internet usage and email conversation (highest privacy intrusion). In Germany, 88.4% of the population above 14 years uses the internet (Verbrauchs- und Medienanalyse 2022: 28). Due to technological progress and availability of internet services, it has become an essential part of people's everyday life (Lyon 2015a). Internet surveillance should be considered very intrusive since it touches possible intimate realms like individuals' private online conversations or browsing habits. Results from other surveys suggest that respondents find the state monitoring e-mails and internet usage intrusive and less acceptable than surveillance via CCTV (e.g., Wester & Giesecke 2019; see also results from ISSP Research Group 2018).

The third dimension varied the *target audience* from (1) suspects of a crime, to (2) certain groups of people who statistically commit crimes more frequently,

[8] The fact that respondents are subject to different victimization probabilities is acknowledged but must be neglected here. I am also aware of the fact that the total number of crimes might be misleading in terms of risk prevalence since it includes crimes of significantly different severity and not all these even impact private persons (e.g., shoplifting). However, while this might possibly lead to an overestimation of prevalence, this does not influence the statistical models since the formulations are identical across levels. In addition, respondents are not informed of the fact that the crime levels are based on actual crime statistics and are thus not deluded.

[9] In Germany, it is compulsory to register one's address with the local residents' registration office.

and to (3) all citizens. While (1) and (3) are the key differentiators between targeted and mass surveillance,[10] the assignment of (2) is less clear. On one hand, limiting the target group of surveillance to specific individuals based on statistical evidence might be rational. For example, authorities might eliminate more crime than through other policies for equivalent disruption and expenditures of resources. On the other hand, using group membership as a denominator for suspiciousness is highly critical since it contradicts liberal values and rights such as fairness, equal treatment before the law, or presumed innocence (Risse & Zeckhauser 2004; Trüdinger 2019: 26). The most prominent example of group-specific profiling is so-called "racial profiling."[11] In my example, I specifically used the wording "groups who commit crimes more frequently." Even though it might be morally debatable, I assume that this target group is somewhere between targeted and mass surveillance in terms of the extensiveness of surveillance. Generally, it is to be assumed that while the understanding of (1) should be equal for everyone, (2) and (3) might depict different groups of people for different respondents.

Financial costs and convenience (the fourth and fifth dimension) have the three levels (1) reliefs, (2) no change, and (3) additional burden. The scenario of governmental policies restricts the content of the dimension in comparison to scenarios that deal for example with individuals' privacy preferences when purchasing products (e.g., Acquisti et al. 2013; Beresford et al. 2012). Tax reliefs/burdens served as a proxy for financial costs (Brockdorff, Appleby-Arnold, Hawellek, et al. 2015; V. K. Smith et al. 2009) while waiting times at airports (e.g., used by Sakano et al. 2016; Viscusi & Zeckhauser 2003) and traffic controls (added to account for non-frequent air travelers) represented convenience factors.[12] The full design is displayed in Table 6.1.

[10] While "suspects of a crime" refers to a legal term—in order for an individual to be officially recognized as a suspect, suspicions must meet the criterion of being deemed "reasonable," as for example delineated in the Rome Statute of the International Court of Justice (Dash & Sharma 2016)—allegedly being objectively descriptive, it is a fact that certain groups are chronically "over-suspected" by law enforcement (Harris 2020) and the public (e.g., Feltes et al. 2018: 606).

[11] The term is used to describe the actions of police or other security institutions to assess suspiciousness of a person on the basis of criteria such as ethnicity, religion, or national origin rather than on basis of specific suspicious facts. Even though it is legally prohibited in many countries, including Germany, and voluminous evidence exists that it fails to secure public safety, it still prevails as common practice (Harris 2020). For a philosophical debate on the subject, see Risse and Zeckhauser (2004).

[12] For daily or frequent transportation, 73.3% of the German population uses a car, 2.3% opts for motorbikes or scooters, and 26.2% chooses a bike. Additionally, 52.0% of Germans occasionally fly (Verbrauchs- und Medienanalyse 2022: 48).

One exemplary vignette looks like this:

> "Please imagine the following scenario: Last year, there were more than one million cases of robbery, theft, and assault in Germany. This means that about every 80th person in Germany was a victim of one of these crimes. One proposal to increase security is the introduction of a nationwide information database. This would store images and videos of public surveillance cameras of suspects of a crime. By establishing the database, other law enforcement costs can be saved and possibly taxes can be reduced. The database should lead to a reduction in time-consuming checks at the airport and traffic controls."

I recognize that the external validity of these scenarios may vary, and their realism can be subjective. However, the issue of internal security has received substantial public and government attention (e.g., Schneider 2020), and databases and data mining are key features of homeland security initiatives worldwide (Seifert 2004). In Germany, an "Anti-terror Database" was introduced in 2006. This database can be accessed by various security authorities and includes various information (such as telecommunications and internet data) on specific individuals (Lang 2021). Although these scenarios are not purely fictitious and have been used by other scholars before (e.g., Lüdemann & Schlepper 2012; Trüdinger & Steckermeier 2017; Ziller & Helbling 2021), I cannot ascertain the extent to which respondents view them as realistic policy options, in particular the conflation with other related effects (i.e., financial costs and convenience).[13] At the same time, individuals are rarely faced with the explicit opportunity to think and agree-disagree on these things. Accordingly, it is difficult to determine how entrenched attitudes on this issue are.

Before the first scenario, respondents receive an intro text and an explanation of what to expect (see Appendix A.4 in the electronic supplementary material). After each presentation of a scenario, they are asked how strongly they agree with the measure on a seven-point Likert scale:

> *Despite all the consequences, how much would you agree with this measure?*
>
> *(1) Fully disagree*
>
> ...
>
> *(7) Fully agree*

[13] Not all forms of robbery, theft, and assault can be addressed with the mentioned forms of surveillance. This might influence the internal validity. Since the formulations are identical across levels, this does not influence the statistical models.

Table 6.1 Vignette dimensions and levels

Level → Dimension ↓	Level 1	Level 2	Level 3
Level of Threat			
Crime Numbers in Germany	*50% of actual figures*	*actual figures*	*200% of actual figures*
	Last year, there were more than **one million cases** of robbery, theft, and assault in Germany. This means that about **every 80th person** in Germany was a victim of one of these crimes.	Last year, there were more than **two million cases** of robbery, theft, and assault in Germany. This means that about **every 40th person** in Germany was a victim of one of these crimes.	Last year, there were more than **four million cases** of robbery, theft, and assault in Germany. This means that about **every 20th person** in Germany was a victim of one of these crimes.
Privacy Intrusion			
	Strength of the intrusion: rather low ⇔ rather high		
Data Collection	The registered addresses	Images and videos of public surveillance cameras	Data on private internet usage and email conversations
Target	Suspects of a crime	Certain groups of people who statistically commit crimes more frequently	All citizens
Other Related Effects			
	Additional impact: rather positive ⇔ rather negative		
Financial costs	Other law enforcement costs can be saved and possibly taxes can be reduced	No further costs incur	Significant costs will be incurred. Taxes may have to be increased for this.
Inconvenience	The database should lead to a reduction in time-consuming checks at the airport and traffic controls.	No other restrictions are associated with it.	Accessing the database may lead to delays at the airport or during traffic controls.

Don't know

To measure subjective feelings of security, I used a five-item battery that assesses fear of crime. Equating these two concepts or using the latter as a proxy for the former is a common practice (Carro et al. 2010: 304).[14] Respondents rated their level of concern regarding (a) physical assault and injury, (b) burglary or break-ins at their homes, (c) robbery and mugging, (d) sexual harassment, and (e) being a victim of a terrorist attack on a seven-point Likert scale. The battery was adapted from the German Victimization Survey (Birkel et al. 2020).[15] The average fear of crime score was computed for each respondent as the mean of the five items, as suggested by Randy L. LaGrange and Kenneth F. Ferraro (1989).

Objective (in)security was assessed by examining the prevalence of criminal activities[16] at the district level (*Landkreis*, NUTS III), based on Police Crime Statistics of the Federal Republic of Germany (as of 2020) (Bundeskriminalamt 2021a; 2021b). The district level was chosen because it is the most disaggregated level with available data. As indicated in Fn. 8, the objective dimension of security is linked to the level of threat in the experiment. While the impact of the latter depends on the experiment's efficacy in manipulation, objective security,

[14] Some authors suggest that within subjective security, there exists not only the *subjective* dimension, which pertains to the fear of becoming a victim of a hypothetical crime but also an *objective* fear of crime stemming from previous experiences of victimization (Allik & Kearns 2017; Solymosi et al. 2015). While this perspective is understandable, I choose to narrow the focus to the fear of crime at this juncture, partly for methodological reasons, allowing me to delineate the duality of objective and subjective uncertainty. Emphasizing the significance of the fear of crime construct further and drawing from discussions on the risk society and modernity (Bauman 1999; Beck 1992; Giddens 1990), empirical evidence is increasingly revealing that the fear of crime is not necessarily the fear of specific offenses but rather an expression of broader feelings of uncertainty and socially constructed anxieties (E. Gray et al. 2008; Jackson 2004; Valente & Valera Pertegas 2018; Vieno et al. 2013).

[15] Kreuter (2002: 49–50) shows that both German and US studies similarly operationalize crime-specific fear and emphasizes the advantage of using a multi-item indicator over a single global indicator (Kreuter 2002: 26–27).

[16] While this is a recognized approach in academia (see, e.g., Burkhardt et al. 2017), it is worth noting that official crime statistics may not always provide an objective reflection of the security situation. This can be related to the extent of unreported crimes, the resources available to law enforcement agencies, as well as political factors that may influence what is defined as criminal and what is not (Buil-Gil et al. 2022). Additionally, other authors also suggest that the clearance rate of crimes may be a meaningful measure of objective security (McGovern 2017; Mosher et al. 2010).

operationalized as the respondents' actual context, is believed to be more comprehensive. Furthermore, the utilization of individual-level data provides greater analytical flexibility in terms of modeling.

Statistical Models

To analyze the effects of the vignette dimensions, I employ a multivariate linear regression model, with the evaluated vignettes nested within respondents. I conduct additional robustness checks considering individual-level characteristics such as age, gender, education, region, and citizenship (see Appendix B.1 in the electronic supplementary material for a summary of all variables).[17] Thereby, I include random slopes for the lower-level variables when including cross-level interactions as recommended by Heisig and Schaeffer (2019). To test hypotheses H5 and H6, I use a three-level model given the district-level crime statistics.[18] Although conceptually similar in content, I differentiate between *threat* (as a dimension within the survey experiment, hypothesis H1) and *objective (in)security* as a contextual variable (hypotheses H5–H6). In all models, continuous variables are standardized by dividing by two standard deviations (as proposed by Gelman 2008). When presenting results involving interactions, I typically report average marginal effects.

6.4 Empirical Results

When assessing the agreement with surveillance measures across all experimental conditions, I discover that 48% of the respondents expressed agreement, indicated by responses above the midpoint on the 7-point scale. In contrast, 32% of the cases indicate disagreement (see Appendix B.1 in the electronic supplementary material). Given that Germans are often viewed as somewhat skeptical of surveillance measures (Ziller & Helbling 2021: 997), I find a relatively high level of approval in the sample.

---

[17] Awareness or non-awareness surrounding the security-surveillance nexus might mediate the attitudes towards related policies. Apart from different levels of interest in politics, individuals might experience different levels of exposure to surveillance measures (for example, due to racial profiling) or have been targeted by (parts of) the proposed security measure. While I cannot control for interest in politics due to the lack of suitable measure, I included citizenship as another control variable in my model. Since the dataset does not contain any additional variables on migration background or religion, no further analyses in this regard can be performed.

[18] 399 of the 401 German districts are represented in the sample.

6.4.1 Assessing the Role of Different Determinants

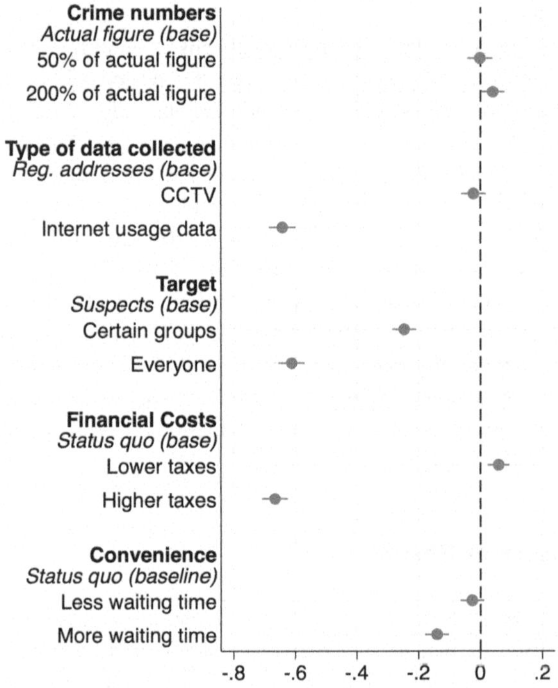

Fig. 6.1 Acceptance of surveillance measures. (*Note:* 95% confidence intervals, N = 4839. Results stem from a two-level linear regression model including post-stratification weights on the individual level. For the underlying model, see Model 2 in Appendix B.2 in the electronic supplementary material)

In Fig. 6.1, I present the effects of different policy conditions on the level of agreement for the fictious measure. We can see that variations in crime figures have no significant impact on the acceptance of surveillance measures. Notably, while a higher number of crimes (200% of the actual figure) lead to a slightly higher acceptance compared to the actual figure (the reference category), this increase is statistically insignificant. Conversely, lowering the number of crimes to 50% of the actual figure does not result in a proportional decrease in acceptance.

In terms of the type of data collected, assessing internet usage data leads to a statistically significant decrease in support for surveillance measures compared to the reference category, which is registered addresses. Interestingly, camera surveillance in public spaces does not significantly differ from the collection of registered addresses. This suggests that respondents do not prioritize the privacy of their behavior in public spaces more highly than the protection of their registered addresses. As for the target of surveillance, the results aligned with my expectations. Targeted surveillance of suspects, the reference category, received higher support in comparison to non-targeted surveillance. Moreover, the collection of data on certain groups of people statistically more likely to commit crimes decreased support. Data collection from everyone, however, exhibited an even higher decrease in support. These findings indicate a clear hierarchy regarding the target of surveillance measures. In contrast, the prioritization of the type of data collected was less distinct. Notably, there was no significant difference between registered addresses and surveillance cameras, with only internet surveillance showing a strong, significant difference. Thus, I tentatively conclude that the more extensive the privacy intervention, the lower the support for a given measure.

Regarding financial costs, I find that, compared to the reference category of "no changes," lower taxes slightly increased the acceptance of surveillance measures. Conversely, higher taxes result in a drastic decrease in acceptance. This aligns with previous studies that have shown the negative effect of the threat of tax increases on the approval of security measures.

Concerning convenience, I observe no significant difference between less waiting time and no changes in waiting time (the reference category). Respondents do not seem to prioritize convenience enhancements. Less waiting time even exhibits a negative coefficient, albeit statistically insignificant. Conversely, an increase in inconvenience manifested as more waiting has a negative effect on the acceptance of a security measure.

The interclass correlation of the model is 0.553, indicating that participants were responsive to variations in the experimental factors. The vignette dimensions account for 55.3% of the variance in acceptance. However, there is also variation between respondents. We know from the literature that acceptance of surveillance measures is influenced by several sociodemographic characteristics. To ensure the robustness of the analysis, I ran an additional model controlling for age, gender, education, region, and citizenship (see Appendix B.2, Model 3 in the electronic supplementary material). This analysis reveals that being female, older age, and living in specific federal states are significantly correlated with acceptance. Importantly, the inclusion of sociodemographic variables does not significantly alter the effects of the vignette dimensions. Surprisingly, contrary to the assumption that Germans, in comparison to those not holding German citizenship, might be less affected by surveillance and hence less opposed to it, in my sample, holding German citizenship is negatively correlated with surveillance approval. Furthermore, I conducted checks for order effects, time spent on the item, and interview quality (Appendix B.2, Model 4 in the electronic supplementary material). These additional survey-specific quality checks reinforced the robustness of the results.[19]

As previously discussed, the extensiveness of surveillance depends on both the type of data collected and the target of surveillance. While the effect of convenience is smaller than the target's and data type's effects, the confidence interval for financial costs overlaps with these two. Peter C. Austin and Janet E. Hux (2002) have shown that overlapping 95% confidence intervals are no sign that the means of two different groups are not statistically different from each other. They instead propose to use the criterion of whether or not two 83% confidence intervals overlap as a method for assessing whether or not two means are significantly different from one another at the $\alpha = 0.05$ level. The respective 83% confidence intervals are presented in Fig. 6.2.

Based on the criterion proposed by Austin and Hux (2002), we see that the effect of more convenience is significantly lower that the effect of targeting "everyone" compared to "suspects" in the target category and than the relative effect of internet usage data compared to registered addresses. The effect of higher taxes, however, is not significantly different to either of the two—even though it comes close with the target dimension. While this allows me to clearly discard hypothesis H4 that suggested that inconvenience has a stronger effect on support for a policy than the extensiveness of the privacy intervention, the narrow overlap between higher taxes and targeting everyone emphasizes the need to delve deeper into the relationship between financial costs and the two dimensions of privacy intrusion to make a clear statement regarding hypothesis H3.

---

[19] I find that the order of the vignettes (i.e., on which of the six positions the vignette is shown) has a significant negative correlation with acceptance, suggesting that the later within the experiment, the lower the acceptance of the proposed policy. However, this effect is only marginal, and it does not significantly alter any of the other effects, neither. Because of the randomization, nothing else was to be expected. As proposed by Auspurg and Hinz (2014: 97), I identified the degree to which the impact of the vignette variables varies among respondents by separately and sequentially estimating random slope models for each vignette variables and find that none of the slopes is significant when compared to the main model. This underlines the robustness of the results.

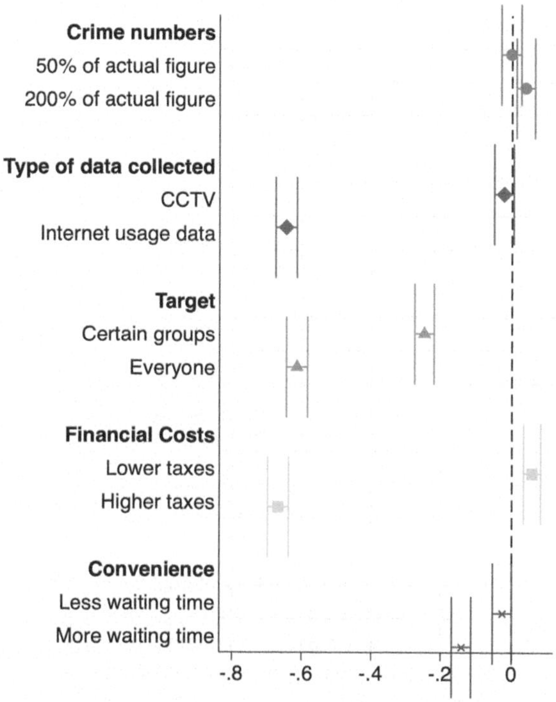

Fig. 6.2 Confidence Intervals of explaining variables in Model 2. (*Note:* 83% confidence intervals, N = 4839. Results stem from a two-level linear regression model including post-stratification weights on the individual level. For the underlying model, see Model 2 in Appendix B.2 in the electronic supplementary material)

As mentioned earlier, I expect that the extensiveness of surveillance measures would depend on the target and data type. To explore this, I compare the effects of the highest coefficients related to the target group. Figure 6.3 displays the mean acceptance for various combinations of tax increase and internet surveillance. I dichotomized both variables, focusing solely on the presence or absence of a specific characteristic. This resulted in dummy variables for tax increase (equals 1 if the cost dimension is "tax increase" and 0 if it is "status quo" or "tax decreases") and internet surveillance (equals 1 if the type of data collected is "internet usage data" and 0 if it is "registered addresses" or "CCTV").

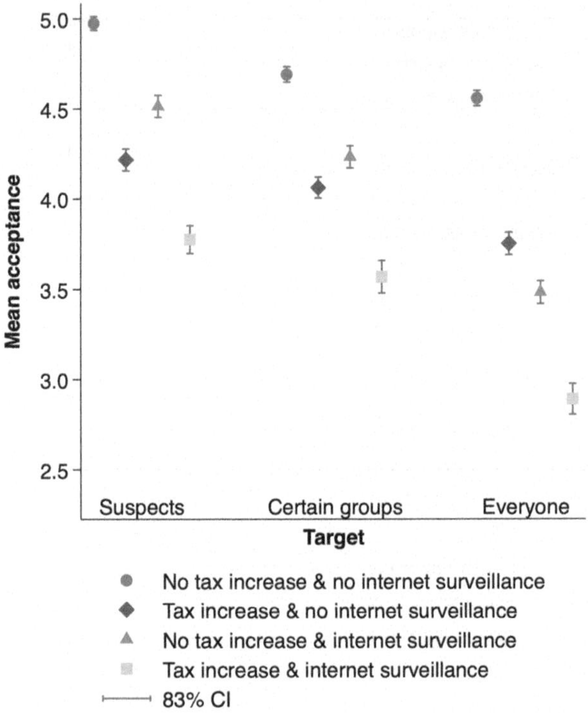

Fig. 6.3 Mean acceptance by groups. (*Note:* 83% confidence intervals, N = 4839. Calculations include post-stratification weights on the individual level)

Not surprisingly, the combination of "no tax increase" (representing either no change in taxes or tax decreases) and "no internet surveillance" (representing either the collection of registered addresses or CCTV)—signified by the circle marker– has the highest mean acceptance among the combinations for all three target groups. Conversely, the combination of "tax increases and internet surveillance"—signified by the square marker—has the lowest mean acceptance.

To further compare the mean acceptance for combinations where only one of the characteristics of interest is present, I examine the targets "suspects" and "certain groups." I find that the mean acceptance is significantly lower for the combination of "tax increase and no internet surveillance"—signified by the diamond marker—than for "no tax increase and internet surveillance"—signified by the triangle marker. However, when the target is "everyone," "tax increase and no internet surveillance" has a significantly higher acceptance than "no tax increase and internet surveillance." Therefore, I conclude that when respondents themselves were not affected by the surveillance measure (i.e., when targeting "suspects" or "certain groups"), tax increases have a stronger negative effect on policy acceptance than more extensive data collection. Alternatively, when respondents were affected themselves, i.e., when mass surveillance is involved, the type of data collected plays a more significant role, with the prevalence of internet surveillance having a stronger negative effect on acceptance than tax increases. In light of this dependency on the target of the surveillance measure, I need to reject hypothesis 3, as financial costs do not consistently have a stronger effect on support for a policy than the level of privacy intrusion.[20]

6.4.2 Focusing on Subjective Versus Objective (In)security

I now turn towards the question to what extent support for state surveillance is contingent on subjective security and/or the objective security situation. In Fig. 6.4, I provide a visual representation of the distribution of crime frequency per 10,000 inhabitants within the sample, ranging from 36 crimes (Berlin) to an outlier district with over 3,000 crimes per 10,000 inhabitants (the city of Suhl in Thuringia).

Figure 6.5 showcases the distribution of the average fear of crime. The alpha coefficient of the five items is .89, indicating high reliability. The distribution is slightly right-skewed. When combined with the mean fear of crime score of 3.3, this suggests that, on average, the sample population tends to be relatively unconcerned about becoming victims of crimes.

While previous studies have hinted at a positive correlation between subjective fear of crime and objective crime prevalence, my data shows only minimal correlations (between .03 and .08 when calculating the average fear of crime at the district level). A bivariate multilevel analysis did not reveal any statistically significant relationship between these two variables on the individual level. The same holds true for the correlations between the individual dimensions (a)–(d) and their corresponding crime figures (Bundeskriminalamt 2021b), with correlations ranging between .03 and .05 (see Appendix B.4 in the electronic supplementary

[20] I have conducted the same group comparison regarding convenience (see Appendix B.3 in the electronic supplementary material). Here, the prevalence of internet surveillance always has a stronger effect on the mean acceptance than whether or not longer waiting times are to come with the measure. However, the difference between the mean acceptance is highest when the respondent is among the surveilled.

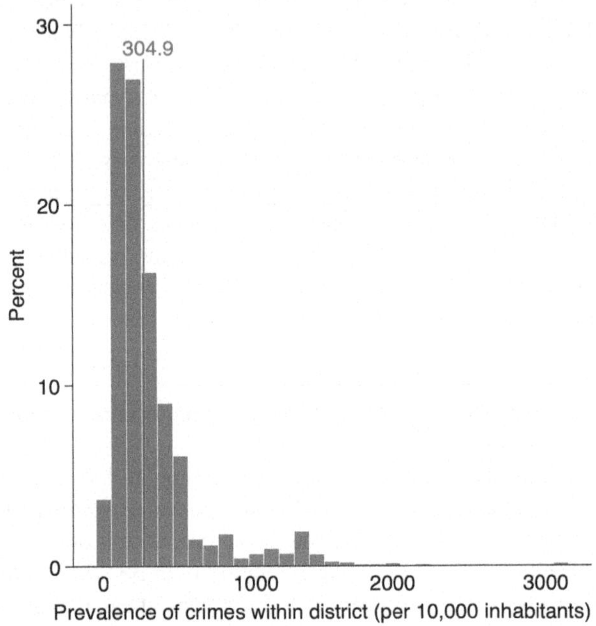

Fig. 6.4 Distribution of objective insecurity within sample. (*Note:* N = 4672.[21] The figure is based on the distribution considering post-stratification weights on the individual level. The line represents the (post-stratification weighted) mean across all respondents)

material). The exception pertains to the dimension related to terrorism. Since the Police Crime Statistics of the Federal Republic of Germany do not provide separate data on terrorist crimes at the district level, I employed figures from the *Global Terrorism Database* (LaFree et al. 2014; National Consortium for the Study of Terrorism and Responses to Terrorism 2023) to proxy the impact at the district level. According to this database, there were 45 victims (i.e., fatalities and injuries) of terrorism in Germany in 2020. The correlation with the individual fear of becoming a victim is lower and even negative (-.01). The missing relationship between subjective fear of terrorism and the risk thereof is in line with

[21] Since the following analyses are not directly related to the ones dealing with the intra-experimental causal effects, I refrained from keeping the sample stable and omitting the respondents with missing values on the subjective (in)security battery for the following analyses.

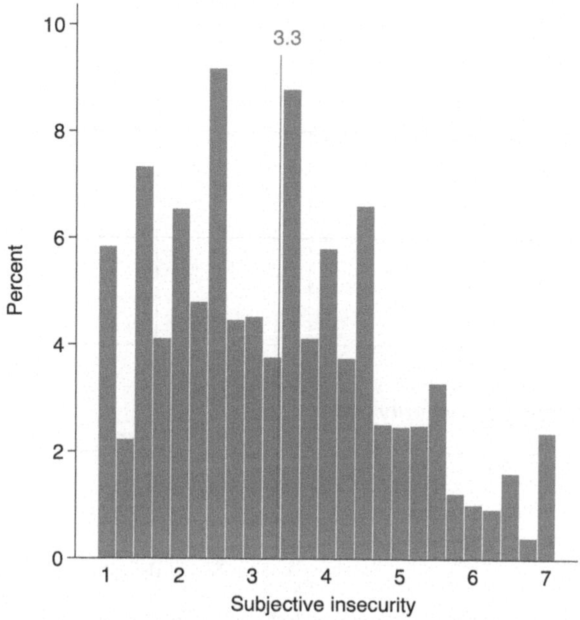

Fig. 6.5 Distribution of subjective insecurity within sample. (*Note:* N = 4672. The figure is based on the distribution considering post-stratification weights on the individual level. The line represents the (post-stratification weighted) mean)

previous studies that have shown that terrorism induces fear on a supra-regional scale, making it less predictable through regional crime rates or victim numbers (G. Norris 2017: 580).

Figure 6.6 illustrates the correlation coefficients of objective and subjective insecurity with acceptance of state surveillance as dependent variable. As expected, subjective insecurity is positively correlated with the acceptance of government security measures, with higher levels of subjective insecurity leading to greater respondent approval. However, the same is not true for objective insecurity, as there is no significant correlation between objective insecurity and the acceptance of governmental security measures.[22] The interaction of the

[22] An alternative operationalization of *objective* insecurity could be the clearance rate (McGovern 2017; Mosher et al. 2010). While the (negative) statistical association between subjective fear of crime and clearance rates is stronger (-.15) than for fear of crime and crime

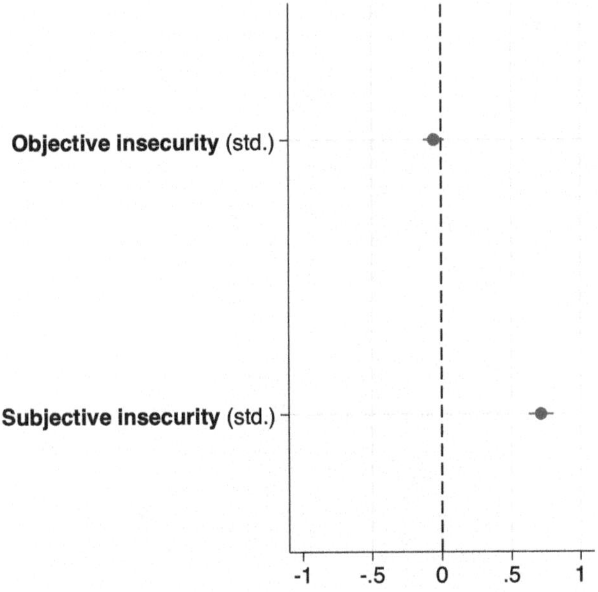

Fig. 6.6 Relationship between objective and subjective insecurity and the acceptance of state surveillance. (*Note:* 95% confidence intervals, N = 4672. Results stem from a three-level linear regression model with vignette dimensions nested within respondents, nested within districts, including post-stratification weights. For the underlying model, see Model 1 in Appendix B.5 in the electronic supplementary material)

two dimensions of security does not yield any significant results (see Appendix B.5, Model 2 in the electronic supplementary material). Next, I delve into how objective and subjective insecurity interact with the main effects of different dimensions in the vignette experiment, focusing particularly on the dimensions related to privacy (type of data collected and target). Figure 6.7 presents the predictive margins of the interaction between objective and subjective security and the three levels of type of data collected.

As anticipated based on the main effects, the slopes of subjective insecurity are significantly steeper than that of objective insecurity. While the latter exhibit a slightly negative trend, it is not statistically significant. For subjective insecurity

prevalence, its effect is likewise not statistically significant. Given that the use of crime rates is the more commonly employed operationalization, I, too, adhere to this in the subsequent analyses.

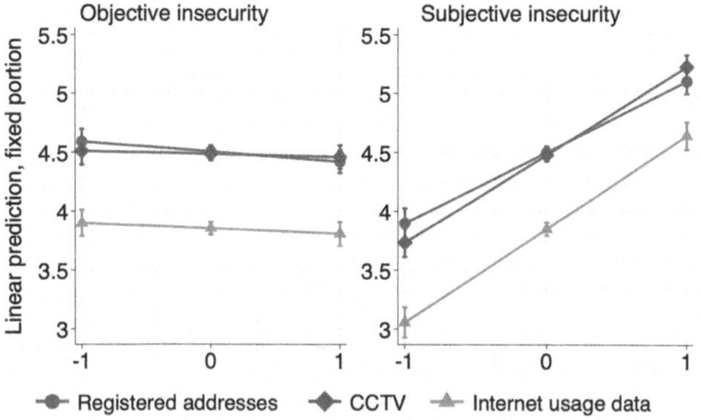

Fig. 6.7 Interactions of type of data collected with insecurity. (*Note:* 95% confidence intervals, N = 4672. Predictive margins with 95% confidence intervals after three-level linear regression model including all respective two-way interactions between objective and subjective security on the one and the three vignette dimensions on the other hand and random slopes on the lower level (namely the vignette dimensions) as well as post-stratification weights on the individual-level. For the underlying model, see Model 3 in Appendix B.5 in the electronic supplementary material)

the slopes for CCTV and internet usage data are nearly parallel, with the increase for registered addresses being somewhat lower. Additionally, the mean acceptance of collecting registered addresses in the case of high subjective security is even lower than that of CCTV, although this difference is not significant.

A similar pattern emerges when examining the target group (see Fig. 6.8). Once again, objective insecurity displays a non-significant negative correlation with the interaction involving the target group and the approval of governmental measures. Conversely, subjective security shows a positive effect for all three levels of target groups, with the most pronounced effect observed for the intermediate category "certain groups." While this category does not significantly differ from "everyone" under low subjective insecurity, it almost reaches the same level as "suspects" under high subjective insecurity.

The respective interaction effects with the other two dimensions (time and cost) do not yield additional insights (see Appendix B.6 in the electronic supplementary material): In all cases, the slopes for objective insecurity remain consistently lower than those for subjective insecurity. Moreover, the latter exhibits nearly parallel trends. As for the "crime figures" dimension, there are no significant differences between treatments, mirroring the findings from their

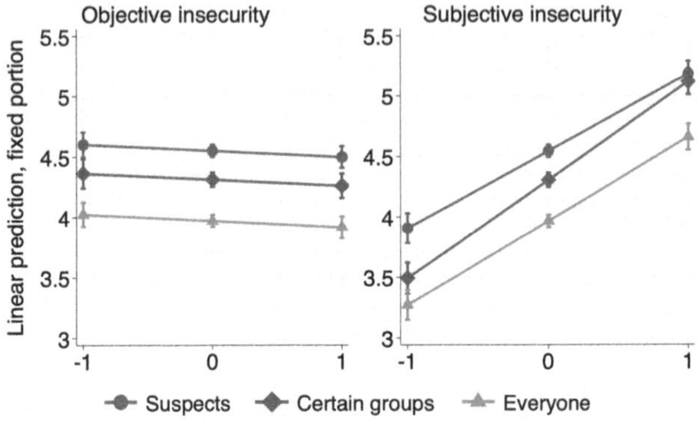

Fig. 6.8 Interactions of target group with insecurity. (*Note:* 95% confidence intervals, N = 4672. Predictive margins with 95% confidence intervals after two-level linear regression model including all respective two-way interactions between objective and subjective security on the one and the three vignette dimensions on the other hand and random slopes on the lower level (namely the vignette dimensions) as well as post-stratification weights on the individual-level. For the underlying model, see Model 3 in Appendix B.5 in the electronic supplementary material)

main effects. Importantly, this holds true regardless of the levels of objective or subjective insecurity.

6.5 Discussion

The study's findings suggest that the variation in crime figures has only a minimal effect on the acceptance of surveillance measures, which leads to the rejection of the hypothesis H1 that higher crime rates would result in greater support for surveillance. There are different possible explanations: (1) It is possible that individuals tend to overestimate the incidence of crime due to media influence and public debates (for Germany, see, e.g.,: Feltes et al. 2018: 607–8), rendering them more reliant on perceived threat for forming their opinions on anti-crime measures (Trüdinger 2019: 33). Respondents might thus perceive all three levels of the presented figures as similar to each other and do thus not ascribe a significant change of the security threat situation to their variation. (2) Respondents might struggle to translate the variation in crime figures into a change in their personal threat levels. (3) The human brain can find it challenging to comprehend very large or very small numbers (Resnick et al. 2017), making it difficult for respondents to perceive a significant variation in the threat situation based on these numbers. I will get back to this point when discussing the results concerning the correlations with respondents' subjective fear of crime and local crime rates. Even though only small in magnitude, the higher crime frame provides significantly higher approval for surveillance, while there is no significant difference in approval with the lower crime frame. The study cannot clarify whether respondents are aware of the actual crime figures, which might lead to a one-sided effect, where an improvement in the security situation does not reduce the demand for surveillance,[23] or, alternatively, that the actual level of crime numbers is crucial for the attitudes.

In terms of the extensiveness of surveillance, the study highlights that the target of surveillance has a more significant impact on acceptance than the type of data collected. This aligns with the idea that privacy concerns are primarily driven by self-interest (Stigler 1980), and approval for surveillance measures is higher when individuals are not among the surveilled. The surveillance of everyone, including the respondent, tends to be less accepted than the surveillance of suspects, assuming that respondents typically do not see themselves as suspects.

However, there are complexities when considering surveillance of "certain groups of people who commit crimes more frequently." There are two facets that need to be discussed: (1) It rather leaves open who is meant. Especially from the field of media studies, we know that there is a discrepancy between reports on the nationality, ethnicity, or origin of perpetrators and actual statistics leading to the prejudice that non-Germans would commit more crimes than Germans—a myth that is not reflected in statistical crime data (Feltes et al. 2018: 606). If we want to speak of certain groups of people who statistically commit crimes more frequently, the German crime statistic shows that perpetrators are on average rather young, more often of male sex, more likely to live in large cities, more likely to belong to lower income and lower education classes, and more likely to be unemployed (Feltes et al. 2018: 607). I cannot say who the respondents were thinking of when presented with this level and whether they identified themselves with this group, thus considering themselves part or non-part of the potentially surveilled. (2) Independently of which group(s) statistically commit crimes more frequently, the approach to precautionary monitor persons who share salient traits and stigmatize them as suspicious contradicts the idea of presumed innocence. This can affect both individuals and society as a whole (Hadjimatheou 2014: 189).

[23] The literature has indicated that, instead of deterring or preventing crime, surveillance merely displaces crime in various forms (M. Clarke 1994) and several studies find surveillance has no effect at all (Ditton & Short 1999; M. Gill et al. 2006; Phillips 1999).

In their assessment of the proposed policy, respondents might thus also include their attitude towards the practice of precautionary surveillance when presented with this specific target group.

Regarding the type of data collected, the study reveals that the collection of internet usage data has a significantly negative effect on acceptance compared to the collection of registered addresses. However, there is no significant difference in acceptance between storing CCTV footage and registered addresses. This finding is somewhat surprising, as one might expect that individuals are more comfortable with authorities having their registered addresses. The normalization of video surveillance in public spaces (Fussey & Coaffee 2012: 203) could contribute to this pattern. When examining the interaction between the type of data collected and the target group, the most intrusive combination, collecting internet data from everyone, has a significant negative impact on acceptance compared to collecting registered addresses from suspects, the least intrusive combination. Thus, it is concluded that the intrusiveness of surveillance measures has a negative effect on acceptance (confirming hypothesis H2).

The scenario of higher taxes significantly decreases acceptance of the proposed policy, and the study observes a stronger public opposition to higher taxes than a desire for tax cuts, in line with the concept of loss aversion and asymmetric responses to price changes. Most studies—albeit not all—find that consumers react more strongly to price increases than they do to price decreases (Ciccone & Soldani 2021: 62) as postulated by Amos Tversky and Daniel Kahneman's prospect theory (1981). It is assumed that humans are loss averse and evaluate assessed losses more strongly than assessed gains. It remains unclear, however, why there is no significant effect between no changes in costs and possible tax decreases. Research on election pledges shows that citizens often assume that politicians rarely keep what they have promised during an election campaign (Dupont et al. 2019: 122). Similarly to election pledges, the mentioning of tax decreases can be regarded as barter object for the citizens' prior action, namely voting for the respective party in the former and accepting data collection in the latter case. Due to their experience with the subjectively stereotypical pledge-breaking politician, respondents might thus be indifferent to the *possible* positive side-effect. Alternatively, the absence of a positive effect for tax decreases could also result from respondents being content with the status quo, not desiring a reduction in internal security budget spending—which would potentially lead to a decrease of services of the government. This is in line with survey evidence on Germans' preferences for government spending priorities which finds that more than 60% of the German population neither opts for spending hikes nor for spending cuts for public safety (Hayo & Neumeier 2019: 4).

In the analysis of the relationship between financial costs and the type of data collected, the study shows that the effect of tax increases (compared to the status quo) is not significantly different from the effect of internet surveillance (compared to collecting registered addresses), leading to the rejection of hypothesis H3. The significance of this relationship is conditional on who is the target of the surveillance measure. When respondents are not among the surveilled (e.g., suspects or certain groups), tax increases have a stronger negative effect on acceptance than internet surveillance. However, when respondents are among the surveilled (e.g., everyone), the type of data collected (internet usage data) becomes more crucial and has a stronger negative impact on acceptance than tax increases. In public discourse, increasing security measures are often justified by the government on the grounds that citizens want more security. If, however, the increase in measures is not to be accompanied at the same time by a passing on of the costs to citizens (as indicated in Brockdorff, Appleby-Arnold, Hawellek, et al.'s (2015) study), this means that other government expenditures would have to be cut. The interplay of these two issues (liberalization of the tax system and focus on law and order) can be found, for example, in the programs of conservative parties. Under these circumstances, an increase in surveillance measures could have additional consequences for coexistence in society. The results highlight the complex interplay of financial costs, tax changes, and self-interest when evaluating surveillance measures.

The study also explores the dimension of convenience (expenditure of time) and its influence on respondents. However, this dimension relies heavily on the assumption that respondents consider their convenience affected by changes in airport or traffic controls. Even though both are relatively common among the German population, not everyone is affected equally, e.g., depending on the frequency of flying or partaking in traffic. In addition, not everyone using individual transportation is experiencing traffic controls. The effects of changes in waiting times are comparatively small and weaker than the effects of the extensiveness of privacy intrusion, leading to the rejection of hypothesis H4. The negative consequence of more waiting time has a stronger (though not statistically significant) effect compared to the positive consequence of less waiting time. This pattern might either be explained by the election pledge effect, where respondents are indifferent to the positive side effect of less waiting time or, alternatively, content with the current waiting time situation. The negative—albeit non-significant—effect of a lower waiting time compared to no changes might even hint towards a suspicion of faster security controls. This is related to Gaskell et al.'s (2004) claim that individuals do not enter into a trade-off when they perceive the measure's usefulness as low (see Sect. 3.3.2).

These findings unveil a striking distinction in how individuals assess surveillance measures based on whether these measures affect themselves or others. In the scenario where privacy is at stake for the individual, concerns over personal privacy weigh heavily in shaping their support for surveillance policies. However, when contemplating measures that do not directly impact them but carry potential financial benefits, individuals prioritize self-interest over abstract values of privacy. This insight raises a fundamental question regarding the nature of individuals' attitudes toward privacy. It appears that many people value privacy primarily as a matter of self-interest (e.g., Stigler 1980), rather than holding it as an intrinsic and abstract good (Rössler 2005). This perspective challenges the idea that privacy is universally cherished as a fundamental value in itself. It implies that, if given the power to make decisions, individuals might be willing to compromise privacy for certain groups—and possibly also foundational values and fundamental human rights in general. This finding adds to the debate on the extent to which individuals' attitudes are driven by self-interest, sociotropic considerations, or even altruism (for an overview, see Dawes et al. 2011; Gilens & Thal 2018).

Furthermore, the research explores the interplay between security and privacy in shaping individuals' attitudes toward surveillance. It underscores the pivotal role of subjective security, as it emerges as a potent factor influencing support for surveillance measures. Individuals who subjectively perceive insecurity are more inclined to accept intrusive surveillance measures. Conversely, the study reveals that objective security, as indicated by crime statistics, does not significantly sway public opinion regarding surveillance measures (confirming hypothesis H5). This is in line with what I have found for hypothesis H1 and raises essential questions about the operationalization of objective security with crime statistics. It also prompts consideration of whether a similar dynamic may apply to public responses to crime, mirroring the observations made in the context of terrorism, where distant events hold greater psychological influence than local incidents (G. Norris 2017: 580).

The significance of subjective insecurity as a predictor of the acceptance of security measures is evident not only in the general analysis but also when looking at dimension-specific effects. Examining the specifics of data collection, the research highlights that the mean acceptance of querying registered addresses grows less strongly with greater levels of insecurity than for the other two types of data. This outcome aligns with the notion that individuals may only be willing to trade off their privacy when they perceive the measure as genuinely useful for enhancing security. Drawing again onto Gaskell et al.'s (2004) that individuals only make trade-offs when they consider a measure as useful (see Sect. 3.3.2), this suggests that under high subjective insecurity, respondents may perceive querying of registered addresses as less effective for ensuring security (or restoring it).

In the context of the target group for surveillance, results suggest that when people feel less insecure, there is no significant difference in their attitudes between the category "certain groups of people who commit crimes more frequently" and "everyone." However, for individuals who experience heightened insecurity, the former category garners significantly more support than the general category "everyone," and it does not differ significantly from the category "suspects." This observation sparks a discussion about the potential ethical implications of surveillance measures based on group affiliations, such as racial profiling. One possible interpretation of the results is that these implications are less important to respondents when they feel insecure, making them more inclined to approve of surveillance measures targeting specific groups compared to those who feel more secure. This way, I can further specify the evidence found in the previous analysis that individuals value privacy in their self-interest but assign less value to it when it concerns others. When people feel relatively secure, they consider the privacy of other non-suspect individuals important, too. However, with subjective insecurity, they perceive privacy less as a foundational value or fundamental human right and no longer significantly differentiate between suspects and people who could be monitored due to certain group affiliations. To date, the literature on the relationship of trust and subjective security is rather unconclusive. On the one hand, the findings seem to contradict the idea that post-materialistic values persist in an atmosphere of insecurity (Inglehart 1981) and, at the same time, empirical results that people who feel insecure have stronger interpersonal communal trust (Vélez et al. 2016). On the other hand, it aligns with (a) studies on trust in insecure environments which reveal that individuals who perceive less security tend to exhibit lower levels of trust in society at large, rendering them more inclined to cast a general suspicion over people (Andrejevic 2004; Marx 1989)[24] and (b) the psychological literature which shows that feelings of security strengthen interpersonal bonds, leading individuals to trust others more readily (Demir 2008).

In conclusion, these multifaceted findings add depth and complexity to the understanding of how self-interest and insecurity intersect with public attitudes toward surveillance. They highlight that privacy may not be an absolute and universally cherished value but is often evaluated primarily through the lens of

---

[24] This viewpoint is further substantiated by arguments put forth by Stutzer and Zehnder (2013), who propose that intensive surveillance can heighten general suspicion, *consequently* eroding communal trust in fellow citizens.

self-interest. The results also underscore the need for further research to unravel the intricate interplay between trust, security, and privacy and its implications for contemporary society.

6.6 Limitations and Future Research

The study acknowledges several limitations, which should be considered in future research.

(1) Survey experiments offer attitude researchers the great advantage that causal effects can be read from them. Compared to classic survey questions, the structured variation of item levels allows the measurement of effects. Nevertheless, survey experiments are not free of shortcomings: In particular, since individual respondents have to be shown a set of several vignettes in order to estimate certain models, researchers are limited in the design of their vignettes in terms of the number of dimensions and levels. Realism is a particular challenge (Auspurg & Hinz 2014: 10). The levels must be formulated in such a way that respondents (a) have an idea of what they are about, (b) a difference between the levels of a dimension is discernible, and (c) any combination is theoretically logical to respondents. In the state surveillance scenario, the variation in financial cost and convenience can only be surveyed in a much more abstract way than in consumer research experiments, where a specific purchase decision is associated with, e.g., discounts for providing data (e.g., as in Beresford et al. 2012), potentially limiting external validity.

(2) The effects observed in the study are relative, making it essential to interpret them in the context of the comparisons made. The effect size and significance of internet usage data refer only to the comparison with registered addresses or CCTV. While the comparison group is easy to interpret for the dimensions context, financial costs, and convenience (no change/status quo versus worsening or improvement), the two dimensions on the invasiveness of surveillance are based on assumptions from the literature, where the subjective perception of the respondents may differ: Individuals might perceive the crime numbers differently and might have a different understanding of what group is referred to, this might be especially problematic for the formulation "certain groups of people who statistically commit crimes more frequently". Similarly, therefore, comparisons of effect sizes should also be made with caution, to say the least.

(3) Some of the results are inconsistent with prior research, such as respondents not differentiating between CCTV and having their addresses stored. Researchers should explore the reasons behind these inconsistencies and investigate whether they are specific to Germany or present in other countries, too.
(4) The finding that individuals seemed to be willing to give up privacy for certain groups invites for future research in several regards. Scholars should (a) explore the driving forces and cognitive processes behind this self-interest driven privacy attitude, (b) investigate whether this finding is Germany-specific or whether it is also prevalent in other countries, potentially focusing on cross-national differences, (c) explore to what extent attitudes towards other foundational values and fundamental human rights might also be mainly driven by self-interest, and (d) look into the societal implications of such understanding of privacy (and other human rights).
(5) Although fear of crime appears to be the standard way of how the literature operationalizes subjective security, studies have shown that fear of crime may encompass an additional dimension, namely, victimization experience. Furthermore, it may not necessarily measure the fear of becoming a victim of a crime but instead serves as an expression of general insecurity. While the latter is advantageous in that it allows me to cover a much broader field and draw more extensive insights, the exact workings of the fear of crime concept are not definitively settled in (psychological) research.
(6) The operationalization of objective security through crime statistics carries two limitations. On one hand, the choice of district levels as the spatial unit is somewhat arbitrary, as this is the lowest level at which data is available. It is difficult to imagine that in a district like Berlin, where more than three million people reside, the objective threat is equal for all residents (see, e.g., Maxfield 1999). On the other hand, and more generally, it raises the question of whether crime statistics can capture individual threat when sociodemographic factors such as age or gender, which have a significant influence on the probability of victimization (Hope & Trickett 2008)—and additionally on the probability filing a police report (Y.-H. Liu et al. 2023)—are disregarded. Thus, the results regarding the influence of "objective" insecurity on the acceptance of privacy intrusions should be interpreted with caution. Following theoretical discussions about how security can be objective (Schneier 2008), future research could address the question of how to measure objective victimization probability, i.e., the "real" risk (Hope & Trickett 2008). Conceivably, multivariate models, such as those that already exist for spatial contexts (e.g., the risk terrain modeling approach, Caplan & Kennedy

2016), could be employed. This is necessary to delve into the question of the correlation between subjective and objective (in)security in detail, focusing specifically on the degree to which subjective insecurity is irrational. Ultimately, this research could propose societal approaches to rationalize subjective security. Since it is a human survival instinct to adapt one's behavior in an uncertain environment (T. O'Brien & Tropp 2015: 137), a systematic mismatch between objective insecurity and its perception could ultimately lead to greater objective insecurity because people do not see the forest for the trees as they are no longer able to identify objectively insecure situations (Zedner 2003).

6.7 Conclusion

This chapter sought to delve deeper into the privacy calculus. It aimed to assess how different factors, such as risks, costs, benefits, and various forms of (in)security, influence the acceptance of privacy invasions. Specifically, I addressed the question: What costs and benefits do individuals consider in their privacy calculus? In contrast to the other two empirical studies, this chapter did not have a cross-national character but focused on the attitudes of German citizens, only. In a nation known for its discerning stance on surveillance (Ziller & Helbling 2021: 997), the findings reveal that a notable proportion of the population expressed a favorable disposition toward such measures. This discovery is particularly striking when contrasted with Germany's broader reputation for skepticism concerning surveillance.

The study employed a factorial survey experiment, a rigorous research methodology, to disentangle the complex web of factors influencing the approval of surveillance policies. I uncovered several crucial insights. A particularly intriguing finding is the role of self-interest in shaping privacy attitudes. The research revealed that, contrary to the notion of privacy as an abstract and universally cherished value, individuals often prioritize their self-interest when evaluating surveillance policies. This leads them to be more willing to compromise privacy when the surveillance does not directly affect them and they are offered money or convenience in advance. This seems to be especially pronounced when people feel insecure. On the other hand, individuals, on average, do not trade their own privacy for money or convenience—countering the idea of an inherent privacy trade-off.

On a more general level, I found a strong negative correlation between the extensiveness of surveillance and citizens' willingness to support it. As surveillance measures become more invasive, their acceptability diminishes. Furthermore, the financial costs and personal convenience associated with these measures emerge as significant determinants of individual support. However, the broader context, including the salience of a security threat, does not seem to sway public opinion. The study also delved into the realms of objective and subjective security. While the objective security situation, as indicated by crime statistics, appeared not to significantly impact the acceptance of surveillance measures, subjective security—the sense of insecurity individuals personally experience—was a powerful driver of approval for intrusive measures. The study thus emphasizes the significance of distinguishing between subjective and objective security. While crime statistics and objective security metrics played a role in the overall assessment of surveillance policies, individuals' personal sense of threat carries more weight in shaping their attitudes than statistical data.

As surveillance technology continues to evolve, and society grapples with the intricate trade-offs between security and privacy, this study provides valuable insights into the attitudes of citizens and their role in shaping policy decisions. Furthermore, it underscores the importance of understanding privacy not just as an abstract principle but as a value that individuals may be willing to trade for perceived personal benefits. While this research offers essential insights into the dynamics of surveillance and privacy, it should be regarded as a foundation for future exploration. The understanding of individual attitudes toward privacy and surveillance remains a relatively uncharted territory, necessitating further research to shed more light on this crucial aspect of our evolving social landscape.

7 Privacy in Different Spheres of Life

So far, I have explored the intricate relationship between privacy and security, with a specific focus on the subjective value of privacy in the context of surveillance aimed at preventing, detecting, or addressing crime and terrorist threats. The prevailing literature, prior to the COVID-19 pandemic, has predominantly centered on state surveillance within this particular sphere of life. However, the landscape of potential threats extends beyond crime and terrorism. People confront diverse objective and subjective risks, and it is widely assumed that individuals view insecurity and threat as undesirable states, motivating them to act in response. As discussed in earlier chapters, there is a belief among some authors that individuals, in their pursuit of security, are occasionally willing to incur costs by sacrificing personal freedom, including their privacy.

In the previous chapters, I delved into the role that the promise of security plays among different populations, and the degree to which privacy decisions hinge on policy formulation and the perceived level of threat. In this chapter, the focus shifts to the fundamental question of whether privacy attitudes are context-specific or whether they can be viewed as a stable personality trait. To address this question, I compare individual privacy attitudes across three distinct spheres of life: terrorism, health concerns, and financial fraud. These three domains are not only frequently cited in surveys as the most significant subjective threats to the public (e.g., Bader et al. 2020; R + V 2022) but also permit the formulation of realistic security promises from the government's perspective.

My analysis is based on data from a pre-registered vignette experiment, which was part of the "Public Attitudes towards the Liberal Script" (PALS) survey,

---

Supplementary Information The online version contains supplementary material available at https://doi.org/10.1007/978-3-658-46462-2_7.

L. Antoine, *The Subjective Value of Privacy*, Wahlen und politische Einstellungen,
https://doi.org/10.1007/978-3-658-46462-2_7

conducted within the Research Cluster "Contestations of the Liberal Script" (SCRIPTS) during 2021/22 (Giebler et al. 2023b). This extensive survey covered 26 countries and included responses from over 50,000 participants. Within the experiment, I sought to gauge how individuals weigh the potential increase in security, presented as experts' expected effectiveness, against privacy invasions in various scenarios. Furthermore, I aimed to determine whether privacy attitudes are sphere-dependent, where individuals make distinct privacy decisions for each sphere, or whether privacy operates as a personality trait that remains relatively consistent across different spheres of life.

The vignette experiment reveals that heightened privacy invasion significantly decreases acceptance of government measures, while promised effectiveness increases acceptance, albeit to a lesser extent than privacy invasion. Notably, acceptance of privacy invasion peaks in the health context, surpassing even terror-related measures. Confirmatory factor analysis indicates that privacy-related attitudes form a consistent latent construct influencing decisions across scenarios. This latent privacy construct strongly predicts privacy-related behavior, demonstrated by its negative impact on providing other private information in the survey, supporting the notion of privacy as a personality trait.

This chapter unfolds as follows: First, I outline the theoretical and empirical approaches that examine the role of spheres of life in privacy decisions. Next, I summarize existing knowledge on public support for surveillance policies and derive hypotheses from the literature. I then provide insights into my data, research design, and methodology, followed by the presentation of my empirical findings. The chapter concludes with a discussion and brief sections on limitations and potential avenues for future research before summarizing my key findings.

7.1 Support for Surveillance Policies

As we have learned before, policies serve to address societal problems through binding decisions (Almond & Powell 1978: 394). Citizens' orientations toward policies illuminate their expectations regarding governmental actions, though the accuracy of citizens' assessments of policy outcomes remains debated (Flynn et al. 2017). Since the late 1970 s, literature has increasingly focused on individuals' privacy choices and associated consequences (R. A. Posner 1978; Stigler 1980), including people's anticipation and evaluation of costs, benefits, and other consequences related to safeguarding their privacy. In this chapter, I will outline the expectations that guide this study. Thereby, I will first focus on overarching explanations for individual support of privacy invasions before turning towards potential sphere-dependent interests in non-disclosure.

7.1.1 Overarching Explanations

To what extent do various spheres of life activate distinct mechanisms in shaping attitudes toward privacy? Public support for surveillance measures is believed to be contingent on the scope of the surveillance (Friedewald, van Lieshout, Rung, et al. 2016). It is chiefly determined by the volume and nature of data collected. Technological advancements have enabled state law enforcement agencies and corporations to amass an ever-expanding array of data types. When it comes to online services, the concept of information sensitivity is employed to describe what individuals are willing to self-disclose. It is posited that individuals attach varying degrees of intimacy to different types of information, with the level of harm resulting from the disclosure being directly linked to the intimacy of the information. This harm can take different forms: material (e.g., loss of financial or other assets), physical (e.g., loss of life or health), or psychological (e.g., loss of social status or relationships) (Mothersbaugh et al. 2012: 77). Individuals are often reluctant to endorse policies that restrict their privacy rights. This reluctance may be rooted in their appreciation of privacy as an intrinsic value (Rössler 2005: 69–70), fear of potential losses (Mothersbaugh et al. 2012: 77), preference for autonomy over security, moral concerns, and self-interest (Stigler 1980). Hence, I posit that

H1a: *The degree of privacy invasion negatively impacts the acceptance of the proposed policy.*

Individuals are inclined to support policies they believe will benefit them (A. Campbell et al. 1960: 208; Margalit 2013: 81). Prior research has demonstrated that the promised or presumed effectiveness of a policy predicts individuals' attitudes and willingness to support it (Drews & van den Bergh 2016; Pavone et al. 2015; PytlikZillig et al. 2018). Perceived effectiveness also hinges on the accuracy of the proposed measure and its validity—i.e., the extent to which the policy addresses a real problem (Sanquist et al. 2008). At the same time, and thereby adding a somewhat theoretical twist, Cayford et al. (2018; 2019) suggest that effectiveness can be viewed as a form of security. Security, in one interpretation, entails providing certainty of expectation, emphasizing the need to minimize uncertainty and maximize predictability so that choices made today can be expected to hold tomorrow (Zedner 2009: 28). There are numerous studies indicating that individuals may be willing to trade private data for the promise of security (see Chap. 5 for the related literature). Therefore, I propose the following hypothesis:

H1b: Effectiveness positively influences the acceptance of surveillance measures.

However, it appears that a stronger perception of effectiveness is also associated with a subjective increase in privacy invasion. Building upon Gaskell et al.'s (2004) considerations, empirical studies (e.g., Pavone & Degli Esposti 2012) have revealed that most individuals fall into two categories: those who trust surveillance measures as effective and who are unconcerned about potential privacy invasions, and those who perceive surveillance measures as ineffective and are apprehensive about privacy invasions. Therefore, individuals often do not engage in a trade-off between privacy and effectiveness (Cayford et al. 2019) leading me to anticipate that effectiveness' effect may be comparatively modest.

7.1.2 Sphere-dependent Interests in Non-disclosure

As discussed in Sect. 2.1.2, the objective value of privacy is not solely determined by the scope of information but is significantly influenced by the specific context in which data is collected. Consequently, different spheres of life trigger distinct interests in non-disclosure or concerns to the contrary. In my study, I aim to compare individual privacy attitudes in the context of state surveillance in different domains.

State surveillance has been on the rise in recent decades, with growing capabilities for governmental institutions to monitor individuals (Marx 2015a; 2016). This development can be attributed not only to technological advancements but also to a shift in governmental rationale (D. Gray 2017: 5). It becomes more and more challenging to compartmentalize these developments into separate spheres as data from various contexts are increasingly interconnected, allowing state institutions to create a more comprehensive profile of their population. Historically, distinct fields of state data collection have been identified in the literature, including tax extraction/social security, public health, and crime prevention: In "Western" states, governments have historically tracked their populations for purposes of tax collection and subsequently to determine eligibility for social security (Rule 2007). Similarly, the historical origins of public health surveillance in Europe can be traced back several centuries (Declich & Carter 1994).

As detailed in Sect. 2.1.3.2, contemporary law enforcement agencies now primarily rely on preventive policing, using data collection and analysis to predict and prevent crimes. Notably, these three fields correspond to areas commonly identified in surveys as posing the most significant subjective threats to the public, including financial fraud, health concerns, and terrorism (e.g., Bader et al. 2020; R + V 2022).[1]

Financial surveillance, health surveillance, and terrorism surveillance were selected to encompass a broad spectrum of state surveillance. I will provide specific details on how I operationalize these three spheres in the data and methodology chapter. Prior to that, I will delve into the specifics of these three domains of state surveillance to refine the hypotheses concerning the spheres of life.

Financial surveillance

In all three spheres of life studied here, fear of data misuse is a potential variable. Regarding financial privacy, understood as the privacy of nonpublic financial information of individuals, persons are believed to have three primary fears: fear of criminals gaining access to personal information for robbery or deception, fear of potential embarrassment due to the exposure of sensitive financial data, and aversion to intrusive marketing practices like unsolicited phone calls or unwanted junk mail (Paul 2001). Discussions on the prevention of financial crimes, such as through domestic transaction reporting requirements, emphasize financial privacy and the right to property as cornerstones of liberal democracies (Michel & Schulp 2022). Financial privacy is significantly influenced by social and cultural factors (e.g., Falsini 2021). Irrespective of whether individuals are actually concealing financial activities, financial matters remain a sensitive and taboo subject in many cultures, with discussions about money typically being discouraged (Whitman 2004: 1190).

---

[1] While it is evident from the literature that surveillance is perceived differently in various countries and cultural contexts (e.g., Capurro 2005; Chiou et al. 2009; Dinev et al. 2006; Farrall 2008; Lowry et al. 2011; Luther & Radovic 2012; Ur & Wang 2013), there is no clear answer as to which spheres of state surveillance are relevant in different contexts. Thus, at this stage, I must assume that the three selected spheres are generally relevant to all countries. This assumption is particularly grounded in the existence of international bodies for data exchange between states for each of the three fields (e.g., the United Nations' Office of Counter-Terrorism, the World Health Organization's International Agency for Research on Cancer, or the OECD's Global Forum on Transparency and Exchange of Information for Tax Purposes). Nevertheless, it is undeniable that the importance of these specific spheres may vary, both in terms of the extent of state activities and subjective perceptions of threat within the population, and that there could potentially be other relevant fields.

Health surveillance

In the context of health privacy—understood as encompassing identifiable information pertaining to past, present, or future physical or mental health, and associated with the provision of healthcare to an individual—a significant concern arises regarding the possible disclosure of this information to insurance companies or potential employers. Such disclosure has the potential to adversely affect individuals in terms of insurance coverage, current or future employment status, or social stigmatization (Lafky & Horan 2011; Willison et al. 2009), especially among minority groups (American Medical Association 2022). It is not without reason that doctors in most countries are subject to a special duty of confidentiality (J. F. Martin 2014).

Terrorism surveillance

In contrast to the other two domains, state surveillance for counterterrorism purposes is considered so comprehensive that specific concerns related to data misuse are not frequently identified in the literature (Lyon 2002). Instead, I need to focus on the most commonly employed forms of surveillance in this context to make inferences about potential fears. When behavior is monitored through cameras or telecommunication interception, individuals have specific fears. Apart from the fear of personal financial or social consequences due to data disclosure, studies have shown that CCTV, in certain spheres of life, increases the fear of crime (e.g., D. Williams & Ahmed 2009) and that awareness of communication interception can potentially result in a "spiral of silence"[2] (Stoycheff 2016). Monitoring public spaces or telecommunications involves considerations of possible racial profiling, which affects not only those who may be targeted but also those who are concerned about its potential impact on freedom of movement and freedom of speech (J. Glaser 2015).

Generating hypotheses

Prior studies, especially in the field of consumer research, have made attempts to measure the monetary value of certain aspects of privacy, often using survey experiments to present participants with trade-offs between privacy and financial gain (Acquisti et al. 2013; 2016; Benndorf & Normann 2018). While financial data have frequently been featured in these experiments, health data and camera surveillance have been less explored in comparative studies. For instance,

[2] The "spiral of silence" theory, developed by Noelle-Neumann (1974), posits that individuals often refrain from expressing minority opinions due to a fear of social isolation or ostracism. This reluctance to speak out creates a self-perpetuating cycle, wherein majority opinions are reinforced, and minority views are suppressed.

Bernado A. Huberman et al. (2005) found that respondents attach greater value to salary information, credit ratings, and savings compared to disclosing their name or body weight. Avi Goldfarb and Catherine Tucker (2012) discovered that respondents are significantly more likely to refuse to disclose their income than, for example, their location data. Jeffrey T. Prince and Scott Wallsten (2022) determined that financial privacy (e.g., sharing bank account balances) was considered the most private in comparison to sharing biometric information, browsing history, or location. From these findings, I propose the following hypothesis:

H1c: Individuals express the greatest privacy concerns in the financial sphere.

While I assume that the perception of privacy invasions as costs and the effectiveness of measures as benefits apply to all three spheres, I expect that the strength of these effects may vary across spheres. The literature suggests that the higher the degree of securitization, the more willing people are to sacrifice their freedoms in exchange for greater security (Dietrich & Crabtree 2019). From extensive research and my findings in previous chapters, I understand that strong securitization effects are particularly pronounced in the realm of counterterrorism (Vultee 2010a). It is also known that individuals tend to emphasize the benefits over the costs (Dienlin & Metzger 2016). However, in securitized spheres, there is an increased awareness of risks, with individuals more carefully weighing the pros and cons of self-disclosure. It has been shown that, in the context of anti-terror surveillance, the type of measures significantly affects support, even when effectiveness is held constant (Brockdorff, Appleby-Arnold, & Fialova 2015). Hence, I propose the following hypothesis:

H1d: The strength of the privacy invasion has the most pronounced effect on acceptance in the terrorism sphere.

At the same time, numerous studies on the COVID-19 pandemic (still prevalent during my data collection) demonstrate that individuals in the health sphere are highly responsive to the effectiveness of measures, primarily focusing on benefits while being less concerned about potential privacy costs (e.g., Kostka & Habich-Sobiegalla 2022; Nguyen et al. 2022). For terrorism, on the other hand, political and public discourses are believed to be highly symbolic, heightening the influence of factors other than effectiveness for citizens policy support (Trüdinger & Ziller 2022; Wenzelburger & Staff 2016). Regarding the financial sphere, as far as I am aware, there is currently no empirical evidence on the impact of effectiveness. Consequently, I anticipate that:

H1e: *The strength of effectiveness has the most pronounced effect on the acceptance in the health sphere.*

7.2 Conceptualizations of Privacy

I have previously detailed the multiplicity of privacy definitions and conceptualizations, see Sect. 2.1. Understandings also vary in terms of where privacy is situated in the cognitive process. One can broadly differentiate between cognate-based and value-based definitions (H. J. Smith et al. 2011).

Cognate-based definitions: Cognate-based definitions describe privacy as an individual's behavior or predisposition to behave in a certain manner. Privacy is perceived as a state of mind (Schoeman 1984; Westin 1967) or an assertion of control (Altman 1975; Westin 1967), emphasizing cognitive, perceptual, and personal traits.

Value-based definitions: In contrast, value-based definitions are influenced by economic and legal viewpoints, treating privacy as a commodity with an economic value or as a fundamental human right that requires safeguarding.[3] In this context, privacy is seen as a social issue that can be managed effectively when considering the respective context (J. F. Taylor et al. 2015).

These differing approaches raise questions about whether privacy is an inherent trait in individuals or whether it is highly context-dependent, influenced by various situations and environments.

7.2.1 Privacy as Personality Trait

The idea that privacy could be considered a personality trait aligns with the widely accepted notion of categorizing individuals into various personality traits, as commonly found in personality psychology (Ajzen 1988; McCrae & Costa 1987). Personality traits are enduring characteristics that give rise to distinct personalities (McCrae et al. 2004). The Big Five or OCEAN model (L. R. Goldberg 1990), which encompasses traits like agreeableness, conscientiousness, emotional stability, extraversion, and openness, is the best-known framework in personality

[3] Here, *value* refers to the positive valence of an issue. The sociological understanding of values as structuring an individual's attitudes, as serving as justifications for behavior (Converse 1964: 211), and as being relatively stable constructs deeply embedded within a person's identity (Rokeach 1973) is more closely related to *cognate-based definitions.*

psychology (Junglas et al. 2008). Research has indicated that the Big Five personality traits, particularly agreeableness, can significantly impact privacy-related decision-making and attitudes, as initially suggested by H. J. Smith et al. (1996; see also Stewart & Segars 2002). Individuals with high agreeableness, known for their sensitivity, trustworthiness, and concern for others, tend to place a higher value on the privacy of their personal information (Junglas et al. 2008; Najafian et al. 2021; Peng & Dutta 2022; Tang et al. 2020; van der Schyff et al. 2020)—while the effects of the other traits vary. However, the application of personality traits in the context of privacy attitudes extends beyond the Big Five model; other traits like risk aversion (e.g., Frik & Gaudeul 2016) and authoritarian dispositions have also been associated with privacy attitudes (e.g., Huq 2013; Rykkja et al. 2011).

Research also explores the question of whether privacy itself can be considered a personality trait. Personality psychology has revisited the idea of individual differences in the willingness to self-disclose personality traits, initially observed in openness with strangers and intimacy among friends (Lewin 1948). However, research on self-disclosure as a personality trait remains inconsistent and inconclusive (J. H. Berg & Derlega 1987). Despite its initial "introduction" as a personality trait (Jourard 1971), challenges in measuring self-disclosure and predicting respondents' self-disclosure led to a reduced emphasis on disclosure as a distinct trait (J. H. Berg & Derlega 1987).

The concept of privacy as a personality trait or stable disposition primarily stems from empirical literature. Westin posits that privacy is a general predisposition and devised a taxonomy of privacy concerns known as the "Privacy Segmentation Index" through a series of evolving questions (Draper 2017; Kumaraguru & Cranor 2005; Margulis 2003). The author (e.g., 1996) categorizes the population into three groups: privacy fundamentalists, privacy pragmatists, and privacy unconcerned. Privacy fundamentalists highly value privacy, resist disclosing personal information, and support strong government regulation for data collection and processing. In contrast, privacy unconcerned individuals readily share personal information with public and privacy organizations, seeing no need for government intervention. The privacy pragmatists, according to Westin, consider the value for themselves and society when deciding to disclose personal information and are often characterized as rational actors (Hoofnagle & Urban 2014). While Westin's work has faced criticism (Hoofnagle & Urban 2014), it has significantly influenced the privacy attitudes debate, and his index has been widely applied in studies (Consolvo et al. 2005; Kuzmanovic & Savic 2020; Kwasny et al. 2008; Malheiros et al. 2013; Woodruff et al. 2014). Some researchers have suggested expanding Westin's three clusters of privacy concern into four (Berendt et al. 2005) or five (Dupree et al. 2016) privacy personas. Many authors consider privacy concerns to be a stable personal disposition and belief that transcends various spheres of life (e.g., Malhotra et al. 2004; Sameer Patil & Kobsa 2005; Schaub & Cranor 2020; H. J. Smith et al. 1996; Taddicken 2014). Nico Ebert et al.'s (2020) findings suggest that privacy concerns and information preferences remain stable across different aspects of life, such as loyalty cards and fitness trackers. Similarly, Gaurav Bansal and Fatemeh M. Zahedi (2014) find that privacy and security trade-offs work similar in the spheres e-commerce, health, and finance.

Various theoretical explanations for these empirical findings exist, ranging from comparing the value of privacy with trust propensity or disposition (Xu et al. 2008) to deriving the personality trait from the "need for privacy" as an individual's consistent preference for self-access or withdrawal from others across situations (Frener et al. 2023). Like other personality traits, it is argued that privacy (value or concern) is both an individually stable trait and can predict behavior, as for example shown by a meta-analysis by Lemi Baruh et al. (2017). Based on this, I propose that individuals value and manage their privacy consistently across various spheres of life and thus hypothesize:

H2a: Privacy value constitutes a personality trait.

7.2.2 Privacy as Non-stable Context-dependent Variable

Conversely, other scholars contest the idea of privacy as a personality trait. Specifically, there is skepticism about the effectiveness of predicting behavior based on privacy attitudes. Despite being widely used and validated, many measures of privacy attitudes have shown to be weak predictors of behavior (Awad & Krishnan 2006; Bandara et al. 2018; Mosteller & Poddar 2017). This observation, often referred to as the "privacy paradox", leads some scholars to question the existence of a general disposition toward privacy. Instead, they argue that privacy concerns are not stable across different aspects of life but are activated or diminished by contextual cues (John et al. 2011). Nissenbaum proposes a contextual understanding of privacy, defining context as "spheres of life" (2004: 119) or "social domains" (2015).[4] Her perspective is grounded in discussions by Pierre Bourdieu and collaborators, who argue that individuals in highly differentiated

[4] *Context* has been interpreted very differently in privacy research and must not always be at odds with cognate definitions: Some scholars understand contextual factors as those

societies navigate a series of autonomous social microcosms, each defined by its unique norms governing roles, expectations, actions, and practices (Bourdieu & Wacquant 1992: 97).

Nissenbaum identifies two types of informational norms. First, norms of appropriateness determine *which information* about individuals is suitable to disclose within a specific sphere of life.[5] The second norm revolves around the respect for sphere-specific norms of information flow, encompassing not only the information itself but also *how* it is conveyed between sender and receiver (Nissenbaum 2004).

While many studies implicitly or explicitly assume that privacy attitudes represent stable predispositions and draw conclusions based on the examination of single aspects of life, some consider the influence of context. For example, several experimental studies (K. Martin & Nissenbaum 2017; K. Martin & Shilton 2016) suggest that the approval of data sharing is contingent on situational factors, such as the secondary use of data for commercial purposes. However, limited research has investigated whether context, understood as different "spheres of life" or "social domains," significantly impacts privacy preferences. In a cross-sectional study on data sharing before and during the COVID-19 pandemic, Frederic Gerdon et al. (2020) demonstrate that individuals are less inclined to share health data compared to location data related to private energy consumption. Still, there are no consistent and significant differences in preferences for sharing with public agencies or private companies, or in the public or private use of the data. Patricia A. Norberg et al. (2007), in an experiment involving US-American students, showed that individuals were hesitant to share certain information for research

psycho-social predispositions that have an influence on privacy decisions: While many studies assume individuals to make rational decisions, a large number of studies (especially on consumer decision behavior) have shown that the decision-making process of individuals is subject to various cognitive biases and heuristics (Acquisti & Grossklags 2005; Gerber et al. 2018). Rationality is further constrained insofar as it can be assumed that most individuals are not autonomous in making their privacy decisions but are significantly influenced by their social environment (Taddicken 2012). Other authors refer to context as the macro-environment to which individuals are exposed. In particular, features of the nation-state, which is the primary lawmaking level in most countries, are used as predictors of privacy attitudes, such that it has been shown that privacy attitudes differ significantly depending on the degree of their country's level of liberal democracy (see Chap. 5). Due to the multifaceted usage of the term *context*, I use Nissenbaum's (2004: 119) circumlocution of "spheres of life" instead.

[5] For example, in the medical sphere, it is appropriate for the patient to share information about their health condition with the doctor, but not vice versa. See also Schoeman's (1984) account, who assigns special value to privacy because the degree of privacy defines the denominator for the degree of different relationships with different people.

purposes but willingly shared it with a bank confederate twelve weeks later. This leads me to the hypothesis conflicting with hypothesis H2a:

H2b: *The value of privacy is contingent upon the sphere of life.*

7.3 Data and Methodology

In this section, I provide details about the data collection, the methodology and the statistical models employed in the study.

Data Collection

The study is part of PALS, a survey conducted in 26 countries (Giebler et al. 2023b).[6] The target population for this survey in all 26 countries comprises permanent residents living in private households aged 18 and older, irrespective of their nationality. The primary mode of survey data collection in most countries was CAWI. Respondents were recruited from an online access panel managed by a survey company. To ensure representativeness, the sample was quota-based, considering factors such as age, education, region of residence, and gender. The quotas were determined based on the "offline population," and the completed interviews align with the population quota. Respondents received a small incentive for their participation. In cases where web-interviews were not feasible, the survey mode was CAPI using a probability sample and a random-walk procedure. The survey was carried out in the most-spoken language(s) in each country, with translations or local adaptations available in over 40 languages. The target sample size was at least 2,000 interviews per country, totaling more than 53,000 interviews. For an overview on the survey countries, see Appendix C.1 in the electronic supplementary material. Respondents with missing values on the outcome variables were excluded from my analysis.

[6] PALS received a positive vote of the Central Ethics Committee of the Presidency of Freie Universität Berlin (ZEA-Nr. 2021–023, 03.11.2021) prior to the data collection.

Methodology

The study employs data from a pre-registered[7] vignette experiment to investigate the multidimensional choices and evaluations made by individuals (Hainmueller et al. 2015: 2395). This method is particularly suitable for understanding attitudes toward topics like surveillance and privacy, which can be complex and sensitive (Dietrich & Crabtree 2019: 347), as has been outlined in more detail in Sect. 6.3. In vignette experiments, respondents are presented with fictional descriptions of situations that systematically differ in several attributes. They are then asked to evaluate each situation based on various criteria such as support, agreement, or perceived usefulness. By varying the situational factors systematically, the effects of individual dimensions can be isolated, allowing researchers to determine the causal impact of relevant situational factors (Auspurg & Hinz 2014).

In this study, each respondent was presented with three fictitious scenarios, each consisting of two dimensions with two levels each. The three scenarios revolve around government measures related to protecting the population from threats in three different spheres of life: future terrorist attacks, an increasing number of cancer deaths, and tax fraud and corruption. The order of the scenarios was randomized. The full design can be found in Table 7.1.

As previously mentioned, I selected three spheres of life to align with existing subjective threats in the population and to be realistic in terms of the potential appropriateness of state surveillance to address these concerns. These scenarios encompass both individual and collective threat components. It is important to note that, given the cross-national nature of my study, the formulation of treatments sometimes had to be somewhat more general to accommodate a variety of national contexts.

The first sphere of life is terrorism, a commonly used example in privacy attitudes research. I vary the strength of privacy intrusion between (1) increasing camera surveillance in public spaces and (2) monitoring telephone calls and Internet activities of everyone without judicial warrant. This distinction reflects the classic differentiation between public and private spaces, assuming that the latter warrant greater protection (Rössler 2005). In addition, monitoring telecommunications is considered a more significant invasion of privacy.

The second sphere concerns health issues, which have gained special prominence, not only due to the COVID-19 pandemic but also because of the

---

[7] The pre-registration for the survey experiment called "Privacy and Security Trade-offs in a Global Context" can be found on Open Science Framework: https://osf.io/xd3ne/?view_only=dc59c71c71ce4e9b807e85f1ff4fcb99.

long-standing debate surrounding the benefits and risks of digitization in healthcare (Dinev et al. 2016). Given the politicization of this topic during the survey and the significant national variations in its handling (Gerdon et al. 2020; Ioannou & Tussyadiah 2021; Kachanoff et al. 2020), I avoided selecting COVID-19 as a scenario. Instead, I chose the cancer threat as a common health concern, prevalent around the world.[8] Government actions to address cancer exist across nations (Nagai & Kim 2017), and respondents are less likely to conflate these actions with COVID-19-related measures due to the noncontagious nature of cancer. I differentiate between targeted surveillance (directed toward specific individuals or groups, in this case, patients) and untargeted surveillance (affecting everyone). While both scenarios can be constructed to support potential medical progress (Zachary et al. 2015), it is evident that examining everyone's health data represents a more substantial privacy intrusion, even if the specifics of the data collected are not fully outlined, compared to increasing data collection only for patients.[9]

The third sphere involves the threat of financial fraud, where various studies have highlighted the sensitivity of financial data (Goldfarb & Tucker 2012; Huberman et al. 2005; Prince & Wallsten 2022). Since financial privacy is often discussed in the context of credit card or e-commerce fraud, constructing a trade-off—i.e., putting too much weight on individual privacy possibly leads to greater insecurity because potentially dubious transactions may go undetected by a supervisory authority (Ballaschk & Paulick 2021)[10]—I address this sensitivity by formulating a scenario in which the trade-off is constructed as a collective threat in the form of tax evasion and corruption.[11] This collective threat manifests

[8] Cancer is the second leading cause of death globally, accounting for an estimated 9.6 million deaths, or one in six deaths, in 2018 (World Health Organization 2023).

[9] It is noteworthy that the final formulation of the first level (target surveillance) includes a justification with "to better understand," whereas this is not the case for the second level (untargeted surveillance), see Table 7.1. This difference could potentially influence the respondents' evaluations. However, this formulation was necessary to enhance the external validity of the scenario.

[10] Obviously, there is no *inherent* trade-off since protecting credit card data may also prevent misuse by ensuring that no one can exploit it.

[11] It is *collective* in the sense that tax fraud and corruption can be seen as anti-social behavior to the disadvantage of the community (Adams & Millie 2021). This financial threat scenario was chosen to be distinguished more prominently from the anti-terrorism scenario, which may also involve the surveillance of illicit financial flows.

when individuals evade taxes or gain unfair advantages through corruption (Storbeck 2002).[12] I distinguish between (1) increasing penalties for not reporting all income and earnings to authorities and (2) monitoring the bank account activities of everyone. The latter, akin to the health concern scenario, represents a classic form of dragnet surveillance affecting all members of society equally, whereas the former entails an implicit increase in privacy intrusion. Raising penalties incentivizes law enforcement agencies to intensify efforts to detect and prosecute financial crimes, potentially involving the monitoring of private data (Ewert & Wagenhofer 2019), thereby leading to increased privacy intrusions or an elevated likelihood of individuals being targeted. Differences in national tax laws among the surveyed countries, i.e., existing competencies of state agencies to access individuals' financial data (EY Global 2023) necessitated this formulation.

In terms of the second treatment, experts' expected effectiveness, I vary analogously between "slightly" and "strongly" in all three spheres of life. The influence of elites on the formation of policy attitudes has been a subject of long-standing study (Zaller 1992). It is established that individuals, particularly on complex issues, rely on information and analyses provided by agents with a legitimate claim to expertise (Lachapelle et al. 2014). Source cues and value predispositions serve as mental shortcuts in this process. Specifically, trust in scientific experts has been demonstrated as a crucial heuristic when shaping public perceptions of risks and general attitudes toward emerging technologies (H. Liu & Priest 2009). Although I acknowledge that the perception of source credibility also plays a crucial role (Druckman 2001), and specifically, despite potential concerns associated with the term "expert," past research indicates that the public generally maintains positive attitudes toward experts and often perceives expertise as independent of the government (Dommett & Pearce 2019).[13] My choice of wording aims to provide an objective evaluation of the measures.

The structure of the vignettes looks like this: The government wants to protect the population of [COUNTRY] against *[sphere of life]*. To do this, it plans to *[privacy intrusion]*. Experts argue that this measure would *[effectiveness]* decrease the threat of *[sphere of life]*.

---

[12] I am aware that this generalized operationalization might encompass super rich tax evaders as well as corruptive and corrupting elites, but respondents may potentially also think of (groups of) individuals who are (accused to) fraudulently taking advantage of social welfare benefits.

[13] For the broad research of what constitutes an expert, their epistemic authority, and their (controversial) role, see, e.g. Goldman (2001) and Quast (2018).

Table 7.1 Vignette dimensions and levels

	Level	*Terrorism*	*Cancer threat*	*Financial fraud*
Sphere of life		future terrorist attacks	an increasing number of deaths from cancer	against tax fraud and corruption
Privacy intrusion	1	increase monitoring of public places with cameras	collect more data to better understand the course of disease of cancer patients	increase penalties for not reporting all income and earnings to the authorities
	2	monitor the telephone calls and Internet activities of everyone without judicial warrant	monitor the medical records of everyone	monitor the bank account activities of everyone
Effectiveness	1	slightly	slightly	slightly
	2	strongly	strongly	strongly

Before the first scenario, respondents receive an intro text and an explanation of what to expect.[14] After each presentation of a scenario, they are asked how strongly they accept the measure on a six-point Likert scale:

Would you consider the government's measure as acceptable or not?

(1) Not acceptable at all

...

(6) Fully acceptable

I prefer not to say.

Don't know

Statistical Models

To analyze the first research question (hypotheses H1a–H1e), I employ a multilevel mixed-effects linear regression model, taking into account the nesting of

[14] "Now, we present you some scenarios how your government might want to deal with different threats and also what experts think about these rules and laws. Please, tell us for each instance whether you consider the government's measures as acceptable or not."

evaluated vignettes within respondents and further nested within countries.[15] I apply post-stratification weights at the individual level and additional weights at the country level to ensure equal representation of all countries in the sample, irrespective of their actual population size (as, e.g., proposed by Welzel 2013: 143). To gain insights into the mechanisms underlying the vignette dimensions, I examine the interaction between privacy intrusion and effectiveness. To explore potential heterogeneity in the effects, I assess if there are significant random slopes on the individual and/or country level for one or more of the three dimensions on a variable-by-variable basis and by conducting Log-Likelihood Ratio Tests as proposed by Hox et al. (2017).

Subsequently, to investigate if the main effects found for hypotheses H1a–H1c hold true for different demographic and contextual groups, I introduce additional variables at both the individual and macro levels. These additional variables include political orientation—measured with the *Short Authoritarianism Scale* (Bizumic & Duckitt 2018)[16]—and trust in government at the individual level as well as liberal democracy—via V-Dem's *Liberal Democracy* Indicator (Coppedge et al. 2022)—at the country level—as outlined in Chap. 3. I also incorporate control variables such as gender, age, and education. For details on the operationalization of these variables, see Appendix C.2 in the electronic supplementary material. Each of these variables is interacted with the vignette dimensions. Thereby, continuous variables are standardized by dividing by two standard deviations (as proposed by Gelman 2008). Following the approach recommended by Heisig and Schaeffer (2019), I include random slopes for the lower-level variables of the cross-level interactions (specifically, the vignette dimensions privacy intrusion, effectiveness, and sphere of life) at the individual level. Additionally, I assess the robustness of the effectiveness dimension by incorporating two supplementary measures from the PALS survey: an index based on four items evaluating individuals' attitudes toward rationality and one item assessing individuals' anti-elitism attitudes since attitudes towards experts are believed to be moderated by

[15] Although my 26 countries might be enough, I calculated an additional model based on REML estimates, as proposed by Elff et al. (2021), see Model 6 in Appendix C.3 in the electronic supplementary material.

[16] I am aware that the degree of Right-Wing Authoritarianism is not conceptually and theoretically equivalent to the left-right continuum—for an overview of the authoritarianism concept, refer to, for example, P. Norris/Inglehart (2019: 69–78). However, multiple studies have indicated that Right-Wing Authoritarianism is essentially synonymous with a preference for right-leaning politicians and parties (Altemeyer 1998; Duckitt & Sibley 2010). At this point, I employ the *Short Authoritarianism Scale*, as it requires the omission of fewer PALS respondents from the analysis due to missing answers compared to using a voting behavior or voting intention-related item.

these (Bertsou & Caramani 2022). To investigate hypotheses 1d and 1e, I include the interaction of privacy invasion and effectiveness with the scenario variable in my baseline model. When presenting results involving interactions, I typically report average marginal effects and provide results from pairwise comparison analyses in certain instances.

To test H2a and H2b, I revert to the unstacked dataset, which means that the items are no longer nested within respondents. Nevertheless, I continue to consider the nesting of respondents within countries and apply weights at both the individual and country levels. I conduct a separate multilevel mixed-effects linear regression analyses for each scenario. I then predict the residuals and perform a confirmatory factor analysis on them. As a robustness check, I conduct separate analyses for countries and use the latent factor from the overall analysis to assess its predictive power for respondents' indication or non-indication of their postal code in a multilevel mixed-effects logistic regression, which can be seen as a proxy for privacy behavior (Sweeney 2000).

7.4 Analysis and Discussion of Results

In this section, I present and discuss the results of the analysis based on the hypotheses outlined earlier. When looking at the overall acceptance of privacy invasions in Fig. 7.1, we see, that acceptance of these intrusions is surprisingly high. Even though most country averages cluster around the middle categories, I find that in a slight majority of countries, the average citizen is acceptant of government privacy invasions, so is the average respondent of PALS.

Overarching explanations

Figure 7.2 shows the effects of privacy intrusion, effectiveness, and sphere of life on the acceptance of fictitious government measures. The results indicate that increasing the degree of privacy intrusion has a significant negative effect on the acceptance of privacy interventions, confirming Hypothesis 1a. Promised effectiveness has a significant positive effect on acceptance, validating Hypothesis 1b. However, the effect size of effectiveness is significantly lower than that of privacy intrusion. Notably, in terms of sphere of life, only cancer threat stands out with significantly higher acceptance of privacy intrusion compared to terrorism and financial fraud. The expectation that financial fraud would have the lowest acceptance was not supported, so Hypothesis 1c is rejected.

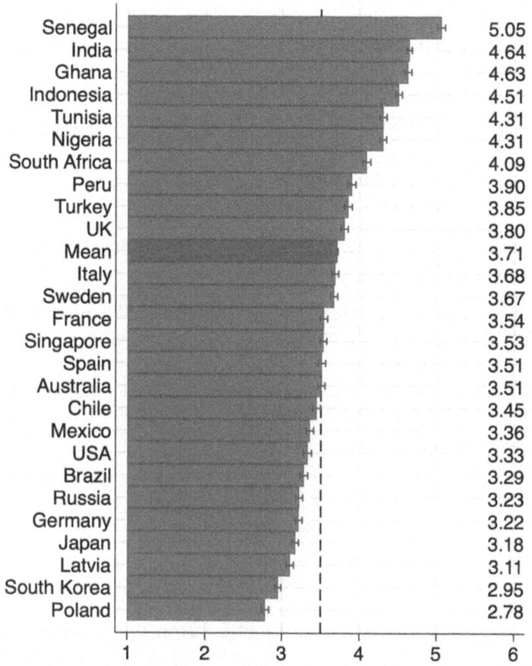

Fig. 7.1 Mean acceptance of privacy invasions by country. (*Note:* The capped spikes indicate the respective 83%-confidence intervals of the average country acceptance to assess the difference of means.[17] N = 49,302. Average acceptance of surveillance measures is calculated as the mean response to the two items. Within each country, post-stratification weights are considered, for the overall mean, I additionally include a weight to adjusting for the different country sample sizes)

Robustness checks

The question now arises as to what extent the effects found are constant across respondents and countries. In a first step, I look at whether there are significant random slopes indicating that the effects are heterogeneous at the individual or country level. I find that except for effectiveness at the individual level, all other variables produce significant random slopes at both the individual and country level (see Appendix C.4 in the electronic supplementary material). To make sense of this heterogeneity, I include interactions with explanatory variables. I know from the previous chapters that the acceptance of security measures and privacy intrusions is moderated by respondent characteristics and their environment. I draw on the analyses conducted in Chap. 5 that investigated to which degree the

[17] Austin and Hux (2002) have shown that overlapping 95% confidence intervals are no sign that the means of two different groups are not statistically different from each other. They instead propose to use the criterion of whether or not two 83% confidence intervals overlap as a method for assessing whether or not two means are significantly different from one another at the $\alpha = 0.05$ level.

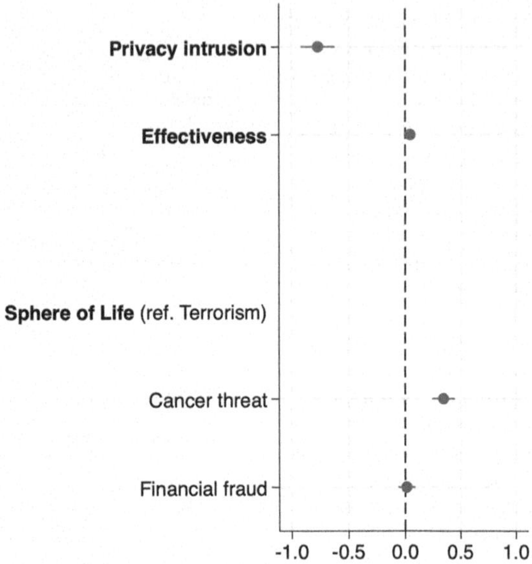

Fig. 7.2 Effects of experimental treatments on the acceptance of the fictious government measures. (*Note:* 95% confidence intervals, N = 49,302. Results stem from a three-level linear regression model including post-stratification weights on the individual level as well as country weights adjusting for the different sample sizes. For the underlying model, see Model 2 in Appendix C.3 in the electronic supplementary material)

effect of a security-based justification is moderated on the micro and macro level and include the same indicators as potential moderators: Political orientation and trust in government on the individual level and liberal democracy on the country level. In addition, I include gender, age, and education as control variables.

Figure 7.3 shows the results of the pairwise comparisons of marginal effects after including interactions of respondents' characteristics with the three treatment dimensions. Consistent with what we observed in Fig. 7.2, I can discern that the group disparities are more pronounced for intrusion compared to effectiveness. The effects of right-wing authoritarianism (RWA) and trust in government are significantly higher when privacy intrusion is more substantial than when it is lower. Taking the main effects into account, this implies that privacy intrusion has a more pronounced negative impact on individuals with lower RWA and lower trust in government compared to those with higher values. For respondents in liberal democracies, too, this negative effect tends to be further amplified. The same trend is evident in the sociodemographic control variables: for women (compared to men), with increasing age, and for individuals with middle to higher levels of education (compared to those with lower education), intrusion has an even more negative effect on acceptance. In the case of effectiveness, only one pairwise comparison is significant: as RWA increases, effectiveness has a significantly reduced

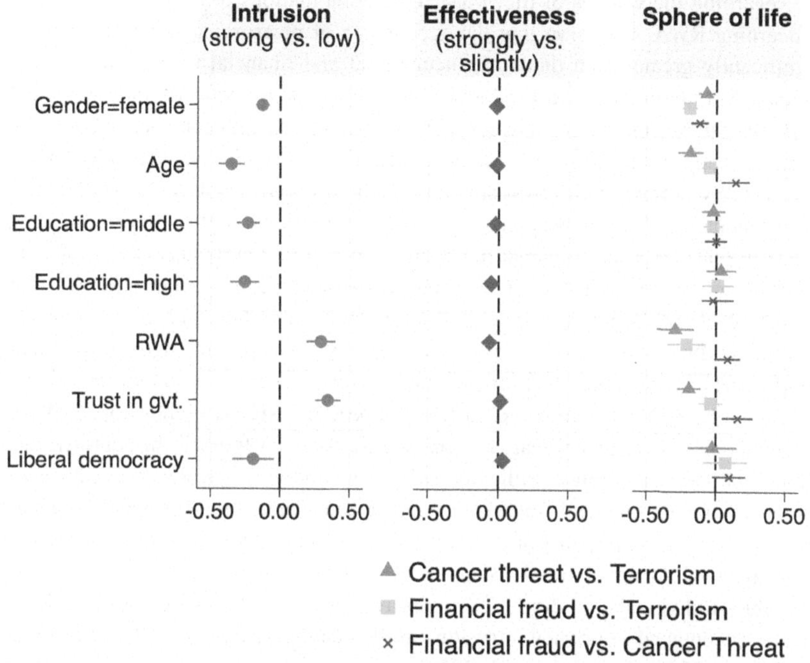

Fig. 7.3 Pairwise comparisons of marginal effects after including interactions of respondents' characteristics with the three treatment dimensions. (*Note:* N = 47,016.[18] The figure shows beta coefficients and respective 95% confidence intervals of pairwise comparisons after average marginal effects have been conducted for each moderator in combination with each vignette dimension. The underlying multilevel regression model includes random slopes for the lower-level variables of the cross-level interactions (namely the vignette dimensions privacy intrusion, effectiveness, sphere of life) as well as post-stratification weights on the individual level as well as country weights adjusting for the different sample sizes. For the underlying model, see Model 3 in Appendix C.3 as well as Appendix C.5 in the electronic supplementary material)

effect. This suggests a negative correlation between authoritarian tendencies and rational thought.

---

[18] Since this analysis serves as a robustness check only, I decided to not omit those respondents with missing values from all analyses, resulting in a slightly lower sample size for this analysis in comparison to all others.

Regarding the spheres of life, I test three combinations of two scenarios each: concerning RWA, I observe that the acceptance of measures against terrorism is significantly greater than that for cancer threat and financial fraud, with no significant distinction between the latter two. This is in line with the literature that finds that authoritarians are always very supportive of anti-terrorism. Compared to less authoritarians who tend adopt more restrictive policy stands (only) when they perceive threat from terrorism (e.g., Hetherington & Suhay 2011). Trust in government significantly correlates with the differentiation between terrorism and cancer threats (measures against the former are more strongly accepted) and with favoring measures against financial fraud over those against cancer threats. The degree of liberal democracy does not significantly correlate with the distinction among the three spheres, nor does educational level. Gender and age, on the other hand, reveal trends where measures against terrorism appear to be more accepted. Additionally, women, compared to men, appear to express higher approval for measures against cancer threats as opposed to financial fraud.[19] In contrast, age shows the opposite trend, with increasing age linked to greater acceptance of measures against financial fraud compared to cancer threats. This result is somewhat surprising. Although I am aware that older individuals are more frequently victimized by financial fraud (Shao et al. 2019), it might have been expected that older individuals, tending to be more reliant on medical care, would exhibit greater acceptance of privacy intrusions in the healthcare domain (Offermann-van Heek et al. 2019; Tsertsidis et al. 2019).

Overall, the non-significance of the effectiveness-dimension is rather surprising. In my view, the result can be interpreted in two ways. On one hand, the finding might be indicative of respondents not making rational decisions. On the other hand, the result could also reflect skepticism towards expertise and elitism in general, with respondents primarily being triggered by the phrase "experts argue." To investigate whether I can make sense of the results, I made use of additional items included in PALS, namely an index based on four items measuring individuals' attitudes towards rationality and one item measuring individuals' anti-elitism. I find, however, that the effect of effectiveness does not significantly vary across levels of rationality or levels of anti-elitism.

Some authors find that perceptions of risks and benefits are not independent of each other suggesting to also investigate a possible interaction of the two factors

[19] From the literature, no specific comparisons of these spheres of life are available. I can only report that studies indicate that women have a lower risk of developing cancer than men (Dorak & Karpuzoglu 2012). Whether this is a result of heightened awareness or counterintuitive to their risk assessment in this study is a question that cannot be answered with the present design.

(Meier & Krämer 2022). I do not find that the effect of effectiveness significantly differs depending on the level of intrusiveness and vice versa (see Appendix C.6 in the electronic supplementary material).

Sphere-dependent interests in non-disclosure

Figure 7.4 explores the average marginal effects of interactions between privacy intrusion and effectiveness with the three spheres of life. This allows me to draw conclusions about the different effects of the two treatments in the three spheres of life. First, as already seen in Fig. 7.2, the changes in the strength of privacy intrusion are significantly larger than changes in effectiveness. As postulated in hypothesis H1d, it can be seen that increasing the privacy intrusion has the largest effect in the terrorism sphere. Thus, the hypothesis can be accepted. Interestingly, however, it turns out that there is no significant difference between cancer threat and financial fraud (as shown by the 83% confidence intervals). The implicit expectation was that the sphere of cancer threat would be more securitized than the sphere of financial fraud, so that the differences should have been larger due to the increase of the privacy intervention. In terms of effectiveness, the results are not in line with my expectations. I had postulated in hypothesis H1e that the effect of effectiveness should be largest in the health sphere. I find, however, that effectiveness enhancement has the greatest effect in the sphere of financial fraud, while it has the lowest effect in the terrorism sphere. The difference between the two spheres of life is significant. The effect of effectiveness in the sphere of cancer threat is between the other two spheres of life. The difference is insignificant in each case. Thus, I must reject hypothesis H1e.

Privacy as personality trait

To find out whether privacy is possibly a personality trait that decisively influences individual privacy decisions across spheres of life, I take a closer look at the relationship between the three spheres. To do so, I use the unstacked dataset and look at the relationship of the three variables first graphically, then statistically, and finally try to calculate a latent factor.

Figure 7.5 shows for all combinations of attitudes towards anti-terrorism measures (x-axis) and measures against cancer threat (y-axis) the mean support for measures in the sphere of financial fraud (color scale from purple to yellow). We see that low values on the x- and y-axis are related to low acceptance of measure against financial fraud and vice versa.

We have learned from the first analysis that the privacy intervention and—even though to a lesser extent, but still statistically significant—promised effectiveness treatments have an effect on the support for government measures. While this

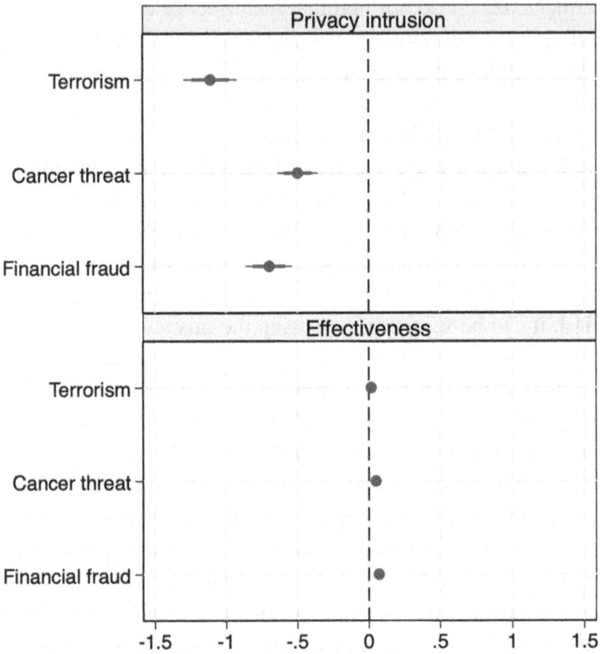

Fig. 7.4 Average marginal effects of the interactions of privacy intrusion and effectiveness with each of the three spheres of life on the acceptance of the fictious government scenarios. (*Note:* N = 49,302, the figure shows beta coefficients and respective 83% and 95% confidence intervals of average marginal effects after a three-level linear regression model including the respective interactions of privacy intrusion and sphere of life as well as effectiveness and sphere of life. The underlying multilevel regression model includes post-stratification weights on the individual level as well as country weights adjusting for the different sample sizes. For the underlying model, see Model 4 in Appendix C.3 in the electronic supplementary material)

is not relevant for the graphic depiction because of the randomization of the treatment dimensions, it needs to be considered when calculating the correlation coefficients by calculating *partial* correlation (Baba et al. 2004). The three variables are correlated with each other at >.4, suggesting a moderate correlation.

To dig deeper into the relationship of the three variables, I estimate a separate model for each of the three scenarios, including the two treatments, i.e., intrusion and effectiveness, as independent variables in each model. I then predict the

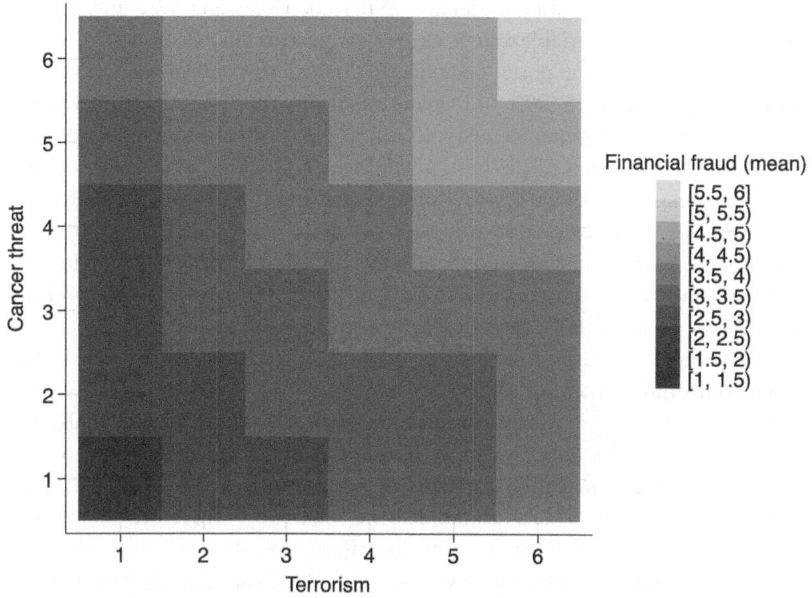

Fig. 7.5 Average support for fictitious government measure in the sphere of financial fraud for each combination of support for the other two spheres of life. (*Note:* N = 49,302, post-stratification weights on the individual level as well as country weights adjusting the different sample sizes. This graph has been created using Ben Jann's (2021) *heatplot* package)

residuals for each scenario. Using these residuals, I conduct a two-level confirmatory factor analysis with standardized coefficients. The results of this analysis suggest that all three items load significantly, with coefficients greater than 0.78 each, on a latent factor. The coefficient of determination (CD) suggests that 69% of the explainable variance of the manifest variables is explained by the latent factor. The standardized root mean squared residual (SRMSR) index is smaller than 0.05 indicating a good fit (Hu & Bentler 1999). This holds true if I consider each country separately (see Appendices F.7 and F.8).

To test the validity of the factor, I use the actual privacy behavior of the respondents as a proxy. During the survey, different socio-demographic information was asked, which could serve as a proxy for privacy behavior. It is assumed that the more individuals value privacy, the less personal information they are willing to disclose about themselves (Joinson et al. 2008). Because some of the socio-demographics were used to quota CAWI respondents and were thus mandatory data, traditional variables such as age or gender are not eligible for this purpose. Instead, I use the postal code query,[20] where respondents had the option not to provide it, of which 4.9% of respondents made use.[21] Results from a multilevel logistic regression indicate a significant negative effect of the latent privacy variable on the indication of the postal code, which provides additional evidence for the existence of a latent privacy attitude, see Fig. 7.6. If we recall that the idea of privacy as a personality trait was discarded partly because of frequent discrepancies between its measurement and predictive power for behavior, the results become even more central. At least in the PALS dataset, privacy-related behavior can be predicted very effectively using the latent privacy construct. I can thus accept hypothesis *H2a Privacy value is a personality trait* while I must decline competing hypothesis *H2b.*

The notion that privacy may be considered a personality trait potentially has direct implications for policy-making. Given that individuals seemingly do not perceive surveillance in various spheres as entirely independent of each other, the negative effects may also accumulate in some way. Therefore, the results contribute to the concept of the "overall surveillance calculus" (*Überwachungsgesamtrechnung*) introduced for the first time by the German Federal Constitutional Court (Friedewald et al. 2022). This concept suggests that surveillance measures, when viewed individually, may appear harmless. However, the assessment of their surveillance potential should always take place in the context of all other surveillance measures.[22] In this regard, policy-makers are urged to consider the overall context of surveillance measures. The fact that respondents apparently do not scrutinize each measure individually but possess relatively stable privacy attitudes can assist policy-makers in anticipating acceptance of measures when attitudes towards existing measures are known. At the same time, the introduction of a new measure may need to be accompanied by the abolition of another measure

[20] Previous research has shown that 87% of the US population can be uniquely identified by gender, postal code and date of birth with postal code being an important factor for identification (Sweeney 2000).

[21] Due to data protection regulations, the postal code was not queried in South Africa and the United Kingdom. These countries were omitted from the analysis.

[22] The current federal government, according to the coalition agreement, aims to heed this call (Sozialdemokratische Partei Deutschlands et al. 2021: 108). Current research projects are examining how to meaningfully implement the approach in practice, see e.g., Friedewald et al. (2022) or Poscher et al. (2021).

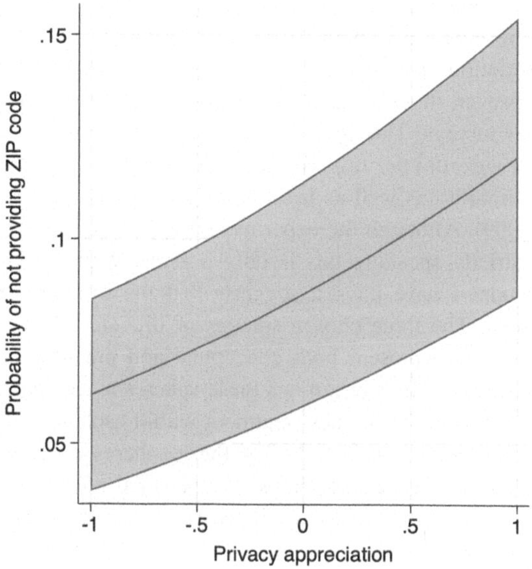

Fig. 7.6 Relationship between privacy trait and privacy behavior. (*Note:* N = 46,876, adjusted marginal mean of the non-provision of the ZIP code for the range of privacy appreciations after multilevel mixed-effects logistic regression model including post-stratification weights on the individual level as well as country weights adjusting the different sample sizes. The privacy appreciation variable is the Gelman-standardized latent construct of a two-level confirmatory factor analysis of the residuals, as described above (Gelman 2008). For the underlying model, see Appendix C.9 in the electronic supplementary material.)

to maintain equilibrium in the subjective overall surveillance calculus. This particularly underscores the importance for policy-makers to thoroughly understand the attitudes of their citizens.

7.5 Limitations and Future research

Certainly, this study is not without limitations. These will be discussed below, along with suggestions for future research.

(1) Survey experiments offer attitude researchers the great advantage that causal effects can be read from them. Compared to classic survey questions, the structured variation of item-levels allows the measurement of effects. Strictly speaking, however, this is not one but three separate *one vignette per respondent* factorial surveys. This form of factorial surveys has several advantages over *multiple vignettes per respondent* factorial surveys. For example, effects of social desirability as well as learning effects are no longer relevant (Auspurg et al. 2009). Although the experimental logic allows me to make causal statements, strictly speaking this is only possible within the vignettes. The analytical model I have chosen suggests that the different spheres of life are comparable. The three chosen spheres of life—terrorism, cancer threat, and financial fraud—present both conceptual and practical differences that merit consideration. The study treats these spheres as comparable, assuming that the varying levels of privacy treatment within each are equivalent. However, a closer examination reveals that these spheres differ substantially in terms of perceived risks, probabilities, and personal relevance to individuals. For example, the probability of an individual developing cancer is significantly higher than becoming a victim of a crime, let alone a terrorist attack (Mueller & Stewart 2021). Public perceptions and politics have contributed to imbalances in the perceived importance of these different threats. While individuals often struggle to assess probabilities accurately (Sunstein 2003), politics can exacerbate this imbalance, with seemingly disproportionate reactions to different threats (Mueller & Stewart 2021). Yet, the study does not delve deeply into how these varying perceptions of probabilities affect the calculus of privacy (Kehr et al. 2015).

(2) In operationalizing the varying levels of privacy invasion within each sphere, the study had to strike a balance between realism[23] and comparability. While I recognize that the study's primary interest is in the direction of the effect rather than exact equivalence of distances, it (implicitly) still assumes that the privacy invasion levels are evenly spaced within each dimension across all three spheres (Auspurg et al. 2009). This simplification may not capture the complexities of how individuals perceive and react to different levels of privacy invasion within different spheres.

[23] While this cannot be quantitatively assessed, the experiment, as part of PALS, underwent several cognitive interviews in which respondents rated the instrument as logical and comprehensible (Giebler et al. 2023b).

(3) The operationalization of financial privacy, encompassing dimensions of tax fraud and corruption, adds an extra layer of complexity compared to the relatively straightforward scenarios in the terrorism and cancer threat scenarios. The two-dimensionality of this sphere introduces the potential for varying interpretations and associations among respondents.[24] While tax fraud and corruption are closely related in many ways (Marjit et al. 2017), the personal relevance and individual associations with these concepts can differ significantly depending on respondents' personal circumstances or contexts (Torgler & Valev 2010). Furthermore, it cannot be determined to what extent the assumption is shared that raising penalties incentivizes law enforcement agencies to intensify efforts in detecting and prosecuting financial crimes, thereby constituting a form of monitoring private data as formulated in the second level of privacy intrusion in this sphere. These nuances may limit comparability with the other two spheres, as respondents may interpret the scenario in ways that are not fully captured by the study's design.

(4) The study's analysis is exclusively focused on state surveillance, assuming that it operates separately from non-state surveillance. However, in practice, distinguishing between state and non-state surveillance is becoming increasingly challenging (Lyon 2015b: 145). Respondents often do not neatly differentiate between these two categories, and their attitudes towards privacy may be influenced by a broader spectrum of surveillance practices, including those carried out by non-state actors (Steinfeld 2017).

(5) On a more general level, the study of attitudes towards surveillance is potentially always limited due to a biased non-response rate: since surveys are themselves essentially a form of surveillance, some individuals might interpret them as a privacy invasion (Haggerty & Gazso 2005; Marx 2007). However, no significant correlation is found between the countries' (proxy

[24] Tax fraud, defined as "illegal and intentional actions taken by individuals to reduce their legally due tax obligations" (Alm 2012: 55), is closely related to collective action and free-rider problems: Although individuals have an inherent interest in the state providing certain (tax-funded) services, it would be rational for each citizen to free-ride since the actual amount they pay has little to do with the level of public services they receive (Di Mauro et al. 2019). In contrast, corruption, can be described as dishonest behavior by those in positions of power. On the one hand, it is corrupt individuals who engage in illegal activities who benefit, as they gain illicit advantages by bribing others. On the other hand, it is those in power who allow themselves to be corrupted.

measures of the) national level of surveillance[25] and the respective non-response or refusal rates in PALS (see Appendix C.10 in the electronic supplementary material).

Based on these limitations, I identify several areas for future research:

(1) Future research should delve into the concept of privacy as a personality trait within the context of various surveillance agents, not limiting the analysis to state surveillance alone. Investigating how individuals' privacy attitudes manifest and interact across different surveillance contexts can provide a more comprehensive understanding of the role of privacy as a personality trait.
(2) Understanding how individuals incorporate probability assessments into their privacy calculus is an important avenue for future exploration. How individuals weigh the likelihood of various threats and privacy invasions in their decision-making process is a critical yet understudied aspect of privacy-related attitudes (Kehr et al. 2015).
(3) To enhance comparability across different spheres, future studies may consider more precise operationalizations that account for the multifaceted associations that respondents may have with particular terms or concepts. By acknowledging and addressing these complexities, future research can provide a more nuanced analysis of privacy attitudes within each sphere of life.
(4) Investigating how multiple surveillance measures interact and accumulate in influencing public opinion is another promising area of research. This can provide valuable insights for policy-makers into the complexities of public attitudes towards surveillance measures and the potential for these attitudes to accumulate over time.
(5) Further research should continue to explore the concept of privacy as a personality trait. Investigating its robustness and implications for public policy and governance can provide valuable insights into how individuals' inherent privacy attitudes shape their responses to a range of privacy-related scenarios and decisions. This ongoing exploration can help bridge the gap between theoretical conceptions of privacy as a personality trait and its practical applications in policy-making and public opinion analysis.

[25] As outlined earlier, I follow Stoycheff et al. (2018: 6) in using *Freedom House's Freedom on the Net Index* as a proxy for state surveillance (Freedom House 2021).

7.6 Conclusion

This chapter has investigated the role of privacy as a personality trait in shaping public attitudes towards state surveillance measures across different spheres of life, including terrorism, cancer threat, and financial fraud. The analysis has provided valuable insights into how individuals' inherent privacy attitudes influence their acceptance of privacy invasions and the effectiveness of government measures. Additionally, the study has explored the interactions between respondents' characteristics and the specific sphere of life in which the surveillance measures are implemented.

The findings revealed several important patterns and implications regarding the relationship between privacy as a personality trait and public attitudes towards state surveillance: The analysis has confirmed that increasing the degree of privacy intrusion has a significant negative effect on the acceptance of privacy interventions. The effectiveness of government measures, as expected, has a significant positive effect on acceptance, although the effect size is lower than that of privacy intrusion. In terms of sphere of life, the results show that the acceptance of privacy intrusion is significantly higher in the context of the cancer threat than in the areas of terrorism and financial fraud, contrary to initial expectations.

The study has identified significant heterogeneity at both the individual and country levels for most effects. Interaction effects with explanatory variables, such as political orientation, trust in government, and liberal democracy, have shed light on how these factors moderate the effects of privacy intrusion and effectiveness. For example, individuals with more authoritarian attitudes tend to be more indifferent about the degree of privacy intrusion but are always supportive of security measures. The sphere of life also interacts with these variables, producing unique patterns in each context.

The analysis of the interactions between privacy intrusion and effectiveness in different spheres of life highlighted the complexities of how individuals weigh privacy and effectiveness in different contexts and challenges initial hypotheses. While privacy intrusion has a more substantial impact than effectiveness, it is not constant among the scenarios and for all individuals.

The study provides evidence to support the concept of privacy as a personality trait. Through confirmatory factor analysis, it demonstrated that privacy-related attitudes can be understood as a latent construct that consistently influences individual privacy decisions across the three spheres. This is supported by the finding that the latent privacy construct significantly predicts privacy-related behavior, such as the willingness to disclose personal information.

The results have important implications for policy-makers. They underline the need to consider the cumulative effects of multiple surveillance measures. Respondents' seemingly stable privacy attitudes indicate that public acceptance of measures can be anticipated more effectively when attitudes towards existing measures are known. Policy-makers should recognize that public acceptance may not be based on the individual merits of each measure but on a broader context.

In conclusion, this chapter offers insights into the role of privacy as a personality trait in shaping public attitudes towards state surveillance measures. It highlights the importance of considering contextual factors, individual characteristics, and the interplay between privacy intrusion and the effectiveness of government measures. By recognizing privacy as a personality trait and understanding its influence, policy-makers can make more informed decisions about surveillance measures and anticipate public responses within a broader context. The findings contribute to the ongoing discourse on privacy, surveillance, and their implications for governance and public policy. Future research in this area can further explore the complexities of privacy attitudes and their interactions with diverse surveillance agents, enabling a more comprehensive understanding of the multifaceted world of privacy-related decision-making.

8 Conclusion

In the age of ubiquitous digital interaction and the post-9/11 idea of preventive justice and citizen's "protection" through state surveillance, the traditional paradigm of privacy is frequently deemed antiquated. The extensive and often overlooked terms and conditions accompanying online platforms serve as a tacit acknowledgment, indicative of a willing surrender of personal data in exchange for the seamless social connectivity these platforms afford. Simultaneously, the individuals' pursuit of security is stirred by the prevailing anxieties of modernity, encompassing a myriad of concerns, ultimately resulting in what appears to be a voluntary acceptance of privacy invasions. Despite sporadic public expressions of concern following security breaches, the prevailing sentiment continues to propagate the notion that privacy is effectively obsolete or, in more dramatic terms, "dead."

This perspective, however, oversimplifies the complex interplay between individual agency, societal expectations, and technological advancements, as this thesis shows. I have found that the relationship between the public and privacy is highly nuanced. Individuals do not appear to take their privacy decisions lightly but rather usually carefully weigh the costs and benefits, rendering a general obituary for privacy inappropriate. In this conclusion of the thesis, the results will first be summarized and discussed. Subsequently, the key contributions to the literature and their scientific and societal implications will be elucidated, followed by an exploration of the limitations of the chosen approach and the identification of potential areas for future research.

L. Antoine, *The Subjective Value of Privacy*, Wahlen und politische Einstellungen,
https://doi.org/10.1007/978-3-658-46462-2_8

8.1 Summary and Discussion of Results

After introducing the research field in *Chap. 1*, Chaps. 2 and 3 systematically reviewed existing research on privacy and security. Notably, the thesis identified a deficiency in the systematic understanding of citizens' perspectives on state surveillance despite its expanding scope. Challenges such as limited cross-referencing, variations in conceptual definitions, overgeneralization of findings, and divergent interpretations of key meta-concepts, such as the privacy-security trade-off, were observed. These challenges impede a clear comprehension of individuals' acceptance of state surveillance. This thesis aimed to rectify these gaps by presenting a more coherent and comprehensive analysis. To achieve this goal, *Chap. 2* systematically identified and scrutinized influential definitions and conceptualizations of privacy to distill a widely acknowledged understanding. A thorough examination highlighted the ubiquity of the *informational* dimension of privacy in all relevant conceptualizations, underscoring its pivotal significance. The deliberate focus on the informational aspect aimed to enhance accessibility for both current and future research, while serving as a model for fostering increased interconnectivity within the research field.

In *Chap. 3, I* conducted a thorough analysis of existing literature concerning the interplay between attitudes toward privacy and security, exploring frameworks such as the privacy calculus theory. Contrary to the widely assumed trade-off paradigm between privacy and security, the findings revealed a nuanced relationship challenging the notion of an inherent trade-off. The research shed light on individuals' willingness to exchange privacy and security for convenience, relationships, and monetary rewards. This nuanced nature of privacy preferences underscores the dynamic relationship between perceived risks and benefits, extending beyond the conventional privacy versus security dichotomy.

Before delving into the empirical contributions, *Chap. 4* presented the conceptual framework and research strategy, elucidating the gaps in the literature identified in the previous two chapters that the thesis aimed to address:

(1) **Lack of Empirical Knowledge:** Limited research on state surveillance, with challenges such as conceptual variations and a lack of systematic understanding, hampers comprehensive insights into public attitudes.
(2) **Lack of Cross-national Studies:** Existing studies predominantly focus on single-country samples, particularly in the USA and Europe, neglecting global perspectives and hindering a holistic understanding of contextual influences on surveillance attitudes.

(3) **Limited Methodological Approaches:** Overreliance on classical surveys and correlational methods limits the establishment of causal relationships, impeding a nuanced understanding of the privacy-security nexus.
(4) **Privacy Calculus within APCO Model:** The role and timing of the privacy calculus within the APCO model are undertheorized, leading to an incomplete understanding of how individuals weigh costs and benefits in privacy decision-making.
(5) **Securitization Theory's Omission of the Audience:** The role of the audience in securitization theory is understudied, impeding a comprehensive understanding of how different individuals and contexts may vary in their susceptibility to security frames.
(6) **Privacy as a Personality Trait:** The debate on whether privacy is a stable personality trait or context-dependent remains unresolved, with limited research on state surveillance, hindering an ample understanding of individual perceptions and evaluations of such measures.

Based on data from the ISSP, *Chap. 5* revealed that, on average, respondents tend to disagree with government privacy invasion. Notably, citizens in India, Belgium, Australia, Norway, Sweden, and France were more accepting of such invasions. In comparing attitudes towards justified and non-justified surveillance measures, the results showed that people tend to be more accepting when the government claims a security reason for invading privacy. However, the extent of approval varied among individuals. Some became more supportive, some remained unchanged, and others became more opposed. The study then considered factors like government support, political orientation, and the level of liberal democracy in a country to explain these changes. Surprisingly, it was only the level of liberal democracy that seemed to play a significant role. Not only was the effect of the security frame more pronounced in democratic countries, but in less democratic countries, the security framing of privacy invasions even led to less approval. Interestingly, individual support for the government and political orientation did not seem to play a big role in whether people accepted security justifications. This challenges previous ideas about how the public views government actions. Concerning individual differences in framing effects, the study revealed that individuals who tend to be opposed to surveillance were more susceptible to accepting privacy invasion when framed as security-enhancing. This finding contradicts the notion that presenting an issue in a specific manner exacerbates divisions among people.

Chapter 6 explored the effect of several costs and benefits on the acceptance of government measures. It utilized data from an original vignette experiment conducted as part of the *Conflict of Values in Germany study* in November 2021, involving around 5000 respondents. Surprisingly, 48% of respondents in Germany expressed agreement with surveillance measures in the sample, contrary to the commonly held perception of Germans as skeptical toward surveillance. The analysis of the dimensions of the vignette experiment revealed nuanced insights. Variations in priming the crime threat scenario had minimal impact on acceptance, suggesting that public opinion was not strongly influenced by fluctuations in crime rates. However, the type of data collected significantly affected support, with more intrusive data types leading to a notable decrease. Similarly, the target of surveillance emerged as a crucial factor, where targeted surveillance of suspects received higher approval than mass surveillance. Financial considerations played a significant role, too, with higher taxes significantly decreasing acceptance. Conversely, convenience enhancements, such as reduced waiting time, did not seem to significantly sway public support for surveillance measures. A detailed exploration of the relationship between financial costs and the type of data collected unveiled that respondents deemed privacy more important when they themselves were (potentially) amongst the surveilled. However, they preferred personal financial incentives over others' privacy. This result questions recent findings indicating that individuals, in their considerations, extend beyond personal benefits to encompass potential advantages for others—a concept termed "other-focus" or "social calculus", discussed in scenarios like sharing location data during the COVID-19 pandemic. The chapter further investigated the exploratory power of subjective versus objective security, highlighting that subjective insecurity positively correlated with acceptance, while objective insecurity, as indicated by crime statistics, did not significantly influence public opinion. At the same time, perceived insecurity significantly influenced the assessment of data types, suggesting that not only intrusiveness but potentially also perceived effectiveness of the measures comes into play when evaluating proposed measures.

Chapter 7 delved into the cross-comparative analysis of public attitudes toward state surveillance measures across different spheres of life, including terrorism, cancer threat, and financial fraud. The study is based on data from an original vignette experiment conducted as part of PALS across 26 countries, encompassing over 50,000 respondents in 2021 and 2022. Surprisingly, there was widespread acceptance of government privacy invasions in many countries, with a slight majority of respondents expressing approval, despite clustering around middle categories. The effects of the treatments of the vignette experiment on the acceptance of fictitious government measures showed that increasing privacy invasion has a significantly negative impact on acceptance and promised effectiveness positively affects acceptance; although its impact was comparatively lower than that of privacy invasion. Notably, acceptance of privacy invasion was highest in the context of the cancer threat, also exceeding acceptance for terror-related measures. Robustness checks revealed significant heterogeneity at both individual and country levels, with interactions of explanatory variables such as political orientation, trust in government, and liberal democracy moderating the effects of privacy invasion and effectiveness. Pairwise comparisons highlighted pronounced group disparities, particularly for privacy invasion, where individuals with lower right-wing authoritarianism, lower trust in government, and in more liberal countries more strongly considered the severity of privacy invasions. While privacy invasion had a more substantial impact than effectiveness, the effects were not constant among scenarios and individuals. Confirmatory factor analysis suggested that privacy-related attitudes could be understood as a latent construct consistently influencing individual decisions across various scenarios. This latent privacy construct significantly predicted privacy-related behavior, as evidenced by its negative effect on providing postal codes in the course of PALS. These results support the idea that privacy could be considered a personality trait.

When comparing the three empirical studies, divergent findings emerged regarding the valuation of privacy. The ISSP revealed a tendency for individuals to reject state invasion of privacy, with only a few countries' average respondents showing moderate approval for state surveillance. On a global scale, respondents generally leaned towards appreciating privacy. However, this trend is not consistent with the *Conflict of Values in Germany study* and PALS. In both, there was a tendency towards approving of state surveillance. One possible explanation for these differences could be the COVID-19 pandemic. While the ISSP took place significantly before the onset of the pandemic, the other two studies were conducted during the "third wave" of the pandemic. At that time, all surveyed countries had implemented extensive measures to contain the pandemic, typically involving invasions of privacy. Some studies suggest that this, perhaps through processes of normalization, has led to altered privacy considerations, with individuals perceiving privacy as less important due to shifted priorities (Cheek et al. 2022; Gerdon et al. 2020; Kampmark 2020).

Comparing rankings between the two cross-comparative studies revealed surprising similarities, especially regarding pairs and trios of countries with nearly identical mean acceptance of measures in both studies such as Sweden and France, USA and Russia, Spain and Chile, as well as Japan, Latvia, and South Korea (the latter trio being amongst the least accepting of privacy invasions in both surveys), or India indicating high average acceptance in both studies. Despite a time lapse of six to seven years and variations in survey formulations and contexts, the consistency between ISSP and PALS suggests relative stability in national privacy attitudes. Notably, Germany consistently occupies a lower position in global acceptance, confirming the assumption that Germans are generally reluctant towards privacy infringements (Brockdorff, Appleby-Arnold, Hawellek, et al. 2015; Trepte & Masur 2017; Trüdinger & Steckermeier 2017; Ziller & Helbling 2021), and underscoring the notion of Germany as a least likely case. This emphasizes the suggestion that the relationships identified in Study 2 could also be present, and perhaps more pronounced, in countries where privacy is less highly regarded.

Significant variations in acceptance exist between countries in both the ISSP and PALS studies, as indicated by the ICC. The degree of liberal democracy seems to play a pivotal role in interpreting these differences. Not only did the susceptibility to the security frame correlate significantly with the degree of democracy, as demonstrated in Study 1, but Study 3 also revealed that the negative effect of the degree of privacy invasion on the acceptance of government measures tends to be more pronounced for respondents from liberal-democratic countries.

All three studies indicated that individuals, on average, consider both costs and benefits. Studies 2 and 3 suggested that individuals are aware of the different degrees of (objective) invasiveness of surveillance and are more likely to reject privacy invasions that theoretically lead to greater disadvantages. This applies to both the type of collected data and, additionally in Study 2, the target of privacy invasion. Simultaneously, self-interest appeared to be a driving factor, as respondents particularly reject measures that affect them directly, but are less opposed to those infringing on the privacy of others. Regarding potential *benefits*, there was a consistent pattern across the three studies, with promises of increased security and effectiveness leading to greater support for government measures. Financial incentives and convenience, however, did not significantly influence respondents. On the other hand, we observed that in addition to reduced privacy, other potential costs and risks were also significantly considered. Study 2, for instance, showed that deterioration in terms of rising costs and reduced convenience has a significant impact on acceptance. This seemingly stronger influence of potential costs is in line with the social-psychological concept of prospect theory (Tversky & Kahneman 1981) and the resulting *bias of loss aversion*, which describes how the pain of losing is psychologically more powerful than the pleasure of gaining.

Interestingly, not all theoretically derived costs and benefits were perceived as such. In Study 1, a fifth of respondents reacted with lower approval to the promise of increased security, and in Study 2, the promise of more convenience was associated with decreased approval. In addition, the positive influence of effectiveness was not universally significant across all spheres of life in Study 3. From the literature, three possible explanations emerge for these results: (1) In Study 1, we observed that particularly in non-liberal democracies, the security frame triggers a negative effect. This suggests that the reference to national security might ring alarm bells, as citizens could interpret this reference as attempts to maintain power against internal opposition, potentially associated with stronger repression. This highlights the delicate relationship between privacy and democracy. (2) Similarly, research on election pledges indicates that citizens often assume politicians rarely keep their promises made during an election campaign (Dupont et al. 2019: 122). Due to their experiences with the subjectively stereotypical pledge-breaking politician, respondents might be indifferent to the possible benefits or may not be willing to significantly support these measures. (3) A third explanation could be that individuals assumed a stronger consideration of the possible negative side effects of benefits. For example, they might believe that decreasing costs could have a negative impact on the resources available for security institutions and, consequently, on personal security—and thus deem this undesirable. Therefore, a cost-benefit analysis is made *within* the benefit component. This is suggested, for instance, by Gaskell et al. (2004). We know, for instance, that many Germans do not prefer tax cuts but are satisfied with the status quo of government spending (Hayo & Neumeier 2019: 4).

All three studies demonstrate significant differences between individuals—not only regarding their general approval of government measures but also in terms of the effects of various elements of hypothetical government measures. The literature indicates a variety of possible antecedents for privacy attitudes (Buck et al. 2022). For Study 1, I selected two individual variables that had been attributed with significant explanatory power in the past: trust in government (van den Broek et al. 2017: 27; Friedewald et al. 2015: 19; Nakhaie & de Lint 2013: 160; Davis & Silver 2004) and political orientation (e.g., Friedewald et al. 2015: 21; van den Broek et al. 2017: 29). However, this thesis could not reveal consistent effects of these variables. While I observed that trust in government is not significantly correlated with susceptibility to the security frame, Study 3 indicated that trust in government moderates the effects of elements of the hypothetical government measures, such that privacy invasion has a more pronounced negative impact on acceptance for individuals with lower trust in government compared to those with higher trust. The same holds for political orientation: while the left-right placement of individuals regarding their voting decision did not show a significant relationship with susceptibility to the security frame, we see that privacy invasion has a more pronounced negative impact on acceptance for non-authoritarian individuals than for those with authoritarian predispositions.

The inclusion of sociodemographic characteristics as control variables suggested, in all three studies, that the models are relatively robust, as the main effects do not significantly change with the addition of these variables. At the same time, I find that age, across all three studies, led to significant associations: older people tend to agree more with state surveillance than younger ones. The effect of being female was significant only in Studies 2 and 3, suggesting that, compared to men, women are more likely to reject privacy invasions, while education had a significant relationship only in Studies 1 and 3, implying that highly educated individuals reject privacy invasions more strongly than less educated ones. This aligns with existing research on the influence of sociodemographic characteristics on privacy.[1]

Race and citizenship are attributed a particular role in the privacy and security nexus (Browne 2015). However, in none of my three studies could I replicate the postulated positive correlation between non-nativeness and the rejection of privacy invasions (Bali 2009: 247; Davis & Silver 2004: 31; Spriggs et al. 2005: 42; Viscusi & Zeckhauser 2003: 107). In Study 2, I even found that non-Germans are less likely to strongly reject privacy invasions compared to Germans. Overall, it became apparent that the influence of moderation variables at the individual level depends significantly on the availability of data. For instance, not only could the influence of trust in government not be verified in Study 2, but also the operationalization of migration background necessarily diverged between the studies.

In Study 2, the influence of security was examined from three perspectives. Firstly, I found that manipulating the security threat within the vignette experiment had little noteworthy impact on the acceptance of hypothetical government measures. Only the threat scenario of higher crime figures had a slightly positive influence on the acceptance of measures. This result contradicts the significant

[1] While most studies find that women are more supportive of so-called "anti-terror measures" (van den Broek et al. 2017: 25; Trüdinger 2018: 94) or state surveillance in general (Trüdinger & Steckermeier 2017: 5), it is important to consider the different contexts in which men and women encounter surveillance (Koskela 2012: 51). For theoretical readings on the relationship between surveillance and gender, see Abu-Laban (2015) and contributions in Dubrofsky/Magnet (2015). Several studies find a positive relationship between age and attitudes towards surveillance (T. H. Bennett & Gelsthorpe 1996: 77; Ditton 2000: 694; Dixon et al. 2003: 18; Honess & Charman 1992: 11; O'Donnell et al. 2010a; Sunil Patil et al. 2015: 14; Schuler & Wolkenstein 2014: 79; Spriggs et al. 2005: 41–42). Similarly, most studies find that education has a negative effect on the acceptance of surveillance measures (van den Broek et al. 2017: 29; Budak et al. 2013: 113; Davis & Silver 2004: 36; Friedewald et al. 2015: 21; Rykkja et al. 2011: 230; H. J. Smith et al. 2011: 999; Trüdinger 2018: 94; Trüdinger & Steckermeier 2017: 5).

effect of the security frame found in Study 1. Apparently, framing urgency in the concrete context works better than in the abstract when only hypothetical crime numbers are mentioned. This underscores the notion expressed in the literature that people may struggle to making sense of very large or very small numbers (Resnick et al. 2017). Secondly, I observed that the objective security situation of respondents, operationalized through crime rates at the district level, had no significant impact on the acceptance of measures. This somewhat emphasizes the cognitive limitations of individuals in rationally perceiving their own environment and transforming this perception into values and behavior (see, e.g., J. Fiske 1996). This becomes particularly apparent in the lack of correlation between objective and subjective insecurity. Thirdly—and conversely—subjective insecurity has a significantly positive correlation with approval of measures. Additionally, the acceptance of specific privacy invasions, such as those targeting a specific group, significantly diverges based on the level of subjective insecurity.

While the influence on privacy may seem paradoxical at first glance, the different framings of security essentially capture the multidimensionality of security. Studies 1 and 3, as well as the manipulation of the crime threat in Study 2, approached security from the perspective of security as social and political practice (Zedner 2003). By framing government measures as relevant to national security, the urgency of the measure was emphasized in line with the securitization theory, which seems to work effectively in my studies. In considering the differentiation between subjective and objective insecurity, Study 2 additionally adds the perspective of security as a state of being. Subjective insecurity is an individual perception (Wolfers 1952), while objective insecurity—at least in my study—acts as a contextual factor. This means that respondents not only need to perceive the context and transfer it to subjective attitudes and behaviors but also before that, somewhat as an additional cognitive act, need to concretize it from the abstract context to their individual level. Therefore, it is not necessarily contradictory that security did not lead to a uniform effect but might be the result of different abstraction levels of security, potentially leading to cognitive overload.

In conclusion, while the three studies do not always identify identical statistical relationships, they complement each other substantively despite different samples, survey contexts, and question formulations. The following section outlines the main contributions of the thesis. This includes addressing the identified research gaps, but also encompasses contributions that emerged during the research process, such as through the comprehensive examination of results.

8.2 Contributions

The thesis has contributed to the literature on the subjective value of privacy on various levels. On a theoretical level, it has refined connections between existing conceptualizations. On a methodological level, it has demonstrated the added value of cross-comparative perspectives and experimental designs. On an empirical level, it has shed light on the individual decision-making processes underlying privacy choices and the extent to which these processes vary among individuals and contexts. In particular, this thesis has made a contribution to highlighting and organizing the hitherto predominantly implicit complexity of subjective values within the privacy-security nexus. Consequently, it aids in revealing the limitations of sometimes overly simplistic theoretical frameworks and can serve as a foundation for adapting them more closely to the (often complex) reality in the future.

In a broad sense, the work, despite limitations imposed by its assumptions, suggests that individuals desire both privacy and security. This does not only align with previous findings by van den Broek et al. (2017: 15) but also seems to support a general finding, namely, that there is no longer a significant security-freedom divide within the population, with two camps favoring either of the groups as for example outlined by Pippa Norris and Ronald Inglehart (2019); instead, respondents tend to appreciate both aspects (Schäfer 2022: 1983). The implication regarding privacy and surveillance is that these values are not intrinsically linked for individuals.

However, this cannot be used as grounds to dismiss the privacy calculus. Clear indications are found in my study that individuals weigh costs and benefits, where the promise of security, holding other factors constant, significantly enhances acceptance of proposed governmental measures. Consequently, the work suggests that the privacy calculus should not be discarded but, on the contrary, should be an integral part of meta-models like the APCO framework. Moreover, the study suggests that potential costs and benefits extend beyond the dichotomy of privacy and security, as individuals also consider other barter objects such as financial costs/savings, increased/decreased inconvenience, or the degree of effectiveness.

Initially compelled by a lack of alternatives, the thesis serves as an example of how consumer research can theoretically and empirically inform the study of state surveillance. Although the methodology does not allow me to determine the level of cognitive effort individuals exerted to fulfill the tasks of the survey experiments,[2] the empirical fact of weighing suggests that assertions about the fundamental inability of "normal" individuals to balance values like security and privacy (Acquisti 2004; Acquisti et al. 2013; Acquisti & Grossklags 2005) may be overly pessimistic. Thus, inadvertently, prior scientific discourse may have falsely aligned with governments that paternalistically question their citizens' ability to make the best decisions for themselves (Allen 2011: 173–94).

My findings indicate that individuals seem to know what is best for themselves. They suggest a strong focus on individual benefit, observing that individuals particularly value privacy when it concerns them directly. Conversely, the privacy of others is not only less appreciated, but privacy invasions are even endorsed if linked to personal financial or non-monetary benefits. This tendency is more pronounced among respondents who feel insecure. Privacy is not perceived as an abstract normative good; rather, personal privacy seems to hold a concrete individual value, being considered as an individual benefit. The finding that the privacy of others is not seen as a personal benefit contradicts the relatively recently discussed dimensions of "other-focus" or "social calculus" (Nabity-Grover et al. 2020).

Regarding security, this study demonstrates that the subjective component has a much stronger impact on the privacy calculus than the objective component. Regardless of the actual insecurity surrounding an individual, their subjective perception influences thinking and behavior. Importantly, the two components do not strongly correlate, meaning some people feel insecure despite objectively having less reason to do so. Until now, no empirical research has so concretely demonstrated this connection concerning the acceptance of state surveillance.

The work contributes further by revealing that the audience matters. As highlighted theoretically by various authors (Balzacq 2005; Côté 2016; Floyd 2010; Salter 2008; M. C. Williams 2010), the success of a securitization move significantly depends on audience acceptance. The empirical result concerning susceptibility to the security frame shows significant differences at the individual level, but particularly at the country level. Notably, security frames have different effects in democratic contexts compared to non-democratic ones, emphasizing the special significance of the relationship between privacy and democracy (Gavison 1980; Lever 2005: 15; Regan 1995: 225; Roberts 2015: 339; Simitis 1987: 734).

Furthermore, this work is one of the first to explore the extent to which privacy in the context of state surveillance could be considered a personality trait.

---

[2] While I can report that the average processing time for the respective tasks in the *Value Conflict in Germany* survey was approximately 50% higher than for a standard Likert scale item with a similarly long text, longer survey duration does not necessarily imply longer deliberation (Rubinstein 2013).

The results indicate that, despite various contextual influences, a common attitude toward privacy invasions underlies the evaluation of different government measures. This suggests that privacy (attitudes) can be regarded as a contextually stable personality trait, contributing significantly to the discussion on the understanding of privacy as contextual integrity (Nissenbaum 2004).

The focus on the informational dimension not only represents a potential limitation of the scope of the findings but can also be seen as important contribution since it allows for reference to and compatibility with a variety of privacy understandings. The lack of mutual reference was identified as one of the main reasons for the lack of systematic knowledge about attitudes towards state surveillance in general (H. Watson et al. 2017). In the systematic analysis of various conceptualizations of privacy, the informational dimension was identified as a component of all prevailing understandings. By explicitly concentrating on this highest common denominator, the study demonstrates empirically as well as methodically-theoretically how our understanding of privacy decisions can be enhanced in the future.

From a methodological perspective, the study demonstrates that expanding the focus from single-country to cross-comparative studies adds significant value to understanding the privacy-security nexus. Analyzing and substantiating country *differences*, such as in terms of level of liberal democracy, and highlighting the stability of certain patterns trough effect *equality*, such as the personality trait observed in all countries, becomes possible through the consideration of heterogeneous contexts.

Simultaneously, the use of survey experiments represents a significant contribution to research, which has previously predominantly relied on correlational studies. It was demonstrated that respondents significantly respond to manipulation—a fundamental condition for the validity of this approach (Auspurg & Hinz 2014). Fractional designs, as used in the Study 2, allow for the consideration of a variety of dimensions and levels without sacrificing exploratory power. Therefore, this approach is particularly suited to illuminate complex decision processes and, most importantly, make causal statements about influences on these processes.

These findings have several potential political implications, briefly discussed here: Firstly, the results overall suggest that governments should take their citizens' attitudes seriously. Especially with technological advancements, states are challenged to regulate commercial interventions more strictly, requiring them to consider their own role in this area. This demand is increasingly being met by courts, evident not only in the judgment of the German Federal Constitutional Court regarding the surveillance balance but also in rulings in other countries.[3]

Since privacy is particularly valued and demanded as a concrete *individual* benefit and not as a social calculus for others, protection must be extended to those who cannot protect themselves, such as children or less tech-savvy older individuals (Livingstone 2018) and to those who are "over-suspected" by law enforcement (Harris 2020) and the public (e.g., Feltes, List, and Bertamini 2018: 606) e.g., due to racialization. The state must fulfill its protective role, concurrently raising awareness about the objective value of privacy or the negative consequences that the loss of others' privacy can have on oneself. On the other hand, this result implies that raising individual concern might increase awareness and political mobilization, which could be significant for the actions of privacy advocates (C. J. Bennett 2008).

The mismatch between subjective and objective privacy, potentially arising from a trend of general uncertainty characterizing modernity (Beck 1992) and political discourse over the past decade, is notable. Particularly, but not exclusively, right-wing parties attempt to gain votes by promising increased security through a focus on "law and order" topics (Hamilton 2023; J. Liu et al. 2023). This inevitably neglects the positive trend of decreasing crime rates. Incumbent governments could focus more on these declining numbers,[4] potentially saving resources and gaining votes through success stories, especially in the face of empty state coffers.

8.3 Limitations and Future Research

The examination of attitudes surrounding state surveillance represents a relatively understudied subject. The present thesis, through its accomplished conceptual framing and well-founded empirical analyses, provides a solid foundation for approaching this nexus in various ways. Nevertheless, this dissertation can at best serve as a starting point for comprehending the subjective value of privacy in its entirety. The following sections highlight some limitations of the work and propose specific avenues for further research.

---

[3] For a detailed overview of European case law on the issue of privacy, see, e.g., Vermeulen (2014).

[4] For a comprehensive overview of research on the issue selection of incumbent parties in election campaigns, see for example Greene (2020).

The conceptualization of privacy in this thesis is limited to the *informational* dimension. This restriction was imposed to establish a common ground and points of connection for as many schools of thought as possible, given the multitude of proposed definitions and conceptualizations, thereby constituting a major contribution of the thesis. Privacy, in this context, is viewed, among other things, as "the other side of the coin" of various forms of privacy (Koops et al. 2017). However, this already implies the existence of another perspective, such as "physical" forms of privacy (see e.g., J. E. Cohen 2008). To better understand the subjective value of privacy, an examination of additional forms of privacy might be necessary. Future research should particularly focus on how individuals understand and experience privacy, drawing initial inspiration from works such as Doris Teutsch et al.'s (2018). This could reveal whether individuals differentiate between various types of privacy and attribute different values to them. At the same time, the detailed examination of various theoretical conceptualizations in this thesis, not only of privacy but also in relation to other concepts such as trade-off or privacy calculus, highlights the necessity of revisiting and potentially revising these frameworks, particularly with regard to developing a shared understanding. In this regard, it is also imperative for the scientific discourse and progress to foster dialogue between empiricists and theorists, especially within specialized research fields, such as surveillance studies.

A significant limitation of this work is its focus on state surveillance. Although the lines between governmental and corporate surveillance are increasingly blurred, distinct logics govern these two areas (Connor & Doan 2021). While there is a wealth of studies, especially in the consumer research domain, addressing corporate surveillance, future research should explore the connection between the subjective appreciation of privacy concerning governments and corporations, for example, investigating whether privacy is a personality trait that extends across these domains or is limited to state surveillance.

To maintain the internal and external validity of the scenarios, specific contexts of state surveillance were singled out, and only selected fictive scenarios were presented within them. The cross-comparative nature required a relatively high level of abstraction. However, state surveillance occurs in various forms beyond these selected contexts, and the representativeness of the chosen scenarios for state surveillance in general could be questioned. Further research is needed to encompass a broader range of state surveillance scenarios, potentially being less abstract.

The external validity of the used items relies solely on conclusions drawn from existing literature or by aligning with already established research instruments. The fact that citizens are generally not informed about—let alone asked for their consent to—state surveillance measures further restricts external validity. Future research should address this aspect more comprehensively, for example through in-depth cognitive interviews in questionnaire design. Given the debate surrounding the privacy paradox (Kokolakis 2017), it is worth considering whether implicit measurements of privacy behavior might contribute to better understand the subjective component of privacy than abstract survey items.

While my analyses suggest that the privacy calculus should not be discarded but, on the contrary, be considered an integral part of meta-models like the APCO framework, the empirical studies could not shed light on the question of where to situate the privacy calculus. Authors differ in their placement within the APCO model. Some position it within the concerns facet, suggesting that concerns develop based on the imaginary weighing of costs and benefits (e.g., Dinev et al. 2015). Others associate it more closely with the outcome, proposing that privacy concerns become part of the privacy calculus, where they are weighed against potential benefits (e.g., H. J. Smith et al. 2011). Again others position the privacy calculus outside the APCO model, considering it as an alternative but relevant pathway (e.g., Jia et al. 2015; Potoglou et al. 2015). While the finding that not only privacy attitudes or concerns, but also the degree of weighing against other goods varies among individuals and contexts, can be considered as evidence supporting the positioning closer to the concerns facet, further (social-psychological) research is necessary to verify this and to investigate the implications of the precise location of the privacy calculus for understanding individual decision-making processes.

The assertion that attitudes toward privacy can be perceived as a relatively stable personality trait is derived from the observation that attitudes were strongly correlated across multiple contexts and that the resulting factor could predict privacy behavior quite well. However, this stability argument is based solely on cross-context observations, not on the variation of the temporal component. Future research should explore the extent to which privacy attitudes remain stable over time, as is observed for other personality traits. Longitudinal studies could be particularly valuable in this regard. Although it has been argued that privacy concerns affect privacy behavior in the long run (Heirman et al. 2013), there are very few longitudinal studies in privacy research (exceptions being Boyd 2011; Dienlin et al. 2023).

The component of objective insecurity in Study 2 was measured through the prevalence of criminality at the smallest possible regional unit (in this case, on the level of districts). Besides general criticism of using crime numbers as a proxy for insecurity (Buil-Gil et al. 2022), it is crucial to note the unequal victimization risk for different groups, e.g., with regard to gender, sexual orientation, and racialization characteristics (Flores et al. 2020). Future research that delves deeper into these differences could potentially provide a better understanding of the weak correlation between objective and subjective security and shed light on a stronger relationship between objective insecurity and the acceptance of privacy invasions.

Furthermore, future research could pay closer attention to the dimension of effectiveness. Explicitly mentioning the effectiveness of a measure as a potential benefit in Study 3 had only a minimal effect on acceptance. This may have been influenced by framing, such as effectiveness *judged by experts*. On the other hand, some results suggest that certain measures may be rejected because they are perceived as not far-reaching enough and potentially ineffective in achieving their goals (for this argument, see, e.g., Gaskell et al. 2004). This suggests that effectiveness was treated too simplistically in this work and should be explored in greater complexity through further research—especially considering that there might be figures on effectiveness of specific measures, allowing for a distinction between an objective and a subjective component, analogous to security.

Finally, statements about the value of privacy are limited in that they are "only" based on responses to previously formulated questionnaire items. Interactive and more flexible data collection methods might be better suited to paint a nuanced picture of the subjective nature of the perception and evaluation of privacy and interventions into it (Green & Zurawski 2015; Pavone & Degli Esposti 2012). Mixed-methods approaches, in particular, could integrate the best of both worlds, the quantitative and the qualitative, to provide a more comprehensive understanding.

While the present study has brought some illumination to the subject, the comprehension of individual attitudes toward privacy and surveillance remains a relatively unexplored area, underscoring the need for further research to provide deeper insights into this pivotal aspect of our evolving social landscape.

Ending on a positive note, this thesis has shown that citizens appear to perceive privacy in a relatively nuanced manner. It is neither glorified as a panacea for all problems nor categorically rejected. This suggests that privacy is not dead but very much alive. Citizens value privacy as one among several goods that need to be weighed against each other. In this context, individuals seem to prioritize personal benefits. However, the fact that privacy is generally perceived as beneficial on average gives hope that through education, the intrinsic value of privacy can be brought more to the forefront. This, in turn, may lead to the protection of those who cannot afford to safeguard their privacy. Increased transparency and control in governmental surveillance activities can not only bolster the legitimacy of such endeavors and democracy itself but also enhance subjective security. Consequently, citizens could indeed attain both: more privacy *and* increased security

References

Abu-Laban, Yasmeen. 2015. "Gendering Surveillance Studies: The Empirical and Normative Promise of Feminist Methodology." *Surveillance & Society* 13 (1): 44–56.

Acquisti, Alessandro. 2004. "Privacy in Electronic Commerce and the Economics of Immediate Gratification." In *Proceedings of the 5th ACM Conference on Electronic Commerce*, 21–29. EC '04. New York, NY, USA: Association for Computing Machinery. https://doi.org/10.1145/988772.988777.

Acquisti, Alessandro. 2009. "Nudging Privacy: The Behavioral Economics of Personal Information." *IEEE Security & Privacy* 7 (6): 82–85.

Acquisti, Alessandro, Laura Brandimarte, and George Loewenstein. 2015. "Privacy and Human Behavior in the Age of Information." *Science, American Association for the Advancement of Science* 347 (6221): 509–14.

Acquisti, Alessandro, and Jens Grossklags. 2005. "Privacy and Rationality in Individual Decision Making." *IEEE Security & Privacy* 3 (1): 26–33.

Acquisti, Alessandro, Leslie K. John, and George Loewenstein. 2012. "The Impact of Relative Standards on the Propensity to Disclose." *Journal of Marketing Research* 49 (2): 160–74.

Acquisti, Alessandro, Leslie K. John, and George Loewenstein. 2013. "What Is Privacy Worth?" *The Journal of Legal Studies* 42 (2): 249–74.

Acquisti, Alessandro, Curtis Taylor, and Liad Wagman. 2016. "The Economics of Privacy." *Journal of Economic Literature* 54 (2): 442–92.

Adams, Jan, and Andrew Millie. 2021. "Everyday Moral Judgements of Anti-Social Behaviour." *Crime Prevention and Community Safety* 23 (1): 56–68.

Adjerid, Idris, Eyal Peer, and Alessandro Acquisti. 2018. "Beyond the Privacy Paradox: Objective versus Relative Risk in Privacy Decision Making." *MIS Quarterly* 42 (2): 465–88.

Adjerid, Idris, Sonam Samat, and Alessandro Acquisti. 2016. "A Query-Theory Perspective of Privacy Decision Making." *The Journal of Legal Studies* 45 (S2): 97–121.

Agerberg, Mattias, and Jacob Sohlberg. 2021. "Personal Proximity and Reactions to Terrorism." *Comparative Political Studies* 54 (14): 2512–45.

Ahmed, Syed Ishtiaque, Md. Romael Haque, Shion Guha, Md. Rashidujjaman Rifat, and Nicola Dell. 2017. "Privacy, Security, and Surveillance in the Global South: A Study of

L. Antoine, *The Subjective Value of Privacy*, Wahlen und politische Einstellungen,
https://doi.org/10.1007/978-3-658-46462-2

Biometric Mobile SIM Registration in Bangladesh." In *Proceedings of the 2017 CHI Conference on Human Factors in Computing Systems*, 906–18. CHI '17. New York, NY, USA: Association for Computing Machinery.

Ainsworth, Mary D. Salter. 2010. "Security and Attachment." In *The Secure Child. Timeless Lessons in Parenting and Childhood Education*, edited by Richard Volpe, 43–54. Toronto: Toronto University Press.

Ajzen, Icek. 1985. "From Intentions to Actions: A Theory of Planned Behavior." In *Action Control: From Cognition to Behavior*, edited by Julius Kuhl and Jürgen Beckmann, 11–39. SSSP Springer Series in Social Psychology. Berlin, Heidelberg: Springer.

Ajzen, Icek. 1988. *Attitudes, Personality and Behaviour*. Chicago: Dorsey.

Ajzen, Icek, and Martin Fishbein. 1980. *Understanding Attitudes and Predicting Social Behavior*. Englewood Cliffs: Pearson.

Aleinikoff, T. Alexander. 1987. "Constitutional Law in the Age of Balancing." *The Yale Law Journal* 96 (5): 943–1005.

Allen, Anita L. 1988. *Uneasy Access: Privacy for Women in a Free Society*. Totowa, N.J: Rowman & Littlefield.

Allen, Anita L. 2011. *Unpopular Privacy: What Must We Hide?* Oxford, New York: Oxford University Press.

Allen, Anita L. 2021. "Privacy and Medicine." In *The Stanford Encyclopedia of Philosophy*, edited by Edward N. Zalta, Spring 2021. Stanford: Metaphysics Research Lab, Stanford University. https://plato.stanford.edu/entries/privacy-medicine/.

Allik, Mirjam, and Ade Kearns. 2017. "'There Goes the Fear': Feelings of Safety at Home and in the Neighborhood: The Role of Personal, Social, and Service Factors." *Journal of Community Psychology* 45 (4): 543–63.

Alm, James. 2012. "Measuring, Explaining, and Controlling Tax Evasion: Lessons from Theory, Experiments, and Field Studies." *International Tax and Public Finance* 19 (1): 54–77.

Almond, Gabriel Abraham, and G. Bingham Powell. 1978. *Comparative Politics: System, Process, and Policy*. Boston: Little, Brown, and Company.

Altemeyer, Bob. 1998. "The Other 'Authoritarian Personality.'" In *Advances in Experimental Social Psychology*, edited by Mark P. Zanna, 30:47–92. New York: Academic Press.

Altman, Irwin. 1975. *The Environment and Social Behavior: Privacy, Personal Space, Territory, Crowding*. Monterey: Brooks/Cole Publishing Company.

American Medical Association. 2022. "Patient Survey Shows Unresolved Tension over Health Data Privacy." American Medical Association. July 25, 2022. https://www.ama-assn.org/press-center/press-releases/patient-survey-shows-unresolved-tension-over-health-data-privacy.

Anderson, Christopher J., and Yuliya V. Tverdova. 2003. "Corruption, Political Allegiances, and Attitudes toward Government in Contemporary Democracies." *American Journal of Political Science* 47 (1): 91–109.

Andrade, Eduardo B., Velitchka Kaltcheva, and Barton Weitz. 2002. "Self-Disclosure on the Web: The Impact of Privacy Policy, Reward, and Company Reputation." *Advances in Consumer Research* 29 (1): 350–53.

Andrejevic, Mark. 2004. "The Work of Watching One Another: Lateral Surveillance, Risk, and Governance." *Surveillance & Society* 2 (4): 479–97.

Andrejevic, Mark. 2007. *iSpy: Surveillance and Power in the Interactive Era*. Lawrence, Kansas: University Press of Kansas.

Ansolabehere, Stephen, and Brian F. Schaffner. 2016. "Taking the Study of Political Behavior Online." In *The Oxford Handbook of Polling and Survey Methods*, edited by Lonna Rae Atkeson and R. Michael Alvarez, 76–96. Oxford: Oxford University Press.

Antoine, Lukas. 2022. "The Power of a Promise: Whom Do Governments' Security Justifications Convince to Accept Surveillance?" *Political Research Exchange* 4 (1): 2101380.

Antoine, Lukas. 2023. "Costs, Inconvenience, or Civil Rights? Investigating Determinants of Public Support for Surveillance." *Surveillance & Society* 21 (4): 409–31.

Aquilina, Kevin. 2010. "Public Security versus Privacy in Technology Law: A Balancing Act?" *Computer Law & Security Review* 26 (2): 130–43.

Aradau, Claudia. 2014. "The Promise of Security: Resilience, Surprise and Epistemic Politics." *Resilience* 2 (2): 73–87.

Arends, J. Frederik M. 2008. "From Homer to Hobbes and Beyond — Aspects of' Security' in the European Tradition." In *Globalization and Environmental Challenges: Reconceptualizing Security in the 21st Century*, edited by Hans G. Brauch, Úrsula Oswald Spring, Úrsula Oswald Mesjasz, John Grin, Pál Dunay, Navnita Chadha Behera, Béchir Chourou, Patricia Kameri-Mbote, and P. H. Liotta, 263–77. Hexagon Series on Human and Environmental Security and Peace. Berlin, Heidelberg: Springer.

Arendt, Hannah. 1998. *The Human Condition*. 2nd ed. Chicago and London: University of Chicago Press.

Arndt, H. W. 1949. "The Cult of Privacy." *The Australian Quarterly* 21 (3): 68–71.

Ashworth, Andrew, and Lucia Zedner. 2014. *Preventive Justice*. Oxford: Oxford University Press.

Auspurg, Katrin, and Thomas Hinz. 2014. *Factorial Survey Experiments*. Los Angeles: SAGE Publications, Inc.

Auspurg, Katrin, Thomas Hinz, and Stefan Liebig. 2009. "Complexity, Learning Effects and Plausibility of Vignettes in the Factorial Survey Design." *Mda: Methods, Data, Analyses* 3 (1): 59–96.

Austin, Peter C. 2010. "Estimating Multilevel Logistic Regression Models When the Number of Clusters Is Low: A Comparison of Different Statistical Software Procedures." *The International Journal of Biostatistics* 6 (1): 1–20.

Austin, Peter C., and Janet E. Hux. 2002. "A Brief Note on Overlapping Confidence Intervals." *Journal of Vascular Surgery* 36 (1): 194–95.

Awad, Naveen Farag, and M. S. Krishnan. 2006. "The Personalization Privacy Paradox: An Empirical Evaluation of Information Transparency and the Willingness to Be Profiled Online for Personalization." *MIS Quarterly* 30 (1): 13–28.

Baba, Kunihiro, Ritei Shibata, and Masaaki Sibuya. 2004. "Partial Correlation and Conditional Correlation as Measures of Conditional Independence." *Australian & New Zealand Journal of Statistics* 46 (4): 657–64.

Bader, Christopher D., Joseph O. Baker, L. Edward Day, and Ann Gordon. 2020. *Fear Itself: The Causes and Consequences of Fear in America*. New York: NYU Press.

Baele, Stéphane J., Travis G. Coan, and Olivier C. Sterck. 2018. "Security through Numbers? Experimentally Assessing the Impact of Numerical Arguments in Security Communication." *The British Journal of Politics and International Relations* 20 (2): 459–76.

Baele, Stéphane J., and Olivier C. Sterck. 2015. "Diagnosing the Securitisation of Immigration at the EU Level: A New Method for Stronger Empirical Claims." *Political Studies* 63 (5): 1120–39.

Baele, Stéphane J., and Catarina P. Thomson. 2017. "An Experimental Agenda for Securitization Theory." *International Studies Review* 19 (4): 646–66.

Bajc, Vida. 2007. "Introduction: Debating Surveillance in the Age of Security." *American Behavioral Scientist* 50 (12): 1567–91.

Baker, Reg, J. Michael Brick, Nancy A. Bates, Mike Battaglia, Mick P. Couper, Jill A. Dever, Krista J. Gile, and Roger Tourangeau. 2013. "Summary Report of the AAPOR Task Force on Non-Probability Sampling." *Journal of Survey Statistics and Methodology* 1 (2): 90–143.

Bakir, Vian. 2015. "News, Agenda Building, and Intelligence Agencies: A Systematic Review of the Field from the Discipline of Journalism, Media, and Communications." *The International Journal of Press/Politics* 20 (2): 131–44.

Baldwin, David A. 1997. "The Concept of Security." *Review of International Studies* 23 (1): 5–26.

Bali, Valentina. 2009. "Tinkering Toward a National Identification System: An Experiment on Policy Attitudes." *Policy Studies Journal* 37 (2): 233–55.

Ball, Kirstie, Sara Degli Esposti, Sally Dibb, Vincenzo Pavone, and Elvira Santiago-Gomez. 2019. "Institutional Trustworthiness and National Security Governance: Evidence from Six European Countries." *Governance* 32 (1): 103–21.

Ballaschk, David, and Jan Paulick. 2021. "The Public, the Private and the Secret: Thoughts on Privacy in Central Bank Digital Currencies." *Journal of Payments Strategy & Systems* 15 (3): 277–86.

Balzacq, Thierry. 2005. "The Three Faces of Securitization: Political Agency, Audience and Context." *European Journal of International Relations* 11 (2): 171–201.

Balzacq, Thierry. 2010a. "A Theory of Securitization: Origins, Core Assumptions, and Variants." In *Securitization Theory. How Security Problems Emerge and Dissolve*, edited by Thierry Balzacq, 1–30. London: Routledge.

Balzacq, Thierry. 2010b. "Enquiries into Methods: A New Framework for Securitization Analysis." In *Securitization Theory. How Security Problems Emerge and Dissolve*, edited by Thierry Balzacq, 31–54. London: Routledge.

Balzacq, Thierry, Sarah Léonard, and Jan Ruzicka. 2016. "'Securitization' Revisited: Theory and Cases." *International Relations* 30 (4): 494–531.

Bandara, Heenkenda Mudiyanselage Ruwan Jayawickrama, Mario Fernando, and Md Shahriar Akter. 2018. "Is the Privacy Paradox a Matter of Psychological Distance? An Exploratory Study of the Privacy Paradox from a Construal Level Theory Perspective." In *Proceedings of the Innovative Behavioral IS Security and Privacy Research*, 3678–87. Waikoloa Village, Hawaii. https://doi.org/10.24251/HICSS.2018.465.

Bannister, Frank. 2005. "The Panoptic State: Privacy, Surveillance and the Balance of Risk." *Information Polity* 10 (1,2): 65–78.

Bansal, Gaurav, and Fatemeh M. Zahedi. 2014. "Trust-Discount Tradeoff in Three Contexts: Frugality Moderating Privacy and Security Concerns." *Journal of Computer Information Systems* 55 (1): 13–29.

Barnard-Wills, David. 2012. *Surveillance and Identity: Discourse, Subjectivity and the State.* Farnham; Burlington: Taylor & Francis Ltd.

Barth, Susanne, and Menno D. T. de Jong. 2017. "The Privacy Paradox—Investigating Discrepancies between Expressed Privacy Concerns and Actual Online Behavior—A Systematic Literature Review." *Telematics and Informatics* 34 (7): 1038–58.
Barton, Allen H. 1968. "Bringing Society Back In: Survey Research and Macro-Methodology." *The American Behavioral Scientist* 12 (2): 1.
Baruh, Lemi, Ekin Secinti, and Zeynep Cemalcilar. 2017. "Online Privacy Concerns and Privacy Management: A Meta-Analytical Review." *Journal of Communication* 67 (1): 26–53.
Bauman, Zygmunt. 1999. *In Search of Politics*. Stanford: Stanford University Press.
Bauman, Zygmunt, Didier Bigo, Paulo Esteves, Elspeth Guild, Vivienne Jabri, David Lyon, and R. B. J. Walker. 2014. "After Snowden: Rethinking the Impact of Surveillance." *International Political Sociology* 8 (2): 121–44.
Beatty, David M. 2004. *The Ultimate Rule of Law*. Oxford, New York: Oxford University Press.
Beck, Ulrich. 1992. *Risk Society: Towards a New Modernity*. London: SAGE.
Behr, Dorothée, and Evi Scholz. 2011. "Questionnaire Translation in Cross-National Survey Research: On the Types and Value of Annotations." *Methoden, Daten, Analysen (Mda)* 5 (2): 157–79.
Bélanger, France, and Robert E. Crossler. 2011. "Privacy in the Digital Age: A Review of Information Privacy Research in Information Systems." *MIS Quarterly* 35 (4): 1017–41.
Belesiotis, Alexandros, George Papadakis, and Dimitrios Skoutas. 2018. "Analyzing and Predicting Spatial Crime Distribution Using Crowdsourced and Open Data." *ACM Transactions on Spatial Algorithms and Systems* 3 (4): 12:1–12:31.
Benamati, John H., Zafer D. Ozdemir, and H. Jeff Smith. 2017. "An Empirical Test of an Antecedents—Privacy Concerns—Outcomes Model." *Journal of Information Science* 43 (5): 583–600.
Benn, Stanley I. 1971. "Privacy, Freedom, and Respect for Persons." In *Privacy and Personality*, edited by John W. Pennock and J. Roland; Chapman, 1–26. New York: Routledge.
Benndorf, Volker, and Hans-Theo Normann. 2018. "The Willingness to Sell Personal Data." *The Scandinavian Journal of Economics* 120 (4): 1260–78.
Bennett, Colin J. 2001. "Privacy in the Political System: Perspectives from Political Science and Economics." A Report Written for the Ethical, Legal and Social Issues (ELSI) Component of the Human Genome Project, U.S. Department of Energy. Victoria: University of Victoria. https://www.colinbennett.ca/wp-content/uploads/2012/06/Privacyin-the-Political-System.pdf.
Bennett, Colin J. 2008. *The Privacy Advocates: Resisting the Spread of Surveillance*. Cambridge: MIT Press.
Bennett, Trevor H., and Loraine Gelsthorpe. 1996. "Public Attitudes Towards CCTV in Public Places." *Studies on Crime and Crime Prevention* 5 (1): 72–90.
Bentham, Jeremy. 1791. *Panopticon Or the Inspection House*.
Bentham, Jeremy. 2007. *An Introduction to the Principles ofMorals and Legislation*. Mineola, N.Y: Dover Publications Inc.
Berendt, Bettina, Oliver Günther, and Sarah Spiekermann. 2005. "Privacy in E-Commerce: Stated Preferences vs. Actual Behavior." *Communications of the ACM* 48 (4): 101–6.
Beresford, Alastair R., Dorothea Kübler, and Sören Preibusch. 2012. "Unwillingness to Pay for Privacy: A Field Experiment." *Economics Letters* 117 (1): 25–27.

Berg, Chris. 2018. *The Classical Liberal Case for Privacy in a World of Surveillance and Technological Change*. Palgrave Studies in Classical Liberalism. Palgrave Macmillan.

Berg, John H., and Valerian J. Derlega. 1987. "Themes in the Study of Self-Disclosure." In *Self-Disclosure: Theory, Research, and Therapy*, edited by Valerian J. Derlega and John H. Berg, 1–8. Perspectives in Social Psychology. Boston, MA: Springer US.

Berlin, Isaiah. 2002. *Liberty: Incorporating Four Essays on Liberty*. Edited by Henry Hardy. 2nd ed. Oxford: Oxford University Press.

Berryessa, Colleen M., and Joel M. Caplan. 2020. "Cognitive and Affective Processing of Risk Information: A Survey Experiment on Risk-Based Decision-Making Related to Crime and Public Safety." *Frontiers in Psychology* 11: 2222.

Bertsou, Eri, and Daniele Caramani. 2022. "People Haven't Had Enough of Experts: Technocratic Attitudes among Citizens in Nine European Democracies." *American Journal of Political Science* 66 (1): 5–23.

Best, Samuel J., Brian S. Krueger, and Jeffrey Ladewig. 2006. "Trends: Privacy in the Information Age." *The Public Opinion Quarterly* 70 (3): 375–401.

Bhatia, Jaspreet, and Travis D. Breaux. 2018. "Empirical Measurement of Perceived Privacy Risk." *ACM Transactions on Computer-Human Interaction* 25 (6): 34:1–34:47.

Bieker, Felix, Benjamin Bremert, and Thilo Hagendorff. 2018. "Die Überwachungs-Gesamtrechnung, Oder: Es Kann Nicht Sein, Was Nicht Sein Darf." In *Die Fortentwicklung Des Datenschutzes: Zwischen Systemgestaltung Und Selbstregulierung*, edited by Alexander Roßnagel, Michael Friedewald, and Marit Hansen, 139–50. DuD-Fachbeiträge. Wiesbaden: Springer Fachmedien.

Biemer, Paul P. 2010. "Total Survey Error: Design, Implementation, and Evaluation." *Public Opinion Quarterly* 74 (5): 817–48.

Bigo, Didier. 2008. "The Field and the Ban-Opticon." In *Terror, Insecurity and Liberty: Illiberal Practices of Liberal Regimes after 9/11*, edited by Didier Bigo and Anastassia Tsoukala, 20–58. London; New York: Taylor & Francis Ltd.

Bigo, Didier. 2010. "Delivering Liberty and Security? The Reframing of Freedom When Associated with Security." In *Europe's 21st Century Challenge*, edited by Didier Bigo, Sergio Carrera, Elspeth Guild, and R.B.J. Walker, 263–87. Farnham: Ashgate.

Bigo, Didier. 2012. "Security, Surveillance and Democracy." In *Routledge Handbook of Surveillance Studies*, edited by Kirstie Ball, Kevin D. Haggerty, and David Lyon, 277–84. New York: Taylor & Francis.

Bigo, Didier, Sergio Carrera, Elspeth Guild, and R. B. J. Walker. 2008. "The Changing Landscape of European Liberty and Security: The Mid-Term Report of the CHALLENGE Project." *International Social Science Journal* 59 (192): 283–308.

Birkel, Christoph, Daniel Church, Dina Hummelsheim-Doss, Nathalie Leitgöb-Guzy, and Dietrich Oberwittler. 2020. *The 2017 German Victimisation Survey Victimisation, Crime-Related Attitudes and Perceptions of Insecurity and Crime in Germany*. Bundeskriminalamt: Wiesbaden.

Bizumic, Boris, and John Duckitt. 2018. "Investigating Right Wing Authoritarianism with a Very Short Authoritarianism Scale." *Journal of Social and Political Psychology* 6 (1): 129–50.

Bjørgo, Tore. 2023. "Introduction to the Special Section on Anti-Government Extremism." *Perspectives on Terrorism* 17 (1): 67–72.

Blackstone, Knight Williamtone. 2001. *Commentaries on the Laws of England: In Four Books*. London: Routledge.

Blatz, W. E. 1966. *Human Security*. Toronto: University of Toronto Press.

Bloustein, Edward J. 1964. "Privacy as an Aspect of Human Dignity: An Answer to Dean Prosser." *New York University Law Review* 39: 962–1007.

Boese, Vanessa A. 2019. "How (Not) to Measure Democracy." *International Area Studies Review* 22 (2): 95–127.

Bogard, William. 2006. "Surveillance Assemblage and Lines of Flight." In *Theorizing Surveillance: The Panopticon and Beyond*, edited by David Lyon, 97–122. Cullompton, Devon: Routledge.

Bogert, Eric, Aaron Schecter, and Richard T. Watson. 2021. "Humans Rely More on Algorithms than Social Influence as a Task Becomes More Difficult." *Scientific Reports* 11 (1): 8028.

Bogomolov, Andrey, Bruno Lepri, Jacopo Staiano, Nuria Oliver, Fabio Pianesi, and Alex Pentland. 2014. "Once Upon a Crime: Towards Crime Prediction from Demographics and Mobile Data." In *Proceedings of the 16th International Conference on Multimodal Interaction*, 427–34. ICMI '14. New York, NY, USA: Association for Computing Machinery. https://doi.org/10.1145/2663204.2663254.

Bok, Sissela. 1984. *Secrets on the Ethics of Concealment and Revelation*. Second Edition. New York: Oxford University Press.

Bol, Nadine, Tobias Dienlin, Sanne Kruikemeier, Marijn Sax, Sophie C Boerman, Joanna Strycharz, Natali Helberger, and Claes H. de Vreese. 2018. "Understanding the Effects of Personalization as a Privacy Calculus: Analyzing Self-Disclosure Across Health, News, and Commerce Contexts." *Journal of Computer-Mediated Communication* 23 (6): 370–88.

Boling, Patricia. 1996. *Privacy and the Politics of Intimate Life*. Ithaca, NY: Cornell University Press.

Bonilla, Tabitha. 2022. *The Importance of Campaign Promises*. Cambridge: Cambridge University Press.

Bonß, Wolfgang. 1995. *Vom Risiko. Unsicherheit Und Ungewißheit in Der Moderne*. Hamburg: Hamburger Edition.

Books, John W., and Charles L. Prysby. 1991. *Political Behavior and the Local Context*. New York: Bloomsbury 3PL.

Booth, Ken. 1991. "Security and Emancipation." *Review of International Studies* 17 (4): 313–26.

Booth, Ken. 2007. *Theory of World Security*. Cambridge Studies in International Relations. Cambridge: Cambridge University Press.

Borah, Porismita. 2011. "Conceptual Issues in Framing Theory: A Systematic Examination of a Decade's Literature." *Journal of Communication* 61 (2): 246–63.

Borel, Jack C. 1964. "Security as a Motivation of Human Behavior." *Archives of General Psychiatry* 10 (2): 105–8.

Bourbeau, Philippe. 2011. *The Securitization of Migration: A Study of Movement and Order*. London: Routledge.

Bourdieu, Pierre, and Loïc J. D. Wacquant. 1992. *An Invitation to Reflexive Sociology*. Chicago, IL: University of Chicago Press.

Boyd, Andrew W. 2011. "A Longitudinal Study of Social Media Privacy Behavior." arXiv. https://doi.org/10.48550/arXiv.1103.3174.

Brettschneider, Corey. 2010. *Democratic Rights: The Substance of Self-Government*. Princeton; Oxford: Princeton University Press.

Brinson, Mary E., and Michael Stohl. 2012. "Media Framing of Terrorism: Implications for Public Opinion, Civil Liberties, and Counterterrorism Policies." *Journal of International and Intercultural Communication* 5 (4): 270–90.

Brockdorff, Noellie, Sandra Appleby-Arnold, and Eva Fialova. 2015. "The Citizens' Perspective: Awareness, Feelings and Acceptance of Surveillance and Surveillance Systems for Fighting Crime in the Czech Republic. A Quantitative Study." RESPECT. Citizens' Awareness of and Attitude towards Surveillance. Valetta: University of Malta. https://www.um.edu.mt/library/oar/handle/123456789/39675.

Brockdorff, Noellie, Sandra Appleby-Arnold, Christian Hawellek, and Andryi Ilyuk. 2015. "The Citizens' Perspective: Awareness, Feelings and Acceptance of Surveillance and Surveillance Systems for Fighting Crime in Germany. A Quantitative Study." RESPECT. Citizens' Awareness of and Attitude towards Surveillance. Valetta: University of Malta. https://doi.org/10.13140/RG.2.2.11042.27847.

Broek, Tijs van den, Merel Ooms, Michael Friedewald, Marc van Lieshout, and Sven Rung. 2017. "Privacy and Security: Citizens' Desires for an Equal Footing." In *Surveillance, Privacy and Security: Citizens' Perspectives*, edited by Michael Friedewald, J. Peter Burgess, Johann Cas, Walter Peissl, and Rocco Bellanova, 15–35. London; New York: Routledge.

Bromberg, Daniel E., Étienne Charbonneau, and Andrew Smith. 2020. "Public Support for Facial Recognition via Police Body-Worn Cameras: Findings from a List Experiment." *Government Information Quarterly* 37 (1): 101415.

Bronitt, Simon. 2008. "Balancing Security and Liberty: Critical Perspectives on Terrorism Law Reform." In *Fresh Perspectives on the "War on Terror,"* edited by Miriam Gani and Penelope Mathew, 65–84. Canberra: ANU Press.

Brosch, Tobias, David Sander, Fabrice Clément, Julien A. Deonna, Ernst Fehr, and Patrik Vuilleumier, eds. 2016. *Handbook of Value: Perspectives from Economics, Neuroscience, Philosophy, Psychology and Sociology*. Oxford, United Kingdom: Oxford University Press.

Brown, Ian, and Douwe Korff. 2009. "Terrorism and the Proportionality of Internet Surveillance." *European Journal of Criminology* 6 (2): 119–34.

Brown, William S. 2000. "Ontological Security, Existential Anxiety and Workplace Privacy." *Journal of Business Ethics* 23 (1): 61–65.

Browne, Simone. 2015. *Dark Matters: On the Surveillance of Blackness*. Durham: Duke University Press.

Bubandt, Nils. 2005. "Vernacular Security: The Politics of Feeling Safe in Global, National and Local Worlds." *Security Dialogue* 36 (3): 275–96.

Büchi, Moritz, Eduard Fosch-Villaronga, Christoph Lutz, Aurelia Tamò-Larrieux, Shruthi Velidi, and Salome Viljoen. 2020. "The Chilling Effects of Algorithmic Profiling: Mapping the Issues." *Computer Law & Security Review* 36: 105367.

Buck, Christoph, Tamara Dinev, and Reza Ghaiumy Anaraky. 2022. "Revisiting APCO." In *Modern Socio-Technical Perspectives on Privacy*, edited by Bart P. Knijnenburg,

Xinru Page, Pamela Wisniewski, Heather Richter Lipford, Nicholas Proferes, and Jennifer Romano, 43–60. Cham: Springer International Publishing.

Budak, Jelena, Ivan-Damir Anić, and Edo Rajh. 2013. "Public Attitudes towards Privacy and Surveillance in Croatia." *Innovation: The European Journal of Social Science Research* 26 (1–2): 100–118.

Budak, Jelena, Edo Rajh, and Vadran Recher. 2017. "Citizens' Privacy Concerns. Does National Culture Matter?" In *Surveillance, Privacy and Security: Citizens' Perspectives*, edited by Michael Friedewald, J. Peter Burgess, Johann Cas, Walter Peissl, and Rocco Bellanova, 36–51. London; New York: Routledge.

Buil-Gil, David, Angelo Moretti, and Samuel H. Langton. 2022. "The Accuracy of Crime Statistics: Assessing the Impact of Police Data Bias on Geographic Crime Analysis." *Journal of Experimental Criminology* 18 (3): 515–41.

Buller, David B., and Judee K. Burgoon. 1996. "Interpersonal Deception Theory." *Communication Theory* 6 (3): 203–42.

Bundeskriminalamt. 2021a. "Police Crime Statistics. Federal Republic of Germany. Report 2020." Wiesbaden. https://www.bka.de/EN/CurrentInformation/Statistics/PoliceCrimeStatistics/2020/pcs2020.html.

Bundeskriminalamt. 2021b. "Polizeiliche Kriminalitätsstatistik 2020—Kreis Falltabellen." Wiesbaden. https://www.bka.de/DE/AktuelleInformationen/StatistikenLagebilder/PolizeilicheKriminalstatistik/PKS2020/PKSTabellen/KreisFalltabellen/kreisfalltabellen_node.html.

Burbank, Matthew J. 1997. "Explaining Contextual Effects on Vote Choice." *Political Behavior* 19 (2): 113–32.

Burke, Anthony. 2006. *Beyond Security, Ethics and Violence: War Against the Other*. Abingdon, Oxon, England ; New York: Routledge.

Burkhardt, Christine, Natalia Delgrande, and Patrice Villettaz. 2017. "Do Police Officers Fear Crime in the Same Way as the Population?: Results of a Local Police Survey on Insecurity and Fear of Crime in Switzerland." In *The Routledge International Handbook on Fear of Crime*, edited by Murray Lee and Gabe Mythen, 282–98. London: Routledge.

Burstein, Paul. 2003. "The Impact of Public Opinion on Public Policy: A Review and an Agenda." *Political Research Quarterly* 56 (1): 29–40.

Büscher, Maximilian, Amina Gutjahr, Gerrit Hornung, Stephan Schindler, Annika Selzer, Indra Spiecker, Sarah Stummer, Thomas Wilmer, and Paul Zurawski. 2022. *Eine explorative Nutzerbefragung zu den Auswirkungen verschiedener Beobachtungssituationen*. Darmstadt: Nationales Forschungszentrum für angewandte Cybersicherheit ATHENE c/o Fraunhofer-Institut für Sichere Informationstechnologie SIT.

Buzan, Barry. 1991. *People States And Fear: National Security Problem in International Relations*. 2nd edition. New York: Longman.

Buzan, Barry, and Ole Wæver. 2003. *Regions and Powers: The Structure of International Security*. Cambridge Studies in International Relations. Cambridge: Cambridge University Press.

Buzan, Barry, Ole Wæver, and Jaap De Wilde. 1997. *Security: A New Framework for Analysis*. UK ed. Boulder, Colo: Lynne Rienner Publishers.

Cameron, William B., and Thomas C. McCormick. 1954. "Concepts of Security and Insecurity." *American Journal of Sociology* 59 (6): 556–64.

Campbell, Angus, Philip E. Converse, Warren E. Miller, and Donald E. Stokes. 1960. *The American Voter*. Chicago: University of Chicago Press.

Campbell, David. 1992. *Writing Security: United States Foreign Policy and the Politics of Identity*. Minneapolis: U of Minnesota Press.

Campbell, Donald T., and H. Laurence Ross. 1968. "The Connecticut Crackdown on Speeding: Time-Series Data in Quasi-Experimental Analysis." *Law & Society Review* 3 (1): 33–53.

Caplan, Joel M., and Leslie W. Kennedy. 2016. *Risk Terrain Modeling: Crime Prediction and Risk Reduction*. Oakland: University of California Press.

Capurro, Rafael. 2005. "Privacy. An Intercultural Perspective." *Ethics and Information Technology* 7 (1): 37–47.

Carro, D., S. Valera, and T. Vidal. 2010. "Perceived Insecurity in the Public Space: Personal, Social and Environmental Variables." *Quality & Quantity* 44 (2): 303–14.

Carter, Emma, Jonathan Paragreen, Guilio Valfrè, and David Fletcher. 2015. "Passenger Acceptance of Counter-Terrorism Security Measures in Stations." *IET Intelligent Transport Systems* 10 (1): 2–9.

Cas, Johann, Rocco Bellanova, J. Peter Burgess, Michael Friedewald, and Walter Peissl. 2017. "Introduction: Surveillance, Privacy and Security." In *Surveillance, Privacy and Security: Citizens' Perspectives*, edited by Michael Friedewald, J. Peter Burgess, Johann Cas, Walter Peissl, and Rocco Bellanova, 1–12. London; New York: Routledge.

Cate, Fred H., and James X. Dempsey, eds. 2017. *Bulk Collection: Systematic Government Access to Private-Sector Data*. Illustrated Edition. Oxford, UK ; New York, NY: Oxford University Press.

Cavoukian, Ann, Michelle Chibba, and Alex Stoianov. 2012. "Advances in Biometric Encryption: Taking Privacy by Design from Academic Research to Deployment." *Review of Policy Research* 29 (1): 37–61.

Cayford, Michelle, and Wolter Pieters. 2018. "The Effectiveness of Surveillance Technology: What Intelligence Officials Are Saying." *The Information Society* 34 (2): 88–103.

Cayford, Michelle, Wolter Pieters, and P.H.A.J.M van Gelder. 2019. "Wanting It All—Public Perceptions of the Effectiveness, Cost, and Privacy of Surveillance Technology." *Journal of Information, Communication and Ethics in Society* 18 (1): 10–27.

Ceyhan, Ayse. 2012. "Surveillance as Biopower." In *Routledge Handbook of Surveillance Studies*, edited by Kristie Ball, Kevin D. Haggerty, and David Lyon, 38–45. London: Routledge.

Chandler, Jennifer. 2009. "Privacy Versus National Security: Clarifying the Trade-Off." In *Lessons from the Identity Trail: Anonymity, Privacy and Identity in a Networked Society*, edited by Ian Kerr, Carole Lucock, and Valerie Stevens, 131–38. Oxford: Oxford University Press.

Cheek, Nathan N., Elena Reutskaja, and Barry Schwartz. 2022. "Balancing the Freedom–Security Trade-Off During Crises and Disasters." *Perspectives on Psychological Science* 17 (4): 1024–49.

Chiou, Andy. 2009. "Cross Cultural Perceptions on Privacy in the United States, Vietnam, Indonesia, and Taiwan." In *Online Consumer Protection: Theories of Human Relativism*, 284–99. IGI Global.

Chiou, Andy, Jeng-chung V. Chen, and Craig Bisset. 2009. "Cross Cultural Perceptions on Privacy in the United States, Vietnam, Indonesia, and Taiwan." In *Online Consumer Protection: Theories of Human Relativism*, edited by Chen Kuanchin and Adam Fadllala, 284–99. New York: IGI Global.

Chong, Daniel. 1996. "Creating Common Frames of Reference on Political Issues." In *Political Persuasion and Attitude Change*, edited by Diana C. Mutz, Richard A. Brody, and Paul M. Sniderman, 196–224. Ann Arbor: University of Michigan Press.

Chong, Dennis, and James N. Druckman. 2007. "A Theory of Framing and Opinion Formation in Competitive Elite Environments." *Journal of Communication* 57 (1): 99–118.

Chong, Dennis, and James N. Druckman. 2013. "Counterframing Effects." *The Journal of Politics* 75 (1): 1–16.

Ciccone, Alice, and Emilia Soldani. 2021. "Stick or Carrot? Asymmetric Responses to Vehicle Registration Taxes in Norway." *Environmental and Resource Economics* 80 (1): 59–94.

Citrin, Jack. 1979. "Do People Want Something for Nothing: Public Opinion on Taxes and Government Spending." *National Tax Journal* 32 (2): 113–29.

Clarke, Michael. 1994. "Blind Eye on the Street." *Police Review* 5: 28–30.

Clarke, Roger. 1999. "Introduction to Dataveillance and Information Privacy, and Definitions of Terms." http://www.rogerclarke.com/DV/Intro.html / https://web.archive.org/web/20220831233024/http://www.rogerclarke.com/DV/Intro.html.

Clarke, Roger. 2006. "What's Privacy. Prepared for a Workshop at the Australian Law Reform Commission on 28 July 2006." http://www.rogerclarke.com/DV/Privacy.html / https://web.archive.org/web/20220831233024/http://www.rogerclarke.com/DV/Privacy.html.

Clarke, Roger. 2015. "A Framework for Analysing Technology's Negative and Positive Impacts on Freedom and Privacy. Appendices." http://www.rogerclarke.com/DV/Biel15-DuD.html / https://web.archive.org/web/20211028075810/http://www.rogerclarke.com/DV/Biel15-DuDA.html.

Cohen, Jean-Louis. 2004. *Regulating Intimacy: A New Legal Paradigm*. Princeton, NJ: Princeton University Press.

Cohen, Julie E. 2008. "Privacy, Visibility, Transparency, and Exposure." *The University of Chicago Law Review* 75 (1): 181–201.

Coleman, James S. 1986. "Social Theory, Social Research, and a Theory of Action." *American Journal of Sociology* 91 (6): 1309–35.

Colquhoun, Patrick. 2012. *A Treatise on the Police of the Metropolis: Containing a Detail of the Various Crimes and Misdemeanors by Which Public and Private Property and Security Are, at Present, Injured and Endangered, and Suggesting Remedies for Their Prevention*. Cambridge Library Collection—British & Irish History, 17th & 18th Centuries. Cambridge: Cambridge University Press.

Connor, Brian T., and Long Doan. 2021. "Government and Corporate Surveillance: Moral Discourse on Privacy in the Civil Sphere." *Information, Communication & Society* 24 (1): 52–68.

Conrad, Frederick G., Mick P. Couper, Roger Tourangeau, and Andrey Peytchev. 2006. "Use and Non-Use of Clarification Features in Web Surveys." *Journal of Official Statistics* 22 (2): 245–69.

Consolvo, Sunny, Ian E. Smith, Tara Matthews, Anthony LaMarca, Jason Tabert, and Pauline Powledge. 2005. "Location Disclosure to Social Relations: Why, When, & What People Want to Share." In *Proceedings of the SIGCHI Conference on Human Factors in Computing Systems*, 81–90. CHI '05. New York, NY, USA: Association for Computing Machinery. https://doi.org/10.1145/1054972.1054985.

Conti, Gregory, Lisa Shay, and Woodrow Hartzog. 2014. "Deconstructing the Relationship Between Privacy and Security." *IEEE Technology and Society Magazine* 33 (2): 28–30.

Converse, Philip E. 1964. "The Nature of Belief Systems in Mass Publics." In *Ideology and Discontent*, edited by David E. Apter, 206–61. New York: Free Press.

Cook, John, and Stephan Lewandowsky. 2016. "Rational Irrationality: Modeling Climate Change Belief Polarization Using Bayesian Networks." *Topics in Cognitive Science* 8 (1): 160–79.

Cooper, James C. 2017. "Anonymity, Autonomy, and the Collection of Personal Data: Measuring the Privacy Impact of Google's 2012 Privacy Policy Change." *George Mason Law & Economics Research Paper* 17 (6).

Coppedge, Michael, John Gerring, Carl H. Knutsen, Staffan I. Lindberg, Svend-Erik Skaaning, Jan Teorell, David Altman, et al. 2022. "V-Dem Dataset 2022." https://doi.org/10.23696/vdemds22.

Coppedge, Michael, John Gerring, Carl Henrik Knutsen, Staffan I. Lindberg, Jan Teorell, Nazifa Alizada, David Altman, et al. 2021. "V-Dem Dataset V11.1." https://doi.org/10.23696/vdemds21.

Coppedge, Michael, Staffan Lindberg, Svend-Erik Skaaning, and Jan Teorell. 2016. "Measuring High Level Democratic Principles Using the V-Dem Data." *International Political Science Review / Revue Internationale de Science Politique* 37 (5): 580–93.

Coppock, Alexander. 2019. "Generalizing from Survey Experiments Conducted on Mechanical Turk: A Replication Approach." *Political Science Research and Methods* 7 (3): 613–28.

Cornesse, Carina, Annelies G. Blom, David Dutwin, Jon A. Krosnick, Edith D. De Leeuw, Stéphane Legleye, Josh Pasek, Darren Pennay, Benjamin Phillips, Joseph W. Sakshaug, Bella Struminskaya, and Alexander Wenz. 2020. "A Review of Conceptual Approaches and Empirical Evidence on Probability and Nonprobability Sample Survey Research." *Journal of Survey Statistics and Methodology* 8 (1): 4–36.

Côté, Adam. 2016. "Agents without Agency: Assessing the Role of the Audience in Securitization Theory." *Security Dialogue* 47 (6): 541–58.

Couper, Mick P., Eleanor Singer, and Richard A. Kulka. 1998. "Participation in the 1990 Decennial Census: Politics, Privacy, Pressures." *American Politics Quarterly* 26 (1): 59–80.

Craven, J. Braxton. 1976. "Personhood: The Right to Be Let Alone." *Duke Law Journal* 25 (4): 699–720.

Cruz, Cesi, Philip Keefi, and Carlos Scartascini. 2016. "The Database of Political Institutions 2015 (DPI2015)." https://publications.iadb.org/en/database-political-institutions-2015-dpi2015.

Culnan, Mary J., and Pamela K. Armstrong. 1999. "Information Privacy Concerns, Procedural Fairness, and Impersonal Trust: An Empirical Investigation." *Organization Science* 10 (1): 104–15.

Cummings, Mary. 2004. "Automation Bias in Intelligent Time Critical Decision Support Systems." In *Proceedings of the AIAA 1st Intelligent Systems Technical Conference*. Chicago: American Institute of Aeronautics and Astronautics. https://doi.org/10.2514/6.2004-6313.

Dalton, Russell J., and Christopher J. Anderson. 2011. *Citizens, Context, and Choice: How Context Shapes Citizens' Electoral Choices*. New York: Oxford University Press.

Dandeker, Christopher. 1994. *Surveillance, Power and Modernity: Bureaucracy and Discipline from 1700 to the Present Day*. Cambridge: Polity.

Dandeker, Christopher. 2005. "Surveillance and Military Transformation: Organizational Trends in Twenty-First-Century Armed Services." In *The New Politics of Surveillance and Visibility*, edited by Kevin D. Haggerty and Richard V. Ericson, 225–49. Toronto: University of Toronto Press.

Dash, Amrutanshu, and Dhruv Sharma. 2016. "Arrest Warrants at the International Criminal Court: Reasonable Suspicion or Reasonable Grounds to Believe?" *International Criminal Law Review* 16 (1): 158–76.

Davis, Darren W., and Brian D. Silver. 2004. "Civil Liberties vs. Security: Public Opinion in the Context of the Terrorist Attacks on America." *American Journal of Political Science* 48 (1): 28–46.

Dawes, Christopher T., Peter John Loewen, and James H. Fowler. 2011. "Social Preferences and Political Participation." *The Journal of Politics* 73 (3): 845–56.

De Leeuw, Edith D., Joop Hox, and Annette Scherpenzeel. 2019. "Mode Effects Versus Question Format Effects: An Experimental Investigation of Measurement Error Implemented in a Probability-Based Online Panel." In *Experimental Methods in Survey Research*, edited by Paul Lavrakas, Michael W. Traugott, Courtney Kennedy, Allyson L. Holbrook, Edith D. De Leeuw, and Brady T. West, 151–65. John Wiley & Sons, Ltd.

Debatin, Bernhard, Jennette P. Lovejoy, Ann-Kathrin Horn, and Brittany N. Hughes. 2009. "Facebook and Online Privacy: Attitudes, Behaviors, and Unintended Consequences." *Journal of Computer-Mediated Communication* 15 (1): 83–108.

DeCew, Judith W. 1997. *In Pursuit of Privacy: Law, Ethics and the Rise of Technology*. Ithaca: Cornell University Press.

Declich, Silvia, and Anne O. Carter. 1994. "Public Health Surveillance: Historical Origins, Methods and Evaluation." *Bulletin of the World Health Organization* 72 (2): 285–304.

Dee, Mike. 2013. "Welfare Surveillance, Income Management and New Paternalism in Australia." *Surveillance & Society* 11 (3): 272–86.

Degli Esposti, Sara, Vincenzo Pavone, and Elvira Santiago-Gómez. 2017. "Aligning Security and Privacy. The Case of Deep Packet Inspection." In *Surveillance, Privacy and Security: Citizens' Perspectives*, edited by Michael Friedewald, J. Peter Burgess, Johann Cas, Walter Peissl, and Rocco Bellanova, 71–90. London; New York: Routledge.

Degli Esposti, Sara, and Elvira Santiago-Gomez. 2015. "Acceptable Surveillance-Orientated Security Technologies: Insights from the SurPRISE Project." *Surveillance & Society* 13 (3/4): 437–54.

Demir, Melikşah. 2008. "Sweetheart, You Really Make Me Happy: Romantic Relationship Quality and Personality as Predictors of Happiness among Emerging Adults." *Journal of Happiness Studies* 9 (2): 257–77.

Dencik, Lina, and Jonathan Cable. 2017. "Digital Citizenship and Surveillance. The Advent of Surveillance Realism. Public Opinion and Activist Responses to the Snowden Leaks." *International Journal of Communication* 11: 763–81.

Dharshing, Samdruk, Stefanie L. Hille, and Rolf Wüstenhagen. 2017. "The Influence of Political Orientation on the Strength and Temporal Persistence of Policy Framing Effects." *Ecological Economics* 142: 295–305.

Di Mauro, Letizia S., Alessandro Pluchino, and Alessio E. Biondo. 2019. "Tax Evasion as a Contagion Game: Evidences from an Agent-Based Model." *The European Physical Journal B* 92 (5): 103.

Dienlin, Tobias, and Johannes Breuer. 2023. "Privacy Is Dead, Long Live Privacy! Two Diverging Perspectives on Current Issues Related to Privacy." *Journal of Media Psychology: Theories, Methods, and Applications* 35 (3): 159–68.

Dienlin, Tobias, Philipp K Masur, and Sabine Trepte. 2023. "A Longitudinal Analysis of the Privacy Paradox." *New Media & Society* 25 (5): 1043–64.

Dienlin, Tobias, and Miriam J. Metzger. 2016. "An Extended Privacy Calculus Model for SNSs: Analyzing Self-Disclosure and Self-Withdrawal in a Representative U.S. Sample." *Journal of Computer-Mediated Communication* 21 (5): 368–83.

Dietrich, Nick, and Charles Crabtree. 2019. "Domestic Demand for Human Rights: Free Speech and the Freedom-Security Trade-Off." *International Studies Quarterly* 63 (2): 346–53.

Dillon, Michael. 1996. *Politics of Security: Towards a Political Phiosophy of Continental Thought*. London ; New York: Taylor & Francis Ltd.

Dinev, Tamara, Valentina Albano, Heng Xu, Alessandro D'Atri, and Paul Hart. 2016. "Individuals' Attitudes Towards Electronic Health Records: A Privacy Calculus Perspective." In *Advances in Healthcare Informatics and Analytics*, edited by Ashish Gupta, Vimla L. Patel, and Robert A. Greenes, 19–50. Cham: Springer International Publishing.

Dinev, Tamara, Massimo Bellotto, Paul Hart, Vincenzo Russo, and Ilaria Serra. 2006. "Internet Users' Privacy Concerns and Beliefs About Government Surveillance: An Exploratory Study of Differences Between Italy and the United States." *Journal of Global Information Management (JGIM)* 14 (4): 57–93.

Dinev, Tamara, and Paul Hart. 2006. "An Extended Privacy Calculus Model for E-Commerce Transactions." *Information Systems Research* 17 (1): 61–80.

Dinev, Tamara, Paul Hart, and Michael R. Mullen. 2008. "Internet Privacy Concerns and Beliefs about Government Surveillance—An Empirical Investigation." *The Journal of Strategic Information Systems* 17 (3): 214–33.

Dinev, Tamara, Allen R. McConnell, and H. Jeff Smith. 2015. "Research Commentary—Informing Privacy Research Through Information Systems, Psychology, and Behavioral Economics: Thinking Outside the 'APCO' Box." *Information Systems Research* 26 (4): 639–55.

Ditton, Jason. 2000. "Crime and the City." *The British Journal of Criminology* 40 (4): 692–709.

Ditton, Jason, and Emma Short. 1999. "Yes, It Works, No, It Doesn't: Comparing the Effects of Open-Street CCTV in Two Adjacent Scottish Town Centres." In *Surveillance of Public Space: CCTV, Street Lighting and Crime Prevention. Crime Prevention Studies*, edited by Kate Painter and Nick Tilley, 371–403. Monsey: Criminal Justice Press.

Dixon, John, Mark Levine, and Rob McAuley. 2003. "Street Drinking Legislation, CCTV and Public Space: Exploring Attitudes towards Public Order Measures. Working Paper." http://citeseerx.ist.psu.edu/viewdoc/download?doi=10.1.1.210.5338&rep=rep1&type=pdf.

Dommett, Katharine, and Warren Pearce. 2019. "What Do We Know about Public Attitudes towards Experts? Reviewing Survey Data in the United Kingdom and European Union." *Public Understanding of Science* 28 (6): 669–78.

Dorak, M. Tevfik, and Ebru Karpuzoglu. 2012. "Gender Differences in Cancer Susceptibility: An Inadequately Addressed Issue." *Frontiers in Genetics* 3 (November): 268.

Dragu, Tiberiu. 2011. "Is There a Trade-off between Security and Liberty? Executive Bias, Privacy Protections, and Terrorism Prevention." *The American Political Science Review* 105 (1): 64–78.

Draper, Nora A. 2017. "From Privacy Pragmatist to Privacy Resigned: Challenging Narratives of Rational Choice in Digital Privacy Debates." *Policy & Internet* 9 (2): 232–51.

Drews, Stefan, and Jeroen C.J.M. van den Bergh. 2016. "What Explains Public Support for Climate Policies? A Review of Empirical and Experimental Studies." *Climate Policy* 16 (7): 855–76.

Druckman, James N. 2001. "On the Limits of Framing Effects: Who Can Frame?" *Journal of Politics* 63 (4): 1041–66.

Dubrofsky, Rachel E., and Shoshana Amielle Magnet, eds. 2015. "Introduction: Feminist Surveillance Studies: Critical Interventions." In *Feminist Surveillance Studies*, 1–17. Durham: Duke University Press.

Duckitt, John, and Chris G. Sibley. 2010. "Personality, Ideology, Prejudice, and Politics: A Dual-Process Motivational Model." *Journal of Personality* 78 (6): 1861–94.

Dunnage, Jonathan. 2016. "Policing and Surveillance." In *The Palgrave Handbook of Mass Dictatorship*, edited by Paul Corner and Jie-Hyun Lim, 119–30. London: Palgrave Macmillan UK.

Dupont, Julia C., Evelyn Bytzek, Melanie C. Steffens, and Frank M. Schneider. 2019. "Which Kind of Political Campaign Messages Do People Perceive as Election Pledges?" *Electoral Studies* 57: 121–30.

Dupree, Janna Lynn, Richard Devries, Daniel M. Berry, and Edward Lank. 2016. "Privacy Personas: Clustering Users via Attitudes and Behaviors toward Security Practices." In *Proceedings of the 2016 CHI Conference on Human Factors in Computing Systems*, 5228–39. CHI '16. New York, NY, USA: Association for Computing Machinery. https://doi.org/10.1145/2858036.2858214.

Dworkin, Ronald. 1977. *Taking Rights Seriously*. Harvard University Press.

Ebert, Nico, Kurt Alexander Ackermann, and Peter Heinrich. 2020. "Does Context in Privacy Communication Really Matter? — A Survey on Consumer Concerns and Preferences." In *Proceedings of the 2020 CHI Conference on Human Factors in Computing Systems*, 1–11. CHI '20. New York, NY, USA: Association for Computing Machinery. https://doi.org/10.1145/3313831.3376575.

Edlund, Jonas, and Arvid Lindh. 2018. "ISSP 2016—Role of Government V: Questionnaire Development Report." https://dbk.gesis.org/dbksearch/file.asp?file=ZA6900_questionnaire_development_report.pdf.

Edlund, Jonas, and Arvid Lindh. 2019. "The ISSP 2016 Role of Government Module: Content, Coverage, and History." *International Journal of Sociology* 49 (2): 99–109.

Edwards, Adam, and Gordon Hughes. 2009. "The Preventive Turn and the Promotion of Safer Communities in England and Wales: Political Inventiveness and Governmental Instabilities." In *Crime Prevention Policies in Comparative Perspective*, edited by Adam Crawford, 62–85. London: Willan publishing Ltd.

Elff, Martin, Jan Paul Heisig, Merlin Schaeffer, and Susumu Shikano. 2021. "Multilevel Analysis with Few Clusters: Improving Likelihood-Based Methods to Provide Unbiased Estimates and Accurate Inference." *British Journal of Political Science* 51 (1): 412–26.

Elueze, Isioma, and Anabel Quan-Haase. 2018. "Privacy Attitudes and Concerns in the Digital Lives of Older Adults: Westin's Privacy Attitude Typology Revisited." *American Behavioral Scientist* 62 (10): 1372–91.

Entman, Robert M. 1993. "Framing: Toward Clarification of a Fractured Paradigm." *Journal of Communication* 43 (4): 51–58.

Ericson, Richard V., and Kevin D. Haggerty. 1997. *Policing the Risk Society*. Toronto: University of Toronto Press.

Etzioni, Amitai. 2000. *The Limits Of Privacy*. New York: Basic Books.

European Parliament. 2022. "Public Opinion Monitoring Unit: Public Opinion on the War in Ukraine. 1 April 2022." https://www.europarl.europa.eu/at-your-service/files/be-heard/eurobarometer/2022/public-opinion-on-the-war-in-ukraine/en-public-opinion-on-the-war-in-ukraine-20220401.pdf.

Evers, Adalbert, and Helga Nowotny. 1987. *Über Den Umgang Mit Unsicherheit: Die Entdeckung Der Gestaltbarkeit von Gesellschaft*. Frankfurt am Main: Suhrkamp.

Ewert, Ralf, and Alfred Wagenhofer. 2019. "Effects of Increasing Enforcement on Financial Reporting Quality and Audit Quality." *Journal of Accounting Research* 57 (1): 121–68.

EY Global. 2023. "Worldwide Personal Tax and Immigration Guide 2022–23." 2023. https://www.ey.com/en_gl/tax-guides/worldwide-personal-tax-and-immigration-guide.

Falsini, Sophie. 2021. "How Social Norms for Men Restrict Women's Financial Inclusion." Consultative Group to Assist the Poor. January 14, 2021. https://www.cgap.org/blog/how-social-norms-for-men-restrict-womens-financial-inclusion.

Farrall, Kenneth N. 2008. "Global Privacy in Flux: Illuminating Privacy across Cultures in China and the U.S." *International Journal of Communication* 2: 993–1030.

Feeley, Malcolm M. 2004. "Actuarial Justice and the Modern State." In *Punishment, Places and Perpetrators*, edited by Gerben Bruinsma, Henk Elffers, and Jan De Keijser, 62–77. Cullompton: Willan.

Feeley, Malcolm M., and Jonathan Simon. 1994. "Actuarial Justice: The Emerging New Criminal Law." In *The Futures of Criminology*, edited by David Nelken, 173–201. London: Sage.

Feltes, Thomas, Katrin List, and Maximilian Bertamini. 2018. "More Refugees, More Offenders, More Crime? Critical Comments with Data from Germany." In *Refugees and Migrants in Law and Policy: Challenges and Opportunities for Global Civic Education*, edited by Helmut Kury and Sławomir Redo, 599–624. Cham: Springer International Publishing.

Ferenbok, Joseph, and Andrew Clement. 2013. "Hidden Changes: From CCTV to 'smart'video Surveillance." In *Eyes Everywhere*, edited by Aaron Doyle, Randy Lippert, and David Lyon, 218–34. London: Routledge.

Fernandes, Teresa, and Marta Costa. 2021. "Privacy Concerns with COVID-19 Tracking Apps: A Privacy Calculus Approach." *Journal of Consumer Marketing* 40 (2): 181–92.

Fernandes, Teresa, and Nuno Pereira. 2021. "Revisiting the Privacy Calculus: Why Are Consumers (Really) Willing to Disclose Personal Data Online?" *Telematics and Informatics* 65: 101717.

Finkelstein, Eric Andrew, Carol Mansfield, Dallas Wood, Brent Rowe, Junxing Chay, and Semra Ozdemir. 2017. "Trade-Offs Between Civil Liberties and National Security: A Discrete Choice Experiment." *Contemporary Economic Policy* 35 (2): 292–311.

Finn, Rachel L., David Wright, and Michael Friedewald. 2013. "Seven Types of Privacy." In *European Data Protection: Coming of Age*, edited by Serge Gutwirth, Ronald Leenes, Paul de Hert, and Yves Poullet, 3–32. Dordrecht: Springer Netherlands.

Fishbein, Martin, and Icek Ajzen. 1975. *Belief, Attitude, Intention and Behavior: An Introduction to Theory and Research*. Reading: Addison-Wesley.

Fiske, John. 1996. *Media Matters: Race & Gender in U.S. Politics*. Minneapolis: University of Minneapolis Press.

Fiske, Susan T., and Shelley E. Taylor. 1984. *Social Cognition*. New York: Random House.

Flores, Andrew R., Lynn Langton, Ilan H. Meyer, and Adam P. Romero. 2020. "Victimization Rates and Traits of Sexual and Gender Minorities in the United States: Results from the National Crime Victimization Survey, 2017." *Science Advances* 6 (40): eaba6910.

Floyd, Rita. 2010. *Security and the Environment: Securitisation Theory and US Environmental Security Policy*. New York: Cambridge University Press.

Floyd, Rita. 2016. "Extraordinary or Ordinary Emergency Measures: What, and Who, Defines the 'Success' of Securitization?" *Cambridge Review of International Affairs* 29 (2): 677–94.

Floyd, Rita, ed. 2019. *The Morality of Security. A Theory of Just Securitization*. Cambridge: Cambridge University Press.

Flynn, Daniel J., Brendan Nyhan, and Jason Reifler. 2017. "The Nature and Origins of Misperceptions: Understanding False and Unsupported Beliefs About Politics." *Political Psychology* 38 (S1): 127–50.

Fonio, Chiara. 2011. "Surveillance under Mussolini's Regime." *Surveillance & Society* 9 (1/2): 80–92.

Foster, Erin D., and Ariel Deardorff. 2017. "Open Science Framework (OSF)." *Journal of the Medical Library Association : JMLA* 105 (2): 203–6.

Foucault, Michel. 1991a. *Discipline and Punish: The Birth of the Prison*. London: Penguin Books.

Foucault, Michel. 1991b. "Governmentality." In *The Foucault Effect: Studies in Governmentality*, edited by Graham Burchell, Colin Gordon, and Peter Miller, 87–104. Chicago: University of Chicago Press.

Fox, Grace, Trevor Clohessy, Lisa van der Werff, Pierangelo Rosati, and Theo Lynn. 2021. "Exploring the Competing Influences of Privacy Concerns and Positive Beliefs on Citizen Acceptance of Contact Tracing Mobile Applications." *Computers in Human Behavior* 121: 106806.

Fraley, Chris R. 2002. "Attachment Stability from Infancy to Adulthood: Meta-Analysis and Dynamic Modeling of Developmental Mechanisms." *Personality and Social Psychology Review* 6 (2): 123–51.

Freedman, Lawrence. 2016. "The Concept of Security." In *The Concept of Security*, edited by Benjamin J. Goold and Lucia Zedner, 3–12. London: Routledge.

Freedom House. 2016. "Freedom on the Net 2016. Silencing the Messenger: Communication Apps Under Pressure." 2016. https://freedomhouse.org/sites/default/files/FOTN_2016_BOOKLET_FINAL.pdf.

Freedom House.2021. "Freedom on the Net 2021. The Global Drive to Control Big Tech." 2021. https://freedomhouse.org/sites/default/files/2021-09/FOTN_2021_Complete_Booklet_09162021_FINAL_UPDATED.pdf.

Frener, Regine, Jana Dombrowski, and Sabine Trepte. 2023. "Development and Validation of the Need for Privacy Scale (NFP-S)." *Communication Methods and Measures* online first: 1–24. https://doi.org/10.1080/19312458.2023.2246014.

Fried, Charles. 1968. "Privacy." *Yale Law Journal* 77 (3): 475–93.

Fried, Charles. 1984. "Privacy [a Moral Analysis]." In *Philosophical Dimensions of Privacy: An Anthology*, edited by Ferdinand David Schoeman, 203–22. Cambridge: Cambridge University Press.

Friedewald, Michael, Peter J. Burgess, Johann Cas, Rocco Bellanova, and Walter Peissl, eds. 2017. *Surveillance, Privacy and Security: Citizens' Perspectives*. London; New York: Routledge.

Friedewald, Michael, Marc van Lieshout, and Sven Rung. 2016. "Modelling the Relationship Between Privacy and Security Perceptions and the Acceptance of Surveillance Practices." In *Privacy and Identity Management. Time for a Revolution? 10th IFIP WG 9.2, 9.5, 9.6/11.7, 11.4, 11.6/SIG 9.2.2 International Summer School, Edinburgh, UK, August 16–21, 2015, Revised Selected Papers*, edited by David Aspinall, Jan Camenisch, Marit Hansen, Simone Fischer-Hübner, and Charles D. Raab, 1–18. IFIP Advances in Information and Communication Technology. Cham: Springer International Publishing.

Friedewald, Michael, Marc van Lieshout, Sven Rung, and Merel Ooms. 2016. "The Context-Dependence of Citizens' Attitudes and Preferences Regarding Privacy and Security." In *Data Protection on the Move: Current Developments in ICT and Privacy/Data Protection*, edited by Serge Gutwirth, Ronald Leenes, and Paul De Hert, 51–74. Law, Governance and Technology Series. Dordrecht: Springer Netherlands.

Friedewald, Michael, Marc van Lieshout, Sven Rung, Merel Ooms, and Jelmer Ypma. 2015. "Privacy and Security Perceptions of European Citizens: A Test of the Trade Off Model." In *Privacy and Identity Management for the Future Internet in the Age of Globalisation*, edited by Jan Camenisch, Simone Fischer-Hübner, and Marit Hansen, 39–53. Heidelberg: Springer VS.

Friedewald, Michael, Alexander Roßnagel, Tamer Bile, Christian L. Geminn, Marit Hansen, Felix Bieker, and Murat Karaboga. 2022. "Zur Einführung Einer Überwachungs-Gesamtrechnung." *Datenschutz Und Datensicherheit—DuD* 46 (9): 572–77.

Frik, Alisa, and Alexia Gaudeul. 2016. "The Relation between Privacy Protection and Risk Attitudes, with a New Experimental Method to Elicit the Implicit Monetary Value of Privacy." *CEGE Discussion Papers* 296: 1–50.

Frik, Alisa, and Alexia Gaudeul. 2020. "A Measure of the Implicit Value of Privacy under Risk." *Journal of Consumer Marketing* 37 (4): 457–72.

Frohman, Larry. 2020. *The Politics of Personal Information: Surveillance, Privacy, and Power in West Germany*. Berghahn Books.

Fussey, Pete, and Jon Coaffee. 2012. "Urban Spaces of Surveillance." In *Routledge Handbook of Surveillance Studies*, edited by Kirstie Ball, Kevin D. Haggerty, and David Lyon, 201–8. New York: Taylor & Francis.

Gaines, Brian J., James H. Kuklinski, and Paul J. Quirk. 2007. "The Logic of the Survey Experiment Reexamined." *Political Analysis* 15 (1): 1–20.

Gallie, Walter B. 1955. "Essentially Contested Concepts." *Proceedings of the Aristotelian Society* 56: 167–98.

Gandy, Oscar H. 1993. *The Panoptic Sort: A Political Economy of Personal Information. Critical Studies in Communication and in the Cultural Industries.* Boulder: Westview Press.

Garcia, Blake E., and Nehemia Geva. 2016. "Security Versus Liberty in the Context of Counterterrorism: An Experimental Approach." *Terrorism and Political Violence* 28 (1): 30–48.

Garland, David. 2002. *The Culture of Control: Crime and Social Order in Contemporary Society.* Chicago, IL: University of Chicago Press.

Gaskell, George, Nick Allum, Wolfgang Wagner, Nicole Kronberger, Helge Torgersen, Juergen Hampel, and Julie Bardes. 2004. "GM Foods and the Misperception of Risk Perception." *Risk Analysis: An Official Publication of the Society for Risk Analysis* 24 (1): 185–94.

Gavison, Ruth. 1980. "Privacy and the Limits of Law." *The Yale Law Journal* 89 (3): 421–71.

Geddes, Barbara. 1990. "How the Cases You Choose Affect the Answers You Get: Selection Bias in Comparative Politics." *Political Analysis* 2: 131–50.

Gellman, Robert, and Pam Dixon. 2011. *Online Privacy: A Reference Handbook.* Santa Barbara, Denver, Oxford: ABC-CLIO.

Gelman, Andrew. 2008. "Scaling Regression Inputs by Dividing by Two Standard Deviations." *Statistics in Medicine* 27 (15): 2865–73.

Gerber, Nina, Paul Gerber, and Melanie Volkamer. 2018. "Explaining the Privacy Paradox: A Systematic Review of Literature Investigating Privacy Attitude and Behavior." *Computers & Security* 77: 226–61.

Gerdon, Frederic, Helen Nissenbaum, Ruben L. Bach, Frauke Kreuter, and Stefan Zins. 2020. "Individual Acceptance of Using Health Data for Private and Public Benefit: Changes During the COVID-19 Pandemic." *Harvard Data Science Review* Special Issue 1.

Gerety, Tom. 1977. "Redefining Privacy." *Harvard Civil Rights-Civil Liberties Law Review* 12 (2): 233–96.

Gerstein, Robert S. 1978. "Intimacy and Privacy." *Ethics* 89 (1): 76–81.

Giddens, Anthony. 1987. *The Nation-State and Violence: Volume 2 of a Contemporary Critique of Historical Materialism.* Berkeley: University of California Press.

Giddens, Anthony. 1990. *The Consequences of Modernity.* Stanford: Stanford University Press.

Giddens, Anthony. 1991. *Giddens, A: Modernity and Self-Identity: Self and Society in the Late Modern Age.* Cambridge: Blackwell Publishers.

Giebler, Heiko, Lukas Antoine, and Rasmus Ollroge. 2024. "Wertekonflikt in Deutschland." http://dx.doi.org/10.17169/refubium-44777.

Giebler, Heiko, Lukas Antoine, Rasmus Ollroge, Jürgen Gerhards, Michael Zürn, Johannes Giesecke, and Macartan Humphreys. 2023a. "Public Attitudes towards the Liberal Script (PALS) Survey: Wave 1." https://doi.org/10.17169/refubium-41265.

Giebler, Heiko, Lukas Antoine, Rasmus Ollroge, Jürgen Gerhards, Michael Zürn, Johannes Giesecke, and Macartan Humphreys. 2023b. "The 'Public Attitudes towards the Liberal

Script' (PALS) Survey. Conceptual Framework, Implementation, and Data." *SCRIPTS Working Paper* 33. https://www.scripts-berlin.eu/publications/working-paper-series/Working-Paper-33-2023/index.html.

Gilens, Martin. 2012. *Affluence and Influence: Economic Inequality and Political Power in America.* Princeton: Princeton University Press.

Gilens, Martin, and Adam Thal. 2018. "Doing Well and Doing Good?: How Concern for Others Shapes Policy Preferences and Partisanship among Affluent Americans." *Public Opinion Quarterly* 82 (2): 209–30.

Gill, Martin, Anthea Rose, Kate Collins, and Martin Hemming. 2006. "Redeployable CCTV and Drug-Related Crime: A Case of Implementation Failure." *Drugs: Education, Prevention and Policy* 13 (5): 451–60.

Gill, Stephen. 1995. "The Global Panopticon? The Neoliberal State, Economic Life, and Democratic Surveillance." *Alternatives* 20 (1): 1–49.

Gilliom, John. 1996. *Surveillance, Privacy, and the Law: Employee Drug Testing and the Politics of Social Control.* Ann Arbor: University of Michigan Press.

Gilliom, John. 2001. *Overseers of the Poor: Surveillance, Resistance, and the Limits of Privacy.* 2nd ed. Chicago: University of Chicago Press.

Glaser, Daryl. 2000. "The Media Inquiry Reports of the South African Human Rights Commission: A Critique." *African Affairs* 99 (396): 373–93.

Glaser, Jack. 2015. *Suspect Race: Causes and Consequences of Racial Profiling.* New York, NY: Oxford University Press.

Glasser, Theodore L., and Charles T. Salmon. 1995. *Public Opinion and the Communication of Consent.* New York/London: Guilford Press.

Goffman, Alice. 2009. "On the Run: Wanted Men in a Philadelphia Ghetto." *American Sociological Review* 74 (3): 339–57.

Goffman, Erving. 1956. *The Presentation of Self in Everyday Life.* Edinburgh: University of Edinburgh, Social Sciences Research Centre.

Goffman, Erving. 1974. *Frame Analysis: An Essay on the Organization of Experience.* Cambridge, MA: Harvard University Press.

Goldberg, Lewis R. 1990. "An Alternative 'Description of Personality': The Big-Five Factor Structure." *Journal of Personality and Social Psychology* 59 (6): 1216–29.

Goldberg, Susan. 2014. *Attachment and Development.* New York: Routledge.

Golder, Matt, and Jacek Stramski. 2010. "Ideological Congruence and Electoral Institutions." *American Journal of Political Science* 54 (1): 90–106.

Goldfarb, Avi, and Catherine Tucker. 2012. "Shifts in Privacy Concerns." *The American Economic Review* 102 (3): 349–53.

Goldman, Alvin I. 2001. "Experts: Which Ones Should You Trust?" *Philosophy and Phenomenological Research* 63 (1): 85–110.

Goold, Benjamin J. 2002. "Privacy Rights and Public Spaces: CCTV and the Problem of the 'Unobservable Observer.'" *Criminal Justice Ethics* 21 (1): 21–27.

Goold, Benjamin J. 2010. "How Much Surveillance Is Too Much? Some Thoughts on Surveillance, Democracy, and the Political Value of Privacy." In *Overvåkning i En Rettsstat—Surveillance in a Constitutional Government*, edited by Dag Wiese Schartum, 38–48. Bergen: Fagbokforlaget.

Gould, Deborah. 2010. "On Affect and Protest." In *Political Emotions*, edited by Janet Staiger, Ann Cvetkovich, and Ann Reynolds, 18–44. New York: Taylor & Francis Ltd.

Goyder, John, and Jean McKenzie Leiper. 1985. "The Decline in Survey Response: A Social Values Interpretation." *Sociology* 19 (1): 55–71.

Gray, David. 2017. *The Fourth Amendment in an Age of Surveillance*. Cambridge: Cambridge University Press.

Gray, Emily, Jonathan Jackson, and Stephen Farrall. 2008. "Reassessing the Fear of Crime." *European Journal of Criminology* 5 (3): 363–80.

Green, Nicola, and Nils Zurawski. 2015. "Surveillance and Ethnography: Researching Surveillance as Everyday Life." *Surveillance & Society* 13 (1): 27–43.

Greenberg, Josh, and Sean Hier. 2009. "CCTV Surveillance and the Poverty of Media Discourse: A Content Analysis of Canadian Newspaper Coverage." *Canadian Journal of Communication* 34 (3): 461–86.

Greene, Zachary. 2020. "Being Heard above the Noise: The Role of Incumbent Issue Diversity in Election Campaigns." *Political Behavior* 42 (2): 487–507.

Gross, Hyman. 1971. "Privacy and Autonomy." In *Privacy and Personality*, edited by John W. Pennock and Roland J. Chapman, 169–81. New York: Routledge.

Gross, Oren. 2009. "Security Vs. Liberty: An Imbalanced Balancing." *Minnesota Legal Studies Research Paper* 9 (42): 1–24.

Gurinskaya, Anna. 2020. "Predicting Citizens' Support for Surveillance Cameras. Does Police Legitimacy Matter?" *International Journal of Comparative and Applied Criminal Justice* 44 (1–2): 63–83.

Gustafson, Kaaryn S. 2012. *Cheating Welfare: Public Assistance and the Criminalization of Poverty*. New York: NYU Press.

Guzik, Keith. 2009. "Discrimination by Design: Predictive Data Mining as Security Practice in the United States' 'War on Terrorism.'" *Surveillance & Society* 7 (1): 3–20.

Guzzini, Stefano. 2000. "A Reconstruction of Constructivism in International Relations." *European Journal of International Relations* 6 (2): 147–82.

Guzzini, Stefano. 2011. "Securitization as a Causal Mechanism." *Security Dialogue* 42 (4–5): 329–41.

Haag, Ernest van den. 1971. "On Privacy." In *Privacy and Personality*, edited by John W. Pennock and J. Roland; Chapman, 149–68. New York: Routledge.

Hadjimatheou, Katerina. 2014. "The Relative Moral Risks of Untargeted and Targeted Surveillance." *Ethical Theory and Moral Practice* 17 (2): 187–207.

Haggerty, Kevin D. 2004. "Technology and Crime Policy: Reply to Michael Jacobson." *Theoretical Criminology* 8 (4): 491–97.

Haggerty, Kevin D. 2009. "Methodology as a Knife Fight: The Process, Politics and Paradox of Evaluating Surveillance." *Critical Criminology* 17 (4): 277–91.

Haggerty, Kevin D., and Amber Gazso. 2005. "The Public Politics of Opinion Research on Surveillance and Privacy." *Surveillance & Society* 3 (2/3): 173–80.

Haider-Markel, Donald P., and Mark R. Joslyn. 2001. "Gun Policy, Opinion, Tragedy, and Blame Attribution: The Conditional Influence of Issue Frames." *The Journal of Politics* 63 (2): 520–43.

Hainmueller, Jens, Dominik Hangartner, and Teppei Yamamoto. 2015. "Validating Vignette and Conjoint Survey Experiments against Real-World Behavior." *Proceedings of the National Academy of Sciences* 112 (8): 2395–2400.

Hallinan, Dara, Michael Friedewald, and Paul McCarthy. 2012. "Citizens' Perceptions of Data Protection and Privacy in Europe." *Computer Law & Security Review* 28 (3): 263–72.

Hamilton, Claire. 2023. "Radical Right Populism and the Sociology of Punishment: Towards a Research Agenda." *Punishment & Society* 25 (4): 888–908.

Hampton, Keith, Lee Rainie, Weixu Lu, Maria Dwyer, Inyoung Shin, and Kristen Purcell. 2014. "Social Media and the 'Spiral of Silence' | Pew Research Center." August 26, 2014. http://www.pewinternet.org/2014/08/26/social-media-and-the-spiral-of-silence/.

Hansen, Lene. 2011. "Theorizing the Image for Security Studies: Visual Securitization and the Muhammad Cartoon Crisis." *European Journal of International Relations* 17 (1): 51–74.

Harborth, David, and Sebastian Pape. 2023. "A Privacy Calculus Model for Contact Tracing Apps: Analyzing the Use Behavior of the German Corona-Warn-App with a Longitudinal User Study." *Computers & Security* 132: 103338.

Harcourt, Bernard. 2003. "The Shaping of Chance: Actuarial Models and Criminal Profiling at the Turn of the Twenty-First Century." *University of Chicago Law Review* 70 (1): 105–28.

Hardin, Russell. 2004. "Civil Liberties in the Era of Mass Terrorism." *The Journal of Ethics* 8 (1): 77–95.

Harris, David A. 2020. "Racial Profiling: Past, Present, and Future?" *Criminal Justice* 10 (34): 10–22.

Hayo, Bernd, and Florian Neumeier. 2019. "Public Preferences for Government Spending Priorities: Survey Evidence from Germany." *German Economic Review* 20 (4): e1–37.

Heirman, Wannes, Michel Walrave, and Koen Ponnet. 2013. "Predicting Adolescents' Disclosure of Personal Information in Exchange for Commercial Incentives: An Application of an Extended Theory of Planned Behavior." *Cyberpsychology, Behavior, and Social Networking* 16 (2): 81–87.

Heisig, Jan P., and Merlin Schaeffer. 2019. "Why You Should Always Include a Random Slope for the Lower-Level Variable Involved in a Cross-Level Interaction." *European Sociological Review* 35 (2): 258–79.

Hendrickson, David C. 2002. "Toward Universal Empire: The Dangerous Quest for Absolute Security." *World Policy Journal* 19 (3): 1–10.

Henkin, Louis. 1974. "Privacy and Autonomy." *Columbia Law Review* 74 (8): 1410–33.

Herbst, Susan. 1992. "Surveys in the Public Sphere: Applying Bourdieu's Critique of Opinion Polls." *International Journal of Public Opinion Research* 4 (3): 220–29.

Herington, Jonathan. 2012. "The Concept of Security." In *Ethics and Security Aspects of Infectious Disease Control*, edited by Michael J. Selgelid and Christian Enemark, 7–26. London: Routledge.

Herington, Jonathan. 2015. "Philosophy: The Concepts of Security, Fear, Liberty, and the State." In *Security: Dialogue across Disciplines*, edited by Philippe Bourbeau, 22–44. Cambridge: Cambridge University Press.

Hetherington, Marc J., and Elizabeth Suhay. 2011. "Authoritarianism, Threat, and Americans' Support for the War on Terror." *American Journal of Political Science* 55 (3): 546–60.

Hibbs, Douglas A. 1979. "The Mass Public and Macroeconomic Performance: The Dynamics of Public Opinion Toward Unemployment and Inflation." *American Journal of Political Science* 23 (4): 705–31.

Higgs, Edward. 2001. "The Rise of the Information State: The Development of Central State Surveillance of the Citizen in England, 1500–2000." *Journal of Historical Sociology* 14 (2): 175–97.

Hobbes, Thomas. 1994. *Leviathan*. Cambridge: Hackett.

Hodgson, Geoffrey M. 2019. "Taxonomic Definitions in Social Science, with Firms, Markets and Institutions as Case Studies." *Journal of Institutional Economics* 15 (2): 207–33.

Hofstede, Geert. 1980. *Culture's Consequences: International Differences in Work-Related Values*. Beverly Hills: SAGE Publications.

Homans, George C. 1961. *Social Behavior: Its Elementary Forms, Revised Ed.* Social Behavior: Its Elementary Forms, Revised Ed. New York: Harcourt.

Honess, Terry, and Elizabeth Charman. 1992. *Closed Circuit Television in Public Places: Its Acceptability and Perceived Effectiveness*. London: Home Office Police Research Group.

Hong, Weiyin, and James Y. L. Thong. 2013. "Internet Privacy Concerns: An Integrated Conceptualization and Four Empirical Studies." *MIS Quarterly* 37 (1): 275–98.

Hoofnagle, Chris Jay, and Jennifer M. Urban, eds. 2014. "Alan Westin's Privacy Homo Economicus." *Wake Forest Law Review* 261: 261–317.

Hope, Tim, and Alan Trickett. 2008. "The Distribution of Crime Victimisation in the Population." *International Review of Victimology* 15 (1): 37–58.

Horn, Gayle. 2005. "Online Searches and Offline Challenges: The Chilling Effect, Anonymity and the New FBI Guidelines." *New York University Annual Survey of American Law* 60: 735–67.

Houston, David J., Nurgul R. Aitalieva, Andrew L. Morelock, and Chris A. Shults. 2016. "Citizen Trust in Civil Servants: A Cross-National Examination." *International Journal of Public Administration* 39 (14): 1203–14.

Hox, Joop J. 2010. *Multilevel Analysis: Techniques and Applications*. 2nd ed. New York: Routledge.

Hox, Joop J., Mirjam Moerbeek, and Rens Van De Schoot. 2017. *Multilevel Analysis: Techniques and Applications*. 3rd edition. New York, NY: Routledge.

Hu, Li-tze, and Peter M. Bentler. 1999. "Cutoff Criteria for Fit Indexes in Covariance Structure Analysis: Conventional Criteria versus New Alternatives." *Structural Equation Modeling* 6 (1): 1–55.

Huberman, Bernado A., Eytan Adar, and Leslie R. Fine. 2005. "Valuating Privacy." *IEEE Security and Privacy* 3 (5): 22–25.

Huckfeldt, R. Robert. 1986. *Politics in Context: Assimilation and Conflict in Urban Neighborhoods*. New York: Algora Publishing.

Huckfeldt, R. Robert, and John Sprague. 1995. *Citizens, Politics and Social Communication: Information and Influence in an Election Campaign*. Cambridge University Press.

Huddy, Leonie, Stanley Feldman, Charles Taber, and Gallya Lahav. 2005. "Threat, Anxiety, and Support of Antiterrorism Policies." *American Journal of Political Science* 49 (3): 593–608.

Huddy, Leonie, Nadia Khatib, and Theresa Capelos. 2002. "Trends: Reactions to the Terrorist Attacks of September 11, 2001." *The Public Opinion Quarterly* 66 (3): 418–50.

Hughes, Kirsty. 2015. "The Social Value of Privacy, the Value of Privacy to Society and Human Rights Discourse." In *Social Dimensions of Privacy: Interdisciplinary Perspectives*, edited by Beate Roessler and Dorota Mokrosinska, 225–43. Cambridge: Cambridge University Press.

Hunt, Chris D.L. 2011. "Conceptualizing Privacy and Elucidating Its Importance: Foundational Considerations for the Development of Canada's Fledgling Privacy Tort." *Queen's Law Journal* 37 (1): 167–219.

Huq, Aziz Z. 2013. "The Political Psychology of Counterterrorism." *University of Chicago, Public Law Working Paper* 9: 71–94.

Iacovetta, Franca. 2000. "The Sexual Politics of Moral Citizenship and Containing 'Dangerous' Foreign Men in Cold War Canada, 1950s-1960s." *Histoire Sociale / Social History* 33 (66): 361–89.

Inglehart, Ronald. 1981. "Post-Materialism in an Environment of Insecurity." *American Political Science Review* 75 (4): 880–900.

Inglehart, Ronald. 1997. *Modernization and Postmodernization: Cultural, Economic, and Political Change in 43 Societies*. Princeton: Princeton University Press.

Inglehart, Ronald, and Christian Welzel. 2004. "What Insights Can Multi-Country Surveys Provide About People and Societies?" *Comparative Politics Newsletter. American Political Science Association* Summer 2004: 1–12.

Inness, Julie. 1996. *Privacy, Intimacy, and Isolation*. Reprint edition. Berlin Heidelberg: Oxford University Press.

Institute for Economics and Peace. 2016. "Global Terrorism Index." Sydney, New York, Brussels and Mexico City. http://economicsandpeace.org/wp-content/uploads/2016/11/Global-Terrorism-Index-2016.2.pdf.

Ioannou, Athina, and Iis Tussyadiah. 2021. "Privacy and Surveillance Attitudes during Health Crises: Acceptance of Surveillance and Privacy Protection Behaviours." *Technology in Society* 67: 101774.

ISSP. 2018a. "International Social Survey Programme ISSP 2016- Role of Government V. Study Monitoring Report." Edited by Dominique Joye and Marlène Sapin. https://dbk.gesis.org/dbksearch/download.asp?id=64690.

ISSP. 2018b. "Role of Government V, Variable Report: Documentation Release 2018/09/19, Related to the International Dataset Archive-Study-No. ZA6900 Version 2.0.0." Edited by GESIS. https://dbk.gesis.org/dbksearch/download.asp?id=64683.

ISSP Research Group. 2018. "International Social Survey Programme: Role of Government V—ISSP 2016." https://doi.org/10.4232/1.13052.

Jäckle, Sebastian, and Julian Schärdel. 2017. "Mehrebenenanalyse." In *Neue Trends in Den Sozialwissenschaften: Innovative Techniken Für Qualitative Und Quantitative Forschung*, edited by Sebastian Jäckle, 147–75. Wiesbaden: Springer Fachmedien.

Jackson, Jonathan. 2004. "Experience and Expression: Social and Cultural Significance in the Fear of Crime." *The British Journal of Criminology* 44 (6): 946–66.

Jackson, Jonathan. 2011. "Revisiting Risk Sensitivity in the Fear of Crime." *Journal of Research in Crime and Delinquency* 48 (4): 513–37.

Jamal, Amaney, and Irfan Nooruddin. 2010. "The Democratic Utility of Trust: A Cross-National Analysis." *The Journal of Politics* 72 (1): 45–59.

Jann, Ben. 2021. "HEATPLOT: Stata Module to Create Heat Plots and Hexagon Plots." https://ideas.repec.org//c/boc/bocode/s458598.html.

Jenkins-Smith, Hank C., and Kerry G. Herron. 2009. "Rock and a Hard Place: Public Willingness to Trade Civil Rights and Liberties for Greater Security." *Politics & Policy* 37 (5): 1095–1129.

Jia, Haiyan, Pamela J. Wisniewski, Heng Xu, Mary Beth Rosson, and John M. Carroll. 2015. "Risk-Taking as a Learning Process for Shaping Teen's Online Information Privacy Behaviors." In *Proceedings of the 18th ACM Conference on Computer Supported Cooperative Work & Social Computing*, 583–99. CSCW '15. New York, NY, USA: Association for Computing Machinery. https://doi.org/10.1145/2675133.2675287.

John, Leslie K., Alessandro Acquisti, and George Loewenstein. 2011. "Strangers on a Plane: Context-Dependent Willingness to Divulge Sensitive Information." *Journal of Consumer Research* 37 (5): 858–73.

Johnston, Les, and Clifford Shearing. 2002. *Governing Security: Explorations of Policing and Justice*. London ; New York: Routledge.

Joinson, Adam N., Carina Paine, Tom Buchanan, and Ulf-Dietrich Reips. 2008. "Measuring Self-Disclosure Online: Blurring and Non-Response to Sensitive Items in Web-Based Surveys." *Computers in Human Behavior* 24 (5): 2158–71.

Jore, Sissel H. 2019. "The Conceptual and Scientific Demarcation of Security in Contrast to Safety." *European Journal for Security Research* 4 (1): 157–74.

Jost, John T., and Orsolya Hunyady. 2005. "Antecedents and Consequences of System-Justifying Ideologies." *Current Directions in Psychological Science* 14 (5): 260–65.

Jost, John T., and Jaime L. Napier. 2011. "The Uncertainty-Threat Model of Political Conservatism." In *Extremism and the Psychology of Uncertainty*, edited by Michael A. Hogg and Danielle L. Blaylock, 90–111. London: Blackwell Publishing Ltd.

Jourard, Sidney M. 1966. "Some Psychological Aspects of Privacy." *Law and Contemporary Problems* 31 (2): 307–18.

Jourard, Sidney M. 1971. *Self Disclosure: An Experimental Analysis of the Transparent Self*. New York: John Wiley & Sons Ltd.

Junglas, Iris A, Norman A Johnson, and Christiane Spitzmüller. 2008. "Personality Traits and Concern for Privacy: An Empirical Study in the Context of Location-Based Services." *European Journal of Information Systems* 17 (4): 387–402.

Kachanoff, Frank J., Yochanan E. Bigman, Kyra Kapsaskis, and Kurt Gray. 2020. "Measuring Realistic and Symbolic Threats of COVID-19 and Their Unique Impacts on Well-Being and Adherence to Public Health Behaviors." *Social Psychological and Personality Science* 12 (5): 603–16.

Kahneman, Daniel, and Amos Tversky. 1979. "Prospect Theory: An Analysis of Decision under Risk." *Econometrica* 47 (2): 263–91.

Kaminska, Olena, and Peter Lynn. 2017. "Survey-Based Cross-Country Comparisons Where Countries Vary in Sample Design: Issues and Solutions." *Journal of Official Statistics* 33 (1): 123–36.

Kampmark, Binoy. 2020. "The Pandemic Surveillance State: An Enduring Legacy of COVID-19." *Journal of Global Faultlines* 7 (1): 59–70.

Kaplan, Seth A., Joseph N. Luchman, and Landon Mock. 2013. "General and Specific Question Sequence Effects in Satisfaction Surveys: Integrating Directional and Correlational Effects." *Journal of Happiness Studies* 14 (5): 1443–58.

Kasper, Debbie V. S. 2005. "The Evolution (Or Devolution) of Privacy." *Sociological Forum* 20 (1): 69–92.

Kasperson, Roger E., Thomas Webler, Bonnie Ram, and Jeannette Sutton. 2022. "The Social Amplification of Risk Framework: New Perspectives." *Risk Analysis* 42 (7): 1367–80.

Kehr, Flavius, Tobias Kowatsch, Daniel Wentzel, and Elgar Fleisch. 2015. "Blissfully Ignorant: The Effects of General Privacy Concerns, General Institutional Trust, and Affect in the Privacy Calculus." *Information Systems Journal* 25 (6): 607–35.

Keiber, Jason. 2015. "Surveillance Hegemony." *Surveillance & Society* 13 (2): 168–81.

Keith, Mark J., Samuel C. Thompson, Joanne Hale, Paul Benjamin Lowry, and Chapman Greer. 2013. "Information Disclosure on Mobile Devices: Re-Examining Privacy Calculus with Actual User Behavior." *International Journal of Human-Computer Studies* 71 (12): 1163–73.

Kelvin, Peter. 1973. "A Social-Psychological Examination of Privacy." *British Journal of Social and Clinical Psychology* 12 (3): 248–61.

Kinnvall, Catarina, Ian Manners, and Jennifer Mitzen. 2018. "Introduction to 2018 Special Issue of European Security: 'Ontological (in)Security in the European Union.'" *European Security* 27 (3): 249–65.

King, Gary, and Christopher J. L. Murray. 2002. "Rethinking Human Security." *Political Science Quarterly* 116: 585–610.

Kitschelt, Herbert. 1994. *The Transformation of European Social Democracy*. Cambridge Studies in Comparative Politics. Cambridge: Cambridge University Press.

Klingemann, Hans-Dieter, Andrea Volkens, Ian Budge, Judith Bara, and Michael D. McDonald. 2006. *Mapping Policy Preferences II: Estimates for Parties, Electors, and Governments in Eastern Europe, European Union, and OECD 1990–2003*. Oxford: Oxford University Press.

Kłosowska, Joanna, Elżbieta A. Bajcar, Helena Bieniek, Justyna Brączyk, Mohsen Joshanloo, Katia Mattarozzi, Arianna Bagnis, et al. 2022. "Development and Cross-National Investigation of a Model Explaining Participation in WHO-Recommended and Placebo Behaviours to Prevent COVID-19 Infection." *Scientific Reports* 12 (October): 17704.

Kluckhohn, Clyde. 1951. "Values and Value-Orientations in the Theory of Action: An Exploration in Definition and Classification." In *Toward a General Theory of Action*, edited by Talcott Parsons and Edward A. Shils, 388–433. Harvard: Harvard University Press.

Knowles, Dudley. 2009. *Political Obligation: A Critical Introduction*. London ; New York: Routledge.

Kohler, Ulrich. 2019. "Possible Uses of Nonprobability Sampling for the Social Sciences." *Survey Methods: Insights from the Field (SMIF)*, April. https://doi.org/10.13094/SMIF-2019-00014.

Kohler, Ulrich, Frauke Kreuter, and Elizabeth A. Stuart. 2019. "Nonprobability Sampling and Causal Analysis." *Annual Review of Statistics and Its Application* 6 (1): 149–72.

Kokolakis, Spyros. 2017. "Privacy Attitudes and Privacy Behaviour: A Review of Current Research on the Privacy Paradox Phenomenon." *Computers & Security* 64: 122–34.

Königs, Peter. 2022. "Government Surveillance, Privacy, and Legitimacy." *Philosophy & Technology* 35 (1): 8.

Koops, Bert-Jaap. 2021. "The Concept of Function Creep." *Law, Innovation and Technology* 13 (1): 29–56.

Koops, Bert-Jaap, Bryce Newell, Tjerk Timan, Ivan Škorvánek, Tomislav Chokrevski, and Maša Galič. 2017. "A Typology of Privacy." *University of Pennsylvania Journal of International Law* 38 (2): 483–575.

Kosinski, Michal, Yoram Bachrach, Pushmeet Kohli, David Stillwell, and Thore Graepel. 2014. "Manifestations of User Personality in Website Choice and Behaviour on Online Social Networks." *Machine Learning* 95 (3): 357–80.

Koskela, Hille. 2012. "'You Shouldn't Wear That Body'—The Problematic of Surveillance and Gender." In *Routledge Handbook of Surveillance Studies*, edited by Kirstie Ball, Kevin D. Haggerty, and David Lyon, 49–56. London: Taylor & Francis.

Kostka, Genia, and Sabrina Habich-Sobiegalla. 2022. "In Times of Crisis: Public Perceptions toward COVID-19 Contact Tracing Apps in China, Germany, and the United States." *New Media & Society* online first (April): 14614448221083285.

Krasnova, Hanna, Sarah Spiekermann, Ksenia Koroleva, and Thomas Hildebrand. 2010. "Online Social Networks: Why We Disclose." *Journal of Information Technology* 25 (2): 109–25.

Kreuter, Frauke. 2002. *Kriminalitätsfurcht: Messung Und Methodische Probleme*. Wiesbaden: VS Verlag für Sozialwissenschaften.

Kriesi, Hanspeter, Edgar Grande, Martin Dolezal, Marc Helbling, Dominic Höglinger, Swen Hutter, and Bruno Wüest. 2012. *Political Conflict in Western Europe*. Cambridge: Cambridge University Press.

Kriesi, Hanspeter, Edgar Grande, Romain Lachat, Martin Dolezal, Simon Bornschier, and Timotheos Frey. 2008. *West European Politics in the Age of Globalization*. Cambridge: Cambridge University Press.

Kroener, Inga, and Daniel Neyland. 2012. "New Technologies, Security and Surveillance." In *Routledge Handbook of Surveillance Studies*, edited by Kirstie Ball, Kevin D. Haggerty, and David Lyon, 141–48. New York: Taylor & Francis.

Krueger, Brian S. 2005. "Government Surveillance and Political Participation on the Internet." *Social Science Computer Review* 23 (4): 439–52.

Krueger, Brian S., Samuel J. Best, and Kristin Johnson. 2020. "Assessing Dimensions of the Security-Liberty Trade-off in the United States." *Surveillance & Society* 18 (1): 104–20.

Kugler, Matthew, and Lior Strahilevitz. 2015. "Surveillance Duration Doesn't Affect Privacy Expectations: An Empirical Test of the Mosaic Theory." *Coase-Sandor Working Paper Series in Law and Economics* 727.

Kuklinski, James H., Paul J. Quirk, Jennifer Jerit, and Robert F. Rich. 2001. "The Political Environment and Citizen Competence." *American Journal of Political Science* 45 (2): 410–24.

Kumaraguru, Ponnurangam, and Lorrie Faith Cranor. 2005. "Privacy Indexes: A Survey of Westin's Studies." Institute for Software Research Int (ISRI) CMU-ISRI-5–138. Pittsburgh: Carnegie Mellon University. https://www.cs.cmu.edu/~ponguru/CMU-ISRI-05-138.pdf.

Kunda, Ziva. 1990. "The Case for Motivated Reasoning." *Psychological Bulletin* 108 (3): 480–98.

Kuzmanovic, Marija, and Gordana Savic. 2020. "Avoiding the Privacy Paradox Using Preference-Based Segmentation: A Conjoint Analysis Approach." *Electronics* 9 (9): 1382.

Kwasny, Michelle N., Kelly E. Caine, Wendy A. Rogers, and Arthur D. Fisk. 2008. "Privacy and Technology: Folk Definitions and Perspectives." *Proceedings of the SIGCHI Conference on Human Factors in Computing Systems. CHI Conference* 2008: 3291–96.

Kymlicka, Will. 1990. *Contemporary Political Philosophy: An Introduction*. Oxford ; New York: Oxford University Press.

Lachapelle, Erick, Éric Montpetit, and Jean-Philippe Gauvin. 2014. "Public Perceptions of Expert Credibility on Policy Issues: The Role of Expert Framing and Political Worldviews." *Policy Studies Journal* 42 (4): 674–97.

Lafky, Deborah Beranek, and Thomas A. Horan. 2011. "Personal Health Records: Consumer Attitudes toward Privacy and Security of Their Personal Health Information." *Health Informatics Journal* 17 (1): 63–71.

LaFree, Gary, Laura Dugan, and Erin Miller. 2014. *Putting Terrorism in Context: Lessons from the Global Terrorism Database*. New York, NY: Routledge.

LaGrange, Randy L., and Kenneth F. Ferraro. 1989. "Assessing Age and Gender Differences in Perceived Risk and Fear of Crime*." *Criminology* 27 (4): 697–720.

Lang, Andrej. 2021. "Non-Judicial Rights Review of Counterterrorism Policies: The Role of Fundamental Rights in the Making of the Counterterrorism Database and the Data Retention Legislation in Germany." *International Journal of Constitutional Law* 19 (2): 634–64.

Laufer, Robert S., and Maxine Wolfe. 1977. "Privacy as a Concept and a Social Issue: A Multidimensional Developmental Theory." *Journal of Social Issues* 33 (3): 22–42.

Laver, Michael, and Ian Budge. 1992. *Party Policy and Government Coalitions*. New York, N.Y: Palgrave Macmillan.

LeBoeuf, Robyn A., and Eldar Shafir. 2003. "Deep Thoughts and Shallow Frames: On the Susceptibility to Framing Effects." *Journal of Behavioral Decision Making* 16 (2): 77–92.

Lee, Murray. 2001. "The Genesis of 'Fear of Crime'." *Theoretical Criminology* 5 (4): 467–85.

Lee, Murray. 2007. *Inventing Fear of Crime: Criminology and the Politics of Fear: Criminology and the Politics of Anxiety*. London: Taylor & Francis Ltd.

Lee, Nam-Jin, Douglas M. McLeod, and Dhavan V. Shah. 2008. "Framing Policy Debates: Issue Dualism, Journalistic Frames, and Opinions on Controversial Policy Issues." *Communication Research* 35 (5): 695–718.

Lee, Namyeon, and Ohbyung Kwon. 2015. "A Privacy-Aware Feature Selection Method for Solving the Personalization–Privacy Paradox in Mobile Wellness Healthcare Services." *Expert Systems with Applications* 42 (5): 2764–71.

Lefebvre, Mathieu, and Anne Stenger. 2020. "Short- & Long-Term Effects of Monetary and Non-Monetary Incentives to Cooperate in Public Good Games: An Experiment." *PLOS ONE* 15 (1): e0227360.

Leffler, Melvyn P. 1990. "National Security." *The Journal of American History* 77 (1): 143–52.

Leman-Langlois, Stéphane. 2002. "The Myopic Panopticon: The Social Consequences of Policing Through the Lens." *Policing and Society* 13 (1): 43–58.

Lever, Annabelle. 2005. "Feminism, Democracy and the Right to Privacy." *Minerva* 9: 1–31.

Lever, Annabelle. 2006. "Privacy Rights and Democracy: A Contradiction in Terms?" *Contemporary Political Theory* 5 (2): 142–62.

Levi, Margaret, and Laura Stoker. 2000. "Political Trust and Trustworthiness." *Annual Review of Political Science* 3 (1): 475–507.

Lewin, Kurt. 1948. *Resolving Social Conflicts: Selected Papers on Group Dynamics [1935–1946]*. New York: Harper.

Lewis, Carol W. 2005. "The Clash between Security and Liberty in the U.S. Response to Terror." *Public Administration Review* 65 (1): 18–30.
Li, Yuan. 2011. "Empirical Studies on Online Information Privacy Concerns: Literature Review and an Integrative Framework." *Communications of the Association for Information Systems* 28 (1).
Li, Yuan. 2012. "Theories in Online Information Privacy Research: A Critical Review and an Integrated Framework." *Decision Support Systems* 54 (1): 471–81.
Lieshout, Marc van, Michael Friedewald, David Wright, and Serge Gutwirth. 2013. "Reconciling Privacy and Security." *Innovation: The European Journal of Social Science Research* 26 (1–2): 119–32.
Lim, Sun Sun, Hichang Cho, and Milagros Rivera Sanchez. 2009. "Online Privacy, Government Surveillance and National ID Cards." *Commun. ACM* 52 (12): 116–20.
Limayem, Moez, Sabine Gabriele Hirt, and Christy M. K. Cheung. 2007. "How Habit Limits the Predictive Power of Intention: The Case of Information Systems Continuance." *MIS Quarterly* 31 (4): 705–37.
Lindsay, David. 2005. "An Exploration of the Conceptual Basis of Privacy and the Implications for the Future of Australian Privacy Law." *Melbourne University Law Review* 29 (1): 131–78.
Lipschutz, Ronnie. 1995. "Negotiating the Boundaries of Difference and Security at Millennium's End." In *On Security*, edited by Ronnie Lipschutz, 212–28. New York: Columbia University Press.
Liu, Hui, and Susanna Priest. 2009. "Understanding Public Support for Stem Cell Research: Media Communication, Interpersonal Communication and Trust in Key Actors." *Public Understanding of Science* 18 (6): 704–18.
Liu, Jiawei, Rosemary J. Avery, Erika F. Fowler, Laura Baum, Sarah E. Gollust, Colleen L. Barry, Brendan Welch, Emmett Tabor, Nathaniel W. Lee, and Jeff Niederdeppe. 2023. "Campaign Advertising and the Cultivation of Crime Worry: Testing Relationships With Two Large Datasets From the 2016 U.S. Election Cycle." *The International Journal of Press/Politics* 28 (1): 70–91.
Liu, Yu-Hsuan, Kevin T Wolff, and Tzu-Ying Lo. 2023. "Big Data in Crime Statistics: Using Google Trends to Measure Victimization in Designated Market Areas across the United States." *Methodological Innovations* online first: 20597991231183962.
Livingstone, Sonia. 2018. "Children: A Special Case for Privacy?" *Intermedia* 46 (2): 18–23.
Loader, Ian, and Richard Sparks. 2007. "Contemporary Landscapes of Crime, Order, and Control: Governance, Risk, and Globalization." In *The Oxford Handbook of Criminology*, edited by Mike Maguire, Rodney Morgan, and Robert Reiner, 83–111. Oxford: Oxford University Press.
Locke, John. 1967. *Locke: Two Treatises of Government*. 2nd ed. Cambridge: Cambridge University Press.
Los, Maria. 2003. "Crime in Transition: The Post-Communist State, Markets and Crime." *Crime, Law and Social Change* 40 (2): 145–69.
Los, Maria. 2005. "Reshaping of Elites and the Privatization of Security: The Case of Poland." *The Journal of Power Institutions in Post-Soviet Societies* 2.
Lowry, Paul, Jinwei Cao, and Andrea Everard. 2011. "Privacy Concerns Versus Desire for Interpersonal Awareness in Driving the Use of Self-Disclosure Technologies: The Case

of Instant Messaging in Two Cultures." *Journal of Management Information Systems* 27 (4): 163–200.

Lüdemann, Christian, and Christina Schlepper. 2012. "The Role of Fear in the Surveillance State in Times of Terrorism: Explaining Attitudes towards New Governmental Security Measures." In *Methods, Theories, and Empirical Applications in the Social Sciences*, edited by Samuel Salzborn, Eldad Davidov, and Jost Reinecke, 263–70. Wiesbaden: VS Verlag für Sozialwissenschaften.

Luebcke, David Martin, and Sybil Milton. 1994. "Locating the Victim: An Overview of Census-Taking, Tabulation Technology, and Persecution in Nazi Germany." *IEEE Annals of the History of Computing* 3 (16): 25–39.

Luhmann, Niklas. 2000. *The Reality of the Mass Media*. Cambridge: Polity Press.

Lundell, Krister. 2012. "Civic Participation and Political Trust: The Impact of Compulsory Voting." *Representation* 48 (2): 221–34.

Lupovici, Amir. 2016. "Securitization Climax: Putting the Iranian Nuclear Project at the Top of the Israeli Public Agenda (2009–2012)." *Foreign Policy Analysis* 12 (3): 413–32.

Luther, Catherine, and Ivanka Radovic. 2012. "Perspectives on Privacy, Information Technology, and Company/Governmental Surveillance in Japan." *Surveillance & Society* 10 (3/4): 263–75.

Lyon, David. 1994. *The Electronic Eye: The Rise of Surveillance Society*. Minneapolis: University of Minnesota Press.

Lyon, David. 2001. *Surveillance Society: Monitoring Everyday Life*. Buckingham: Open University Press.

Lyon, David. 2002. *Surveillance as Social Sorting: Privacy, Risk and Automated Discrimination*. London, New York: Routledge.

Lyon, David. 2003. "Surveillance after September 11, 2001." In *The Intensification of Surveillance: Crime, Terrorism and Warfare in the Information Age*, edited by Kirstie Ball and Frank Webster, 16–25. London ; Sterling, VA: Pluto Press.

Lyon, David. 2007a. "Surveillance, Security and Social Sorting: Emerging Research Priorities." *International Criminal Justice Review* 17 (3): 161–70.

Lyon, David. 2007b. *Surveillance Studies: An Overview*. Cambridge, Malden: Polity.

Lyon, David. 2015a. *Surveillance after Snowden*. Oxford: Polity Press.

Lyon, David. 2015b. "The Snowden Stakes: Challenges for Understanding Surveillance Today." *Surveillance & Society* 13 (2): 139–52.

Maas, Cora J. M., and Joop J. Hox. 2005. "Sufficient Sample Sizes for Multilevel Modeling." *Methodology* 1 (3): 86–92.

Macnish, Kevin. 2018. "Government Surveillance and Why Defining Privacy Matters in a Post-Snowden World." *Journal of Applied Philosophy* 35 (2): 417–32.

Macnish, Kevin. 2020. "Mass Surveillance: A Private Affair?" *Moral Philosophy and Politics* 7 (1): 9–27.

Magi, Trina J. 2011. "Fourteen Reasons Privacy Matters: A Multidisciplinary Review of Scholarly Literature." *The Library Quarterly: Information, Community, Policy* 81 (2): 187–209.

Malheiros, Miguel, Sören Preibusch, and M. Angela Sasse. 2013. "'Fairly Truthful': The Impact of Perceived Effort, Fairness, Relevance, and Sensitivity on Personal Data Disclosure." In *Trust and Trustworthy Computing*, edited by Michael Huth, N. Asokan,

Srdjan Čapkun, Ivan Flechais, and Lizzie Coles-Kemp, 250–66. Lecture Notes in Computer Science. Berlin, Heidelberg: Springer. https://doi.org/10.1007/978-3-642-38908-5_19.

Malhotra, Naresh K., Sung S. Kim, and James Agarwal. 2004. "Internet Users' Information Privacy Concerns (IUIPC): The Construct, the Scale, and a Causal Model." *Information Systems Research* 15 (4): 336–55.

Manderson, Lenore. 1999. "Public Health Developments in Colonial Malaya: Colonialism and the Politics of Prevention." *American Journal of Public Health* 89 (1): 102–7.

Maréchal, Nathalie. 2015. "First They Came for the Poor: Surveillance of Welfare Recipients as an Uncontested Practice." *Media and Communication* 3 (3): 56–67.

Margalit, Yotam. 2013. "Explaining Social Policy Preferences: Evidence from the Great Recession." *American Political Science Review* 107 (1): 80–103.

Margulis, Stephen T. 2003. "On the Status and Contribution of Westin's and Altman's Theories of Privacy." *Journal of Social Issues* 59 (2): 411–29.

Marjit, Sugata, Marcel Thum, and André Seidel. 2017. "Tax Evasion, Corruption and Tax Loopholes." *German Economic Review* 18 (3): 283–301.

Marthews, Alex, and Catherine E. Tucker. 2017. "Government Surveillance and Internet Search Behavior." *Working Paper*, 1–53.

Martin, Jean F. 2014. "Privacy and Confidentiality." In *Handbook of Global Bioethics*, edited by Henk A.M.J. ten Have and Bert Gordijn, 119–37. Dordrecht: Springer Netherlands.

Martin, Kirsten, and Helen Nissenbaum. 2017. "Measuring Privacy: An Empirical Test Using Context to Expose Confounding Variables." *Science and Technology Law Review* 18 (1).

Martin, Kirsten, and Katie Shilton. 2016. "Putting Mobile Application Privacy in Context: An Empirical Study of User Privacy Expectations for Mobile Devices." *The Information Society* 32 (3): 200–216.

Marx, Gary T. 1989. "Commentary: Some Trends and Issues in Citizen Involvement in the Law Enforcement Process." *Crime & Delinquency* 35 (3): 500–519.

Marx, Gary T. 2002. "Technology and Social Control: The Search for the Illusive Silver Bullet." In *International Encyclopedia of the Social & Behavioral Sciences*, edited by Neil J. Smelser and Paul B. Baltes, 15506–11. Amsterdam: Elsevier.

Marx, Gary T. 2007. "Surveys and Surveillance." In *Envisioning the Survey Interview of the Future*, edited by Frederick G. Conrad and Michael F. Schober, 254–66. New York: John Wiley & Sons, Ltd.

Marx, Gary T. 2015a. "Coming to Terms. The Kalaidoscope of Privacy and Surveillance." In *Social Dimensions of Privacy: Interdisciplinary Perspectives*, edited by Beate Roessler and Dorota Mokrosinska, 32–49. Cambridge: Cambridge University Press.

Marx, Gary T. 2015b. "Surveillance Studies." In *International Encyclopedia of the Social & Behavioral Sciences*, edited by James D. Wright, 2nd ed., 733–41. Oxford: Elsevier.

Marx, Gary T. 2016. *Windows Into the Soul: Surveillance and Society in an Age of High Technology*. Chicago: University of Chicago Press.

Mas-Colell, Andreu, Michael Dennis Whinston, and Jerry R. Green. 1995. *Microeconomic Theory*. New York: Oxford University Press.

Maslow, Abraham H. 1943. "A Theory of Human Motivation." *Psychological Review* 50 (4): 370–96.

Mau, Steffen. 2022. *Sorting Machines: The Reinvention of the Border in the 21st Century*. Medford: Polity.

Mau, Steffen, Jan Mewes, and Nadine M. Schöneck. 2012. "What Determines Subjective Socio-Economic Insecurity? Context and Class in Comparative Perspective." *Socio-Economic Review* 10 (4): 655–82.

Maxfield, Michael G. 1999. "The National Incident-Based Reporting System: Research and Policy Applications." *Journal of Quantitative Criminology* 15 (2): 119–49.

McCrae, Robert R., and Paul T. Costa. 1987. "Validation of the Five-Factor Model of Personality Across Instruments and Observers." *Journal of Personality and Social Psychology* 52 (1): 81–90.

McCrae, Robert R., Paul T. Costa, Martina Hřebíčková, Tomáš Urbánek, Thomas A. Martin, Valery E. Oryol, Alexey A. Rukavishnikov, and Ivan G. Senin. 2004. "Age Differences in Personality Traits across Cultures: Self-report and Observer Perspectives." *European Journal of Personality* 18 (2): 143–57.

McCulloch, Jude, and Sharon Pickering. 2009. "Pre-Crime and Counter-Terrorism: Imagining Future Crime in the 'War on Terror.'" *The British Journal of Criminology* 49 (5): 628–45.

McCulloch, Jude, and Dean Wilson. 2015. *Pre-Crime: Pre-Emption, Precaution and the Future.* Abingdon; New York: Taylor & Francis Ltd.

McGovern, Alyce. 2017. "Policing, Performance Indicators and Fear of Crime." In *The Routledge International Handbook on Fear of Crime*, edited by Murray Lee and Gabe Mythen, 299–311. London: Routledge.

McMullan, John L. 1998. "The Arresting Eye: Discourse, Surveillance and Disciplinary Administration in Early English Police Thinking." *Social & Legal Studies* 7 (1): 97–128.

McSweeney, Bill. 1999. *Security, Identity and Interests: A Sociology of International Relations.* Cambridge Studies in International Relations. Cambridge: Cambridge University Press.

Meier, Yannic, and Nicole C. Krämer. 2022. "The Privacy Calculus Revisited: An Empirical Investigation of Online Privacy Decisions on Between- and Within-Person Levels." *Communication Research*, 00936502221102101.

Menges, Leonhard. 2020. "Did the NSA and GCHQ Diminish Our Privacy? What the Control Account Should Say." *Moral Philosophy and Politics* 7 (1): 29–48.

Menichelli, Francesca. 2017. "Beyond the Trade-off between Privacy and Security? Organizational Routines and Individual Strategies at the Security Check." In *Surveillance, Privacy and Security: Citizens' Perspectives*, edited by Michael Friedewald, J. Peter Burgess, Johann Cas, Walter Peissl, and Rocco Bellanova, 91–103. London; New York: Routledge.

Mercer, Andrew W., Frauke Kreuter, Scott Keeter, and Elizabeth A. Stuart. 2017. "Theory and Practice in Nonprobability Surveys." *Public Opinion Quarterly* 81 (S1): 250–71.

Merolla, Jennifer L., and Elizabeth J. Zechmeister. 2009. *Democracy at Risk: How Terrorist Threats Affect the Public.* Chicago: University of Chicago Press.

Michaelson, Christopher. 2006. "Balancing Civil Liberties against National Security? A Critique of Counterterrorism Rhetoric." *University of New South Wales Law Journal* 29 (2): 1–21.

Michel, Norbert J., and Jennifer J. Schulp. 2022. "Revising the Bank Secrecy Act to Protect Privacy and Deter Criminals." *CATO Institute. Policy Analysis* 932.

Miguel, Edward, Colin Camerer, Katherine Casey, Jacob Cohen, Kevin M. Esterling, Alan Gerber, Rachel Glennerster, et al. 2014. "Promoting Transparency in Social Science Research." *Science* 343 (6166): 30–31.

Mikulincer, Mario, and Phillip R. Shaver. 2003. "The Attachment Behavioral System in Adulthood: Activation, Psychodynamics, and Interpersonal Processes." In *Advances in Experimental Social Psychology, Vol. 35*, 53–152. San Diego, CA, US: Elsevier Academic Press.

Mill, John Stuart. 1871. *Utilitarianism.* London: Longmans, Green, Reader, and Dyer.

Miller, Kevin. 2014. "Total Surveillance, Big Data, and Predictive Crime Technology: Privacy's Perfect Storm." *Journal of Technology Law & Policy* 19 (1): 105–46.

Milne, George R., and Mary Ellen Gordon. 1993. "Direct Mail Privacy-Efficiency Trade-Offs within an Implied Social Contract Framework." *Journal of Public Policy & Marketing* 12 (2): 206–15.

Milne, Sara, Claire Lomax, and Mark H. Freeston. 2019. "A Review of the Relationship between Intolerance of Uncertainty and Threat Appraisal in Anxiety." *The Cognitive Behaviour Therapist* 12: e38.

Miltgen, Caroline Lancelot, and H. Jeff Smith. 2019. "Falsifying and Withholding: Exploring Individuals' Contextual Privacy-Related Decision-Making." *Information & Management* 56 (5): 696–717.

Miratrix, Luke W., Jasjeet S. Sekhon, Alexander G. Theodoridis, and Luis F. Campos. 2018. "Worth Weighting? How to Think About and Use Weights in Survey Experiments." *Political Analysis* 26 (3): 275–91.

Mironenko Enerstvedt, Olga. 2017. "Legal Principles of Privacy and Data Protection." In *Aviation Security, Privacy, Data Protection and Other Human Rights: Technologies and Legal Principles*, edited by Olga Mironenko Enerstvedt, 157–202. Law, Governance and Technology Series. Cham: Springer International Publishing.

Mishra, Sushma, Peter J. Draus, Gregory J. Leone, and Donald J. Caputo. 2012. "An Exploration of Student Attitudes on Privacy/Security Issues: Facebook Usage Concerns and Expectations." *Issues In Information Systems* 13 (1): 340–49.

Moineddin, Rahim, Flora I. Matheson, and Richard H. Glazier. 2007. "A Simulation Study of Sample Size for Multilevel Logistic Regression Models." *BMC Medical Research Methodology* 7 (1): 34.

Mokrosinska, Dorota. 2019. "On the Individual, Social, and Political Value of Privacy." In *Privatsphäre 4.0: Eine Neuverortung Des Privaten Im Zeitalter Der Digitalisierung*, edited by Hauke Behrendt, Wulf Loh, Tobias Matzner, and Catrin Misselhorn, 107–22. Stuttgart: J.B. Metzler.

Moore, Adam D. 2003. "Privacy: Its Meaning and Value." *American Philosophical Quarterly* 40 (3): 215–27.

Moore, Adam D. 2008. "Defining Privacy." *Journal of Social Philosophy* 39 (3): 411–28.

Moore, Adam D. 2011. "Privacy, Security, and Government Surveillance: Wikileaks and the New Accountability." *Public Affairs Quarterly* 25 (2): 141–56.

Moore, Barrington. 1984. *Privacy: Studies in Social and Cultural History.* Armonk; New York: Taylor & Francis Inc.

Morgan, Patrick M. 1992. "Safeguarding Security Studies." *Arms Control* 13 (3): 464–79.

Mosher, Clayton J., Terance D. Miethe, and Timothy C. Hart. 2010. *The Mismeasure of Crime.* Thousand Oaks: SAGE Publications.

Mosteller, Jill, and Amit Poddar. 2017. "To Share and Protect: Using Regulatory Focus Theory to Examine the Privacy Paradox of Consumers' Social Media Engagement and Online Privacy Protection Behaviors." *Journal of Interactive Marketing* 39 (1): 27–38.

Mothersbaugh, David L., William K. Foxx, Sharon E. Beatty, and Sijun Wang. 2012. "Disclosure Antecedents in an Online Service Context: The Role of Sensitivity of Information." *Journal of Service Research* 15 (1): 76–98.

Mueller, John, and Mark G. Stewart. 2021. "Terrorism and Bathtubs: Comparing and Assessing the Risks." *Terrorism and Political Violence* 33 (1): 138–63.

Mullinix, Kevin J., Thomas J. Leeper, James N. Druckman, and Jeremy Freese. 2015. "The Generalizability of Survey Experiments." *Journal of Experimental Political Science* 2 (2): 109–38.

Munk, Timme Bisgaard. 2017. "100,000 False Positives for Every Real Terrorist: Why Anti-Terror Algorithms Don't Work." *First Monday* 22 (9).

Murphy, Michael P. A. 2020. "The Securitization Audience in Theologico-Political Perspective: Giorgio Agamben, Doxological Acclamations, and Paraconsistent Logic." *International Relations* 34 (1): 67–83.

Nabity-Grover, Teagen, Christy M.K. Cheung, and Jason Bennett Thatcher. 2020. "Inside out and Outside in: How the COVID-19 Pandemic Affects Self-Disclosure on Social Media." *International Journal of Information Management* 55: 102188.

Nagai, Hiroki, and Young Hak Kim. 2017. "Cancer Prevention from the Perspective of Global Cancer Burden Patterns." *Journal of Thoracic Disease* 9 (3): 448–51.

Nagel, Thomas. 1998. "Concealment and Exposure." *Philosophy & Public Affairs* 27 (1): 3–30.

Nagy, Veronika. 2017. "How to Silence the Lambs? Constructing Authoritarian Governance in Post-Transitional Hungary." *Surveillance & Society* 15 (3/4): 447–55.

Najafian, Shabnam, Amra Delic, Marko Tkalcic, and Nava Tintarev. 2021. "Factors Influencing Privacy Concern for Explanations of Group Recommendation." In *Proceedings of the 29th ACM Conference on User Modeling, Adaptation and Personalization*, 14–23. Utrecht Netherlands: ACM. https://doi.org/10.1145/3450613.3456845.

Nakhaie, Reza, and Willem de Lint. 2013. "Trust and Support for Surveillance Policies in Canadian and American Opinion." *International Criminal Justice Review* 23 (2): 149–69.

Nam, Taewoo. 2019. "What Determines the Acceptance of Government Surveillance? Examining the Influence of Information Privacy Correlates." *The Social Science Journal* 56 (4): 530–44.

National Consortium for the Study of Terrorism and Responses to Terrorism. 2019. "Global Terrorism Database." 2019. https://www.start.umd.edu/gtd/.

National Consortium for the Study of Terrorism and Responses to Terrorism. 2023. "Global Terrorism Database: Search Results—Date: (Between 2020–01–01 and 2020–12–31) All Incidents Regardless of Doubt. Country: (Germany)." 2023. https://www.start.umd.edu/gtd/search/Results.aspx?expanded=no&casualties_type=b&casualties_max=&start_year=2020&start_month=1&start_day=1&end_year=2020&end_month=12&end_day=31&dtp2=all&success=yes&country=75&ob=GTDID&od=desc&page=1&count=50#results-table.

Nehf, James. 2003. "Recognizing the Societal Value in Information Privacy." *Washington Law Review* 78 (1): 1.

Neocleous, Mark. 2007. “Security, Liberty and the Myth of Balance: Towards a Critique of Security Politics.” *Contemporary Political Theory* 6 (2): 131–49.

Neocleous, Mark. 2008. *Critique of Security*. Edinburgh: Edinburgh University Press.

Ng-Kruelle, Grace, Paul A. Swatman, Douglas S. Rebne, and J. Felix Hampe. 2002. “The Price of Convenience.” *Quarterly Journal of Electronic Commerce* 3 (3): 273–85.

Nguyen, Tin Trung, Minh Tu Tran Hoang, and Minh Tuan Phung. 2022. “‘To Our Health!’ Perceived Benefits Offset Privacy Concerns in Using National Contact-Tracing Apps.” *Library Hi Tech* 41 (1): 174–91.

Nisbett, Richard E., and Lee Ross. 1980. *Human Inference: Strategies and Shortcomings of Social Judgment*. Englewood Cliffs: Prentice-Hall.

Nissenbaum, Helen. 2004. “Privacy as Contextual Integrity.” *Washington Law Review* 79 (1): 119.

Nissenbaum, Helen. 2009. *Privacy in Context: Technology, Policy, and the Integrity of Social Life*. Stanford: Stanford University Press.

Nissenbaum, Helen. 2015. “Respect for Context as a Benchmark for Privacy Online: What It Is and Isn’t.” In *Social Dimensions of Privacy: Interdisciplinary Perspectives*, edited by Beate Roessler and Dorota Mokrosinska, 278–302. Cambridge: Cambridge University Press.

Nissenbaum, Helen. 2018. “Respecting Context to Protect Privacy: Why Meaning Matters.” *Science and Engineering Ethics* 24 (3): 831–52.

Noelle-Neumann, Elisabeth. 1974. “The Spiral of Silence A Theory of Public Opinion.” *Journal of Communication* 24 (2): 43–51.

Norberg, Patricia A., Daniel R. Horne, and David A. Horne. 2007. “The Privacy Paradox: Personal Information Disclosure Intentions versus Behaviors.” *Journal of Consumer Affairs* 41 (1): 100–126.

Norris, Clive. 2007. “The Intensification and Bifurcation of Surveillance in British Criminal Justice Policy.” *European Journal on Criminal Policy and Research* 13 (1): 139–58.

Norris, Gareth. 2017. “Authoritarianism and Privacy: The Moderating Role of Terrorism.” *Surveillance & Society* 15 (3/4): 573–81.

Norris, Pippa, and Ronald Inglehart. 2019. *Cultural Backlash: Trump, Brexit, and Authoritarian Populism*. Cambridge: Cambridge University Press.

Norris, Pippa, Montague Kern, and Marion Just. 2004. “Framing Terrorism.” In *Framing Terrorism: The News Media, the Government and the Public*, edited by Pippa Norris, Montague Kern, and Marion Just, 3–26. New York; London: Routledge.

O’Brien, David M. 1979. *Privacy, Law, and Public Policy*. New York, N.Y.: Praeger.

O’Brien, Thomas, and Linda R. Tropp. 2015. “Psychology: The Phenomenology of Human Security.” In *Security: Dialogue across Disciplines*, edited by Philippe Bourbeau, 137–55. Cambridge: Cambridge University Press.

O’Donnell, Aisling T., Jolanda Jetten, and Michelle K. Ryan. 2010a. “Watching over Your Own: How Surveillance Moderates the Impact of Shared Identity on Perceptions of Leaders and Follower Behaviour.” *European Journal of Social Psychology* 40 (6): 1046–61.

O’Donnell, Aisling T., Jolanda Jetten, and Michelle K. Ryan. 2010b. “Who Is Watching over You? The Role of Shared Identity in Perceptions of Surveillance.” *European Journal of Social Psychology* 40 (1): 135–47.

Oesch, Daniel, and Line Rennwald. 2018. "Electoral Competition in Europe's New Tripolar Political Space: Class Voting for the Left, Centre-Right and Radical Right." *European Journal of Political Research* 57 (4): 783–807.

Offermann-van Heek, Julia, Eva-Maria Schomakers, and Martina Ziefle. 2019. "Bare Necessities? How the Need for Care Modulates the Acceptance of Ambient Assisted Living Technologies." *International Journal of Medical Informatics* 127: 147–56.

Office of the Privacy Commissioner of Canada Communications. 2009. "Canadians and Privacy. Final Report." Gatineau, Quebec. https://www.priv.gc.ca/en/opc-actions-and-decisions/research/explore-privacy-research/2009/ekos_2009_01/.

Olson, Kristen, Jolene D. Smyth, Rachel Horwitz, Scott Keeter, Virginia Lesser, Stephanie Marken, Nancy A. Mathiowetz, et al. 2021. "Transitions From Telephone Surveys to Self-Administered and Mixed-Mode Surveys: Aapor Task Force Report." *Journal of Survey Statistics and Methodology* 9 (3): 381–411.

O'Malley, Pat. 2004. *Risk, Uncertainty and Government*. London ; Portland, Or: Routledge.

O'Malley, Pat, and Steven Hutchinson. 2007. "Reinventing Prevention: Why Did 'Crime Prevention' Develop So Late?" *The British Journal of Criminology* 47 (3): 373–89.

Paccagnella, Omar. 2011. "Sample Size and Accuracy of Estimates in Multilevel Models." *Methodology* 7 (3): 111–20.

Parent, William A. 1983a. "A New Definition of Privacy for the Law." *Law and Philosophy* 2 (3): 305–38.

Parent, William A. 1983b. "Privacy, Morality, and the Law." *Philosophy & Public Affairs* 12 (4): 269–88.

Parent, William A. 1983c. "Recent Work on the Concept of Privacy." *American Philosophical Quarterly* 20 (4): 341–55.

Park, Hyeon Ho, Gyeong Seok Oh, and Seung Yeop Paek. 2012. "Measuring the Crime Displacement and Diffusion of Benefit Effects of Open-Street CCTV in South Korea." *International Journal of Law, Crime and Justice* 40 (3): 179–91.

Patel, Tina Girishbhai. 2012. "Surveillance, Suspicion and Stigma: Brown Bodies in a Terror-Panic Climate." *Surveillance & Society* 10 (3/4): 215–34.

Patil, Sameer, and Alfred Kobsa. 2005. "Uncovering Privacy Attitudes and Practices in Instant Messaging." In *Proceedings of the 2005 ACM International Conference on Supporting Group Work*, 109–12. GROUP '05. New York, NY, USA: Association for Computing Machinery. https://doi.org/10.1145/1099203.1099220.

Patil, Sunil, Hui Lu, Catherine L Saunders, Dimitris Potoglou, and Neil Robinson. 2016. "Public Preferences for Electronic Health Data Storage, Access, and Sharing — Evidence from a Pan-European Survey." *Journal of the American Medical Informatics Association* 23 (6): 1096–1106.

Patil, Sunil, Bhanu Patruni, Hui Lu, Fay Dunkerley, James Fox, Dimitris Potoglou, and Neil Robinson. 2015. "Public Perception of Security and Privacy. PACT Project, Deliverable 4.2." PACT Project, Deliverable 4.2. Cambridge: RAND Corporation. https://www.rand.org/content/dam/rand/pubs/research_reports/RR700/RR704/RAND_RR704.pdf.

Patil, Sunil, Dimitris Potoglou, Hui Lu, Neil Robinson, and Peter Burge. 2014. "Trade-off Across Privacy, Security and Surveillance in the Case of Metro Travel in Europe." *Transportation Research Procedia* 1 (1): 121–32.

Paul, Pamela. 2001. "Mixed Signals." *American Demographics* 23 (7): 44.

Pavlou, Paul A. 2011. "State of the Information Privacy Literature: Where Are We Now And Where Should We Go?" *MIS Quarterly* 35 (4): 977–88.

Pavone, Vincenzo, and Sara Degli Esposti. 2012. "Public Assessment of New Surveillance-Oriented Security Technologies: Beyond the Trade-off between Privacy and Security." *Public Understanding of Science* 21 (5): 556–72.

Pavone, Vincenzo, Sara Degli Esposti, and Elvira Santiago-Gomez. 2013. "D 2.2—Draft Report on Key Factors. Surveillance, Privacy and Security: A Large Scale Participatory Assessment of Criteria and Factors Determining Acceptability and Acceptance of Security Technologies in Europe." Brussels: European Union. http://surprise-project.eu/wp-content/uploads/2013/10/SurPRISE-D2.2-Draft-Report-on-Key-Factors.pdf.

Pavone, Vincenzo, Sara Degli Esposti, and Elvira Santiago-Gómez. 2015. "Key Factors Affecting Acceptance and Acceptability of Surveillance-Orientated Security Technologies (SOSTs)." SurPRISE project, Deliverable 2.4. Brussels: European Union. https://www.researchgate.net/publication/271700613_Key_factors_affecting_acceptance_and_acceptability_of_Surveillance-orientated_Security_Technologies_SOSTs.

Peceny, Mark, Caroline C. Beer, and Shannon Sanchez-Terry. 2002. "Dictatorial Peace?" *The American Political Science Review* 96 (1): 15–26.

Peffley, Mark A., and Jon Hurwitz. 1985. "A Hierarchical Model of Attitude Constraint." *American Journal of Political Science* 29 (4): 871–90.

Peng, Mei-Hui, and Bireswar Dutta. 2022. "Impact of Personality Traits and Information Privacy Concern on E-Learning Environment Adoption during COVID-19 Pandemic: An Empirical Investigation." *Sustainability* 14 (13): 8031.

Penney, Jonathon W. 2016. "Chilling Effects: Online Surveillance and Wikipedia Use." *Berkeley Technology Law Journal* 31 (1): 117.

Penney, Jonathon W. 2017. "Internet Surveillance, Regulation, and Chilling Effects Online: A Comparative Case Study." *Internet Policy Review* 6 (2).

Percy, Sarah. 2007. *Regulating the Private Security Industry*. Milton Park, Abingdon, Oxon: Routledge.

Petersen, Julie K. 2012. *Introduction to Surveillance Studies*. Boca Raton: CRC Press.

Phelps, Joseph, Glen Nowak, and Elizabeth Ferrell. 2000. "Privacy Concerns and Consumer Willingness to Provide Personal Information." *Journal of Public Policy & Marketing* 19 (1): 27–41.

Phillips, Coretta. 1999. "A Review of CCTV Evaluations: Crime Reduction Effects and Attitudes To Its Use." *Crime Prevention Studies* 10: 123–55.

Pizzi, Gabriele, and Daniele Scarpi. 2020. "Privacy Threats with Retail Technologies: A Consumer Perspective." *Journal of Retailing and Consumer Services* 56: 102160.

Plangger, Kirk, and Matteo Montecchi. 2020. "Thinking Beyond Privacy Calculus: Investigating Reactions to Customer Surveillance." *Journal of Interactive Marketing* 50: 32–44.

Pomfret, Liam, Josephine Previte, and Len Coote. 2020. "Beyond Concern: Socio-Demographic and Attitudinal Influences on Privacy and Disclosure Choices." *Journal of Marketing Management* 36 (5–6): 519–49.

Porcedda, Maria G. 2017. "The Manifold Significance of Citizens' Legal Recommendations on Privacy, Security and Surveillance." In *Surveillance, Privacy and Security: Citizens' Perspectives*, edited by Michael Friedewald, J. Peter Burgess, Johann Cas, Walter Peissl, and Rocco Bellanova, 199–211. London; New York: Routledge.

Poscher, Ralf, Michael Kilchling, and Lukas Martin Landerer. 2021. "Ein Überwachungsbarometer Für Deutschland. Entwicklung Eines Konzeptes Zur Periodischen Erfassung Staatlicher Überwachungsmaßnahmen." *Zeitschrift Für Das Gesamte Sicherheitsrecht* 4 (6): 225–32.

Posner, Eric A., and Adrian Vermeule. 2007. *Terror in the Balance: Security, Liberty, and the Courts*. New York: Oxford University Press Inc.

Posner, Richard A. 1978. "The Right of Privacy." *Sibley Lecture Series* 12 (3): 393–422.

Posner, Richard A. 2006. *Not a Suicide Pact: The Constitution in a Time of National Emergency*. New York ; Oxford: OXFORD UNIV PR.

Potoglou, Dimitris, Juan-Francisco Palacios, and Claudio Feijóo. 2015. "An Integrated Latent Variable and Choice Model to Explore the Role of Privacy Concern on Stated Behavioural Intentions in E-Commerce." *Journal of Choice Modelling* 17: 10–27.

Potoglou, Dimitris, Neil Robinson, Chong W. Kim, Peter Burge, and Richard Warnes. 2010. "Quantifying Individuals' Trade-Offs between Privacy, Liberty and Security: The Case of Rail Travel in UK." *Transportation Research Part A: Policy and Practice* 44 (3): 169–81.

Preibusch, Sören. 2013. "Guide to Measuring Privacy Concern: Review of Survey and Observational Instruments." *International Journal of Human-Computer Studies* 71 (12): 1133–43.

Prince, Jeffrey T., and Scott Wallsten. 2022. "How Much Is Privacy Worth around the World and across Platforms?" *Journal of Economics & Management Strategy* 31 (4): 841–61.

Putnam, Robert D. 1966. "Political Attitudes and the Local Community." *American Political Science Review* 60 (3): 640–54.

Pyszczynski, Thomas A. 2004. "What Are We So Afraid Of? A Terror Management Theory Perspective on the Politics of Fear." *Social Research* 71 (4): 827–48.

Pyszczynski, Thomas A., Sheldon Solomon, and Jeff Greenburg. 2002. *In the Wake of 9–11: The Psychology of Terror*. Washington: American Psychological Association.

PytlikZillig, Lisa M., Myiah J. Hutchens, Peter Muhlberger, Frank J. Gonzalez, and Alan J. Tomkins. 2018. "Policy Acceptance." In *Deliberative Public Engagement with Science: An Empirical Investigation*, edited by Lisa M. PytlikZillig, Myiah J. Hutchens, Peter Muhlberger, Frank J. Gonzalez, and Alan J. Tomkins, 89–116. SpringerBriefs in Psychology. Cham: Springer International Publishing.

Quast, Christian. 2018. "Towards a Balanced Account of Expertise." *Social Epistemology* 32 (6): 397–419.

Quinn, Kelly. 2016. "Why We Share: A Uses and Gratifications Approach to Privacy Regulation in Social Media Use." *Journal of Broadcasting & Electronic Media* 60 (1): 61–86.

R+V. 2022. "Im Langzeitvergleich: „Die Ängste der Deutschen"." 2022. https://www.ruv.de/newsroom/themenspezial-die-aengste-der-deutschen/langzeitvergleich.

Raab, Charles D. 1999. "From Balancing to Steering: New Directions for Data Protection." In *Visions of Privacy*, edited by Colin J. Bennett and Rebecca Grant, 68–94. Toronto: University of Toronto Press.

Rachels, James. 1975. "Why Privacy Is Important." *Philosophy & Public Affairs* 4 (4): 323–33.

Rainie, Lee, and Maeve Duggan. 2016. "Privacy and Information Sharing." Pew Research Center. https://www.pewresearch.org/wp-content/uploads/sites/9/2016/01/PI_2016.01.14_Privacy-and-Info-Sharing_FINAL.pdf.

Raudenbush, Stephen W., and Anthony S. Bryk. 2002. *Hierarchical Linear Models: Applications and Data Analysis Methods*. 2nd ed. Thousand Oaks: SAGE Publications.

Reddick, Christopher G., Akemi Takeoka Chatfield, and Patricia A. Jaramillo. 2015. "Public Opinion on National Security Agency Surveillance Programs: A Multi-Method Approach." *Government Information Quarterly* 32 (2): 129–41.

Rediger, Arielle. 2017. "Always-Listening Technologies: Who Is Listening and What Can Be Done About It?" *Loyola Consumer Law Review* 29 (2): 229.

Regan, Priscilla M. 1995. *Legislating Privacy: Technology, Social Values, and Public Policy*. Chapel Hill: University of North Carolina Press.

Reiman, Jeffrey H. 1976. "Privacy, Intimacy, and Personhood." *Philosophy & Public Affairs* 6 (1): 26–44.

Reiman, Jeffrey H. 1995. "Driving to the Panopticon: A Philosophical Exploration of the Risks to Privacy Posed by the Highway Technology of the Future." *Santa Clara High Technology Law Journal* 11 (1): 27.

Remster, Brianna, and Rory Kramer. 2018. "Race, Space, and Surveillance: Understanding the Relationship between Criminal Justice Contact and Institutional Involvement." *Socius* 4: 1–16.

Resnick, Ilyse, Nora S. Newcombe, and Thomas F. Shipley. 2017. "Dealing with Big Numbers: Representation and Understanding of Magnitudes Outside of Human Experience." *Cognitive Science* 41 (4): 1020–41.

Risse, Mathias, and Richard Zeckhauser. 2004. "Racial Profiling." *Philosophy & Public Affairs* 32 (2): 131–70.

Roberts, Andrew. 2015. "A Republican Account of the Value of Privacy." *European Journal of Political Theory* 14 (3): 320–44.

Robinson, Neil, Dimitris Potoglou, Chong Woo Kim, Peter Burge, and Richard Warnes. 2010. "Security, At What Cost?: Quantifying People's Trade-Offs across Liberty, Privacy and Security." Santa Monica: RAND Corporation. https://www.rand.org/pubs/technical_reports/TR664.html.

Rokeach, Milton. 1973. *The Nature of Human Values*. New York: Free Press.

Rose, Ellen. 2005. "Data Users versus Data Subjects: Are Consumers Willing to Pay for Property Rights to Personal Information?" In *Proceedings of the 38th Annual Hawaii International Conference on System Sciences*, 180. Big Island, HI, USA: IEEE. https://doi.org/10.1109/HICSS.2005.184.

Rosen, Jeffrey. 2000. *The Unwanted Gaze: The Destruction of Privacy in America*. New York: Random House.

Rössler, Beate. 2005. *The Value of Privacy*. Cambridge: Polity.

Rössler, Beate. 2015. "Should Personal Data Be a Tradable Good? On the Moral Limits of Markets in Privacy." In *Social Dimensions of Privacy: Interdisciplinary Perspectives*, edited by Beate Rössler and Dorota Mokrosinska, 141–61. Cambridge: Cambridge University Press.

Rössler, Beate. 2018. "Three Dimensions of Privacy." In *The Handbook of Privacy Studies*, edited by Bart Sloot and Aviva Groot, 137–42. Amsterdam University Press.

Roßnagel, Alexander. 2010. "Die„Überwachungs-Gesamtrechnung"-Das BVerfG Und Die Vorratsdatenspeicherung." *Neue Juristische Wochenschrift: NJW* 63 (18): 1238–42.

Roßnagel, Alexander, Tamer Bile, Christian Geminn, Marit Hansen, Felix Bieker, and Murat Karaboga. 2022. “On the Introduction of a Surveillance Calculus in Germany.” *Forum Privacy and Self-Determined Life in the Digital World—Policy Paper*, 1–12.

Rosso, Mark, ABM Nasir, and Mohsen Farhadloo. 2020. “Chilling Effects and the Stock Market Response to the Snowden Revelations.” *New Media & Society* 22 (11): 1976–95.

Rubinstein, Ariel. 2013. “Response Time and Decision Making: An Experimental Study.” *Judgment and Decision Making* 8 (5): 540–51.

Ruddock, Philip. 2004. “A New Framework : Counter-Terrorism and the Rule of Law.” *The Sydney Papers* 16 (2): 112–21.

Rule, James B. 2007. *Privacy in Peril: How We Are Sacrificing a Fundamental Right in Exchange for Security and Convenience*. Oxford ; New York: Oxford University Press.

Ryan, Mary K. 2018. “Government Surveillance: Racism and Civic Virtue in the United States.” In *Surveillance, Race, Culture*, edited by Susan Flynn and Antonia Mackay, 43–59. Cham: Springer International Publishing.

Rykkja, Lise H., Per Lægreid, and Anne Lise Fimreite. 2011. “Attitudes towards Anti-Terror Measures: The Role of Trust, Political Orientation and Civil Liberties Support.” *Critical Studies on Terrorism* 4 (2): 219–37.

Sackett, Lee. 1993. “A Post-Modern Panopticon: The Royal Commission into Aboriginal Deaths in Custody.” *Australian Journal of Social Issues* 28 (3): 229–44.

Sætra, Henrik Skaug. 2019. “Freedom under the Gaze of Big Brother: Preparing the Grounds for a Liberal Defence of Privacy in the Era of Big Data.” *Technology in Society* 58: 101160.

Sætra, Henrik Skaug. 2022. “The Ethics of Trading Privacy for Security: The Multifaceted Effects of Privacy on Liberty and Security.” *Technology in Society* 68: 101854.

Sakano, R., Kofi Obeng, and K. Fuller. 2016. “Airport Security and Screening Satisfaction: A Case Study of U.S.” *Journal of Air Transport Management* 55: 129–38.

Salter, Mark B. 2008. “Securitization and Desecuritization: A Dramaturgical Analysis of the Canadian Air Transport Security Authority.” *Journal of International Relations and Development* 11 (4): 321–49.

Sandel, Michael J. 1998. *Democracy's Discontent—America in Search: America in Search of a Public Philosophy*. Cambridge, Mass.: The Belknap Press.

Sanders, Carrie B., and Stacey Hannem. 2012. “Policing ‘the Risky’: Technology and Surveillance in Everyday Patrol Work.” *Canadian Review of Sociology/Revue Canadienne de Sociologie* 49 (4): 389–410.

Sanquist, Thomas F., Heidi Mahy, and Frederic Morris. 2008. “An Exploratory Risk Perception Study of Attitudes Toward Homeland Security Systems.” *Risk Analysis* 28 (4): 1125–33.

Scanlon, Thomas. 1975. “Thomson on Privacy.” *Philosophy and Public Affairs* 4 (4): 315–22.

Schäfer, Armin. 2022. “Cultural Backlash? How (Not) to Explain the Rise of Authoritarian Populism.” *British Journal of Political Science* 52 (4): 1977–93.

Schakel, Wouter. 2021. “Unequal Policy Responsiveness in the Netherlands.” *Socio-Economic Review* 19 (1): 37–57.

Schaub, Florian, and Lorrie Faith Cranor. 2020. “Usable and Useful Privacy Interfaces.” *An Introduction to Privacy for Technology Professionals*, 176–299.

Scherer, Philipp, and Sigrid Roßteutscher. 2019. “Wertorientierungen Und Wertewandel.” In *Politikwissenschaftliche Einstellungs-Und Verhaltensforschung*, edited by Oscar W.

Gabriel, Jürgen Maier, and Thorsten Faas, 207–29. Baden-Baden: Nomos Verlagsgesellschaft mbH & Co. KG.
Schneider, Steffen. 2020. "Democracy and Security in Germany before and after Reunification." In *Routledge Handbook of Democracy and Security*, edited by Leonard Weinberg, Elizabeth Francis, and Eliot Assoudeh, 97–108. London: Routledge.
Schneier, Bruce. 2001. "Protecting Privacy and Liberty." *Nature* 413 (6858): 773–773.
Schneier, Bruce. 2008. "The Psychology of Security." In *Proceedings of Progress in Cryptology—AFRICACRYPT 2008*, edited by Serge Vaudenay, 50–79. Lecture Notes in Computer Science. Berlin, Heidelberg: Springer. https://doi.org/10.1007/978-3-540-68164-9_5.
Schoeman, Ferdinand David. 1984. "Privacy: Philosophical Dimensions of the Literature." In *Philosophical Dimensions of Privacy: An Anthology*, edited by Ferdinand David Schoeman, 1–33. Cambridge: Cambridge University Press.
Schoeman, Ferdinand David. 1992. *Privacy and Social Freedom*. Cambridge Studies in Philosophy and Public Policy. Cambridge: Cambridge University Press.
Schoonhoven, Bas van, Arnold Roosendaal, and Noor Huijboom. 2014. "Privacy Versus Collective Security." In *Privacy and Identity Management for Emerging Services and Technologies*, edited by Marit Hansen, Jaap-Henk Hoepman, Ronald Leenes, and Diane Whitehouse, 93–101. IFIP Advances in Information and Communication Technology. Berlin, Heidelberg: Springer. https://doi.org/10.1007/978-3-642-55137-6_7.
Schulan, Alexander. 2019. "Behavioural Economics of Security." *European Journal for Security Research* 4 (2): 273–86.
Schuler, Magdalena, and Larissa Wolkenstein. 2014. "Psychologie Und Sicherheitstechnologie." In *Sicherheit Und Offene Gesellschaft. Herausforderungen, Methoden Und Praxis Einer Gesellschaftspolitischen Sicherheitsforschung*, edited by Hans-Helmuth Gander and Gisela Riescher, 77–106. Baden-Baden: Nomos.
Schwartz, Paul M. 2005. "Privacy Inalienability and the Regulation of Spyware." *Berkeley Technology Law Journal* 20 (3): 1269–82.
Schyff, Karl van der, Stephen Flowerday, and Paul Benjamin Lowry. 2020. "Information Privacy Behavior in the Use of Facebook Apps: A Personality-Based Vulnerability Assessment." *Heliyon* 6 (8): e04714.
Sears, David O., Richard R. Lau, Tom R. Tyler, and Harris M. Allen. 1980. "Self-Interest vs. Symbolic Politics in Policy Attitudes and Presidential Voting." *American Political Science Review* 74 (3): 670–84.
Seifert, Jeffrey W. 2004. "Data Mining and the Search for Security: Challenges for Connecting the Dots and Databases." *Government Information Quarterly* 21 (4): 461–80.
Selinger, Evan, and Hyo Joo (Judy) Rhee. 2021. "Normalizing Surveillance." *SATS* 22 (1): 49–74.
Shaddy, Franklin, Ayelet Fishbach, and Itamar Simonson. 2021. "Trade-Offs in Choice." *Annual Review of Psychology* 72 (1): 181–206.
Shao, Jingjin, Qianhan Zhang, Yining Ren, Xiying Li, and Tian Lin. 2019. "Why Are Older Adults Victims of Fraud? Current Knowledge and Prospects Regarding Older Adults' Vulnerability to Fraud." *Journal of Elder Abuse & Neglect* 31 (3): 225–43.
Siegel, David A. 2013. "Will You Accept the Government's Friend Request? Social Networks and Privacy Concerns." *PLOS ONE* 8 (11): e80682.

Simitis, Spiros. 1987. "Reviewing Privacy In an Information Society." *University of Pennsylvania Law Review* 135 (3): 707.

Simmel, Arnold. 1971. "Privacy Is Not an Isolated Freedom." In *Privacy and Personality*, edited by John W. Pennock and J. Roland; Chapman, 71–87. New York: Routledge.

Simmons, Ric. 2016. "Quantifying Criminal Procedure: How to Unlock the Potential of Big Data in Our Criminal Justice System." *Michigan State Law Review* 947: 947–1017.

Simon, Robert. 2020. "Is There a Trade-off Between Freedom and Safety? A Philosophical Contribution to a Covid-19 Related Discussion." *Philosophy Study* 10 (7): 445–53.

Simone, Maria A. 2009. "Give Me Liberty and Give Me Surveillance: A Case Study of the US Government's Discourse of Surveillance." *Critical Discourse Studies* 6 (1): 1–14.

Singer, Eleanor, John Van Hoewyk, and Randall J. Neugebauer. 2003. "Attitudes and Behavior: The Impact of Privacy and Confidentiality Concerns on Participation in the 2000 Census." *The Public Opinion Quarterly* 67 (3): 368–84.

Sjöstedt, Roxanna. 2019. "Assessing Securitization Theory: Theoretical Discussions and Empirical Developments." In *Securitization Revisited: Contemporary Applications and Insights*, edited by Michael J. Butler, 28–46. London: Routledge.

Smith, Adam. 1978. *Lectures on Jurisprudence.* Oxford: Oxford University Press.

Smith, Graham M. 2005. "Into Cerberus' Lair: Bringing the Idea of Security to Light." *The British Journal of Politics and International Relations* 7 (4): 485–507.

Smith, H. Jeff, Tamara Dinev, and Heng Xu. 2011. "Information Privacy Research: An Interdisciplinary Review." *MIS Quarterly* 35 (4): 989–1015.

Smith, H. Jeff, Sandra J. Milberg, and Sandra J. Burke. 1996. "Information Privacy: Measuring Individuals' Concerns about Organizational Practices." *MIS Quarterly* 20 (2): 167–96.

Smith, Patrick Taylor. 2020. "A Neo-Republican Theory of Just State Surveillance." *Moral Philosophy and Politics* 7 (1): 49–71.

Smith, V. Kerry, Carol Mansfield, and Laurel Clayton. 2009. "Valuing a Homeland Security Policy: Countermeasures for the Threats from Shoulder Mounted Missiles." *Journal of Risk and Uncertainty* 38 (3): 215–43.

Snijders, Tom A. B., and Roel Bosker. 2011. *Multilevel Analysis: An Introduction to Basic and Advanced Multilevel Modeling.* Second Edition. Los Angeles: SAGE Publications Ltd.

Solove, Daniel J. 2002. "Conceptualizing Privacy." *California Law Review* 90 (4): 1087–1155.

Solove, Daniel J. 2006. "A Taxonomy of Privacy." *University of Pennsylvania Law Review* 154 (3): 477–560.

Solove, Daniel J. 2007. "'I've Got Nothing to Hide' and Other Misunderstandings of Privacy." *San Diego Law Review* 44: 745–72.

Solove, Daniel J. 2008a. "Data Mining and the Security-Liberty Debate." *The University of Chicago Law Review* 74 (1): 343–62.

Solove, Daniel J. 2008b. *Understanding Privacy.* Cambridge, Mass: Harvard University Press.

Solove, Daniel J. 2011. *Nothing to Hide: The False Tradeoff Between Privacy and Security.* New Haven ; London: Yale University Press.

Solymosi, Reka, Kate Bowers, and Taku Fujiyama. 2015. "Mapping Fear of Crime as a Context-Dependent Everyday Experience That Varies in Space and Time." *Legal and Criminological Psychology* 20 (2): 193–211.

Sozialdemokratische Partei Deutschlands, Bündnis '90/Die Grünen, and Freie Demokraten. 2021. "Mehr Fortschritt Wagen—Bündnis Für Freiheit, Gerechtigkeit Und Nachhaltigkeit. Koalitionsvertrag 2021–2025." Berlin. https://www.bundesregierung.de/breg-de/service/gesetzesvorhaben/koalitionsvertrag-2021-1990800.

Spiekermann, Sarah, Jens Grossklags, and Bettina Berendt. 2001. "E-Privacy in 2nd Generation E-Commerce: Privacy Preferences versus Actual Behavior." In *Proceedings of the 3rd ACM Conference on Electronic Commerce*, 38–47. EC '01. New York, NY, USA: Association for Computing Machinery. https://doi.org/10.1145/501158.501163.

Spriggs, Angela, Javier Argomaniz, Martin Gill, and Jane Bryan. 2005. "Public Attitudes Towards CCTV: Results From the Pre-Intervention Public Attitude Survey Carried Out in Areas Implementing CCTV." 10/05. Home Office Online Report. London: Home Office. http://doi.apa.org/get-pe-doi.cfm?doi=10.1037/e635042007-001.

Stahl, Titus. 2020. "Privacy in Public: A Democratic Defense." *Moral Philosophy and Politics* 7 (1): 73–96.

Stallen, Pieter Jan M., and Arend Tomas. 1988. "Public Concern About Industrial Hazards." *Risk Analysis* 8 (2): 237–45.

Stegmueller, Daniel. 2013. "How Many Countries for Multilevel Modeling? A Comparison of Frequentist and Bayesian Approaches." *American Journal of Political Science* 57 (3): 748–61.

Steinfeld, Nili. 2017. "Track Me, Track Me Not: Support and Consent to State and Private Sector Surveillance." *Telematics and Informatics* 34 (8): 1663–72.

Sterrett, David, Dan Malato, Jennifer Benz, Trevor Tompson, and Ned English. 2017. "Assessing Changes in Coverage Bias of Web Surveys in the United States." *Public Opinion Quarterly* 81 (S1): 338–56.

Stevic, Anja, Desirée Schmuck, Anna Koemets, Melanie Hirsch, Kathrin Karsay, Marina F. Thomas, and Jörg Matthes. 2022. "Privacy Concerns Can Stress You out: Investigating the Reciprocal Relationship between Mobile Social Media Privacy Concerns and Perceived Stress." *Communications* 47 (3): 327–49.

Stewart, Kathy A., and Albert H. Segars. 2002. "An Empirical Examination of the Concern for Information Privacy Instrument." *Information Systems Research* 13 (1): 36–49.

Stigler, George J. 1980. "An Introduction to Privacy in Economics and Politics." *The Journal of Legal Studies* 9 (4): 623–44.

Storbeck, Jürgen. 2002. "The Hiding of Wealth." *Journal of Financial Crime* 9 (4): 372–79.

Stoycheff, Elizabeth. 2016. "Under Surveillance: Examining Facebook's Spiral of Silence Effects in the Wake of NSA Internet Monitoring." *Journalism & Mass Communication Quarterly* 93 (2): 296–311.

Stoycheff, Elizabeth, G. Scott Burgess, and Maria Clara Martucci. 2018. "Online Censorship and Digital Surveillance: The Relationship between Suppression Technologies and Democratization across Countries." *Information, Communication & Society* 23 (4): 474–90.

Stoycheff, Elizabeth, Juan Liu, Kai Xu, and Kunto Wibowo. 2018. "Privacy and the Panopticon: Online Mass Surveillance's Deterrence and Chilling Effects." *New Media & Society* 21 (3): 602–19.

Stritzel, Holger. 2007. "Towards a Theory of Securitization: Copenhagen and Beyond." *European Journal of International Relations* 13 (3): 357–83.

Stritzel, Holger. 2014. *Security in Translation*. London: Palgrave Macmillan UK.

Stutzer, Alois, and Michael Zehnder. 2013. "Is Camera Surveillance an Effective Measure of Counterterrorism?" *Defence and Peace Economics* 24 (1): 1–14.

Sun, Yongqiang, Nan Wang, Xiao-Liang Shen, and Jacky Xi Zhang. 2015. "Location Information Disclosure in Location-Based Social Network Services: Privacy Calculus, Benefit Structure, and Gender Differences." *Computers in Human Behavior* 52: 278–92.

Sunstein, Cass R. 2003. "Terrorism and Probability Neglect." *Journal of Risk and Uncertainty* 26 (2/3): 121–36.

Sunstein, Cass R. 2005. *Laws of Fear: Beyond the Precautionary Principle*. The Seeley Lectures. Cambridge: Cambridge University Press.

Sunstein, Cass R. 2007. "On the Divergent American Reactions to Terrorism and Climate Change." *Columbia Law Review* 107 (2): 503–57.

Suzor, Nicolas, Kylie Pappalardo, and Natalie McIntosh. 2017. "The Passage of Australia's Data Retention Regime: National Security, Human Rights, and Media Scrutiny." *Internet Policy Review* 6 (1): 1–16.

Svenonius, Ola, and Fredrika Björklund. 2018. "Explaining Attitudes to Secret Surveillance in Post-Communist Societies." *East European Politics* 34 (2): 123–51.

Sweeney, Latanya. 2000. "Simple Demographics Often Identify People Uniquely." *Carnegie Mellon University, Data Privacy Working Paper* 3: 1–34.

Swire, Peter. 2006. "Privacy and Information Sharing in the War on Terrorism." *Villanova Law Review* 51 (4): 951.

Taddicken, Monika. 2012. "Privacy, Surveillance, and Self-Disclosure in the Social Web: Exploring the User's Perspective via Focus Groups." In *Internet and Surveillance: The Challenges of Web 2.0 and Social Media*, edited by Christian Fuchs, Kees Boersma, Anders Albrechtslund, and Marisol Sandoval, 255–72. New York: Routledge.

Taddicken, Monika. 2014. "The 'Privacy Paradox' in the Social Web: The Impact of Privacy Concerns, Individual Characteristics, and the Perceived Social Relevance on Different Forms of Self-Disclosure." *Journal of Computer-Mediated Communication* 19 (2): 248–73.

Tajfel, Henry, and John C. Turner. 1979. "An Integrative Theory of Intergroup Conflict." In *The Social Psychology of Intergroup Relations*, edited by William G. Austin and Stephen Worchel, 33–47. Monterey, Calif: Brooks/Cole Pub. Co.

Tang, Jie, Umair Akram, and Wenjing Shi. 2020. "Why People Need Privacy? The Role of Privacy Fatigue in App Users' Intention to Disclose Privacy: Based on Personality Traits." *Journal of Enterprise Information Management* 34 (4): 1097–1120.

Tausendpfund, Markus. 2020. "Mehrebenenanalyse." In *Fortgeschrittene Analyseverfahren in Den Sozialwissenschaften: Ein Überblick*, edited by Markus Tausendpfund, 119–64. Grundwissen Politik. Wiesbaden: Springer Fachmedien.

Taylor, Isaac. 2017. "Data Collection, Counterterrorism and the Right to Privacy." *Politics, Philosophy & Economics* 16 (3): 326–46.

Taylor, Jennifer Fries, Jodie Ferguson, and Pamela Scholder Ellen. 2015. "From Trait to State: Understanding Privacy Concerns." *Journal of Consumer Marketing* 32 (2): 99–112.

Teutsch, Doris, Philipp K. Masur, and Sabine Trepte. 2018. "Privacy in Mediated and Nonmediated Interpersonal Communication: How Subjective Concepts and Situational Perceptions Influence Behaviors." *Social Media + Society* 4 (2): 2056305118767134.

Thierer, Adam. 2013. "Technopanics, Threat Inflation, and the Danger of an Information Technology Precautionary Principle." *Minnesota Journal of Law, Science & Technology* 14 (1): 309.

Thomas, William I. 1923. "The Unadjusted Girl: With Cases and Standpoint for Behavior Analysis." *Criminal Science Monographs* 1 (4): 1–257.

Thompson, Nik, Tanya McGill, Anna Bunn, and Rukshan Alexander. 2020. "Cultural Factors and the Role of Privacy Concerns in Acceptance of Government Surveillance." *Journal of the Association for Information Science and Technology* 71 (9): 1129–42.

Torgler, Benno, and Neven T. Valev. 2010. "Gender and Public Attitudes Toward Corruption and Tax Evasion." *Contemporary Economic Policy* 28 (4): 554–68.

Toshkov, Dimiter, Lars Mäder, and Anne Rasmussen. 2020. "Party Government and Policy Responsiveness. Evidence from Three Parliamentary Democracies." *Journal of Public Policy* 40 (2): 329–47.

Tourangeau, Roger, Kenneth A. Rasinski, Norman Bradburn, and Roy D'Andrade. 1989. "Carryover Effects in Attitude Surveys." *The Public Opinion Quarterly* 53 (4): 495–524.

Trepte, Sabine, and Philipp K. Masur. 2017. "Privacy Attitudes, Perceptions, and Behaviors of the German Population." Forum Privatheit Und Selbstbestimmtes Leben in Der Digitalen Welt. Karlsruhe: Fraunhofer ISI. https://www.forum-privatheit.de/forum-privatheit-de/texte/veroeffentlichungen-des-forums/Trepte_Masur_2017_Research_Report_Hohenheim.pdf.

Trepte, Sabine, Michael Scharkow, and Tobias Dienlin. 2020. "The Privacy Calculus Contextualized: The Influence of Affordances." *Computers in Human Behavior* 104: 106115.

Trüdinger, Eva-Maria. 2018. "Sicherheit Aus Vertrauen? Der Einfluss Politischen Und Sozialen Vertrauens Auf Präferenzen Für Staatliche Antiterrormaßnahmen." In *Freiheit Oder Sicherheit? Ein Spannungsverhältnis Aus Sicht Der Bürgerinnen Und Bürger*, edited by Markus Steinbrecher, Heiko Biehl, Evelyn Bytzek, and Ulrich Rosar, 77–100. Schriftenreihe Des Zentrums Für Militärgeschichte Und Sozialwissenschaften Der Bundeswehr. Wiesbaden: Springer Fachmedien.

Trüdinger, Eva-Maria. 2019. "Perceptions of Threat and Policy Attitudes: The Case of Support for Anti-Terrorism Policies in Germany." Habilitation, Stuttgart: Universität Stuttgart. https://elib.uni-stuttgart.de/bitstream/11682/11010/3/Truedinger_Habil_Thesis_Threat_Policy_Att_2019.pdf.

Trüdinger, Eva-Maria. 2020. "Policy-Orientierungen." In *Politikwissenschaftliche Einstellungs- Und Verhaltensforschung. Handbuch Für Wissenschaft Und Studium*, edited by Thorsten Faas, Oscar W. Gabriel, and Jürgen Maier, 309–25. Baden-Baden: Nomos.

Trüdinger, Eva-Maria, and Leonie C. Steckermeier. 2017. "Trusting and Controlling? Political Trust, Information and Acceptance of Surveillance Policies: The Case of Germany." *Government Information Quarterly* 34 (3): 421–33.

Trüdinger, Eva-Maria, and Conrad Ziller. 2022. "Considered Effective? How Policy Evaluations and Threat Perceptions Affect Support for Surveillance in the Context of Terrorism." *Politics & Policy* 50 (5): 894–912.

Tsapogas, Dimitris. 2017. "The Importance of Social and Political Context in Explaining Citizens' Attitudes towards Electronic Surveillance and Political Participation." In *Surveillance, Privacy and Security: Citizens' Perspectives*, edited by Michael Friedewald, J. Peter Burgess, Johann Cas, Walter Peissl, and Rocco Bellanova, 212–32. London; New York: Routledge.

Tsertsidis, Antonios, Ella Kolkowska, and Karin Hedström. 2019. "Factors Influencing Seniors' Acceptance of Technology for Ageing in Place in the Post-Implementation Stage: A Literature Review." *International Journal of Medical Informatics* 129: 324–33.

Turner, John C., Michael A. Hogg, Penelope J. Oakes, Stephen D. Reicher, and Margaret S. Wetherell. 1987. *Rediscovering the Social Group: A Self-Categorization Theory*. Rediscovering the Social Group: A Self-Categorization Theory. Cambridge: Basil Blackwell.

Tversky, Amos, and Daniel Kahneman. 1974. "Judgment under Uncertainty: Heuristics and Biases." *Science* 185 (4157): 1124–31.

Tversky, Amos, and Daniel Kahneman. 1981. "The Framing of Decisions and the Psychology of Choice." *Science* 211 (4481): 453–58.

Tversky, Amos, and Itamar Simonson. 1993. "Context-Dependent Preferences." *Management Science* 39 (10): 1179–89.

UNECE. 2015. "Conference of European Statisticians. Recommendations for the 2020 Censuses of Population and Housing." New York; Geneva: United Nations Economic Commission for Europe. https://www.unece.org/fileadmin/DAM/stats/publications/2015/ECE CES41_EN.pdf.

United Nations Development Programme. 1994. "Human Development Report 1994." New York: United Nations. https://hdr.undp.org/content/human-development-report-1994.

Ur, Blase, and Yang Wang. 2013. "A Cross-Cultural Framework for Protecting User Privacy in Online Social Media." In *Proceedings of the 22nd International Conference on World Wide Web*, 755–62. WWW '13 Companion. Rio de Janeiro: ACM. https://doi.org/10.1145/2487788.2488037.

Vagle, Jeffrey L. 2017. *Being Watched: Legal Challenges to Government Surveillance*. new York: NYU Press.

Valente, Riccardo, and Sergi Valera Pertegas. 2018. "Ontological Insecurity and Subjective Feelings of Unsafety: Analysing Socially Constructed Fears in Italy." *Social Science Research* 71: 160–70.

Van Heek, Julia, Katrin Arning, and Martina Ziefle. 2016. "'How Fear of Crime Affects Needs for Privacy Safety'. Acceptance of Surveillance Technologies in Smart Cities." In *Proceedings of the 5th International Conference on Smart Cities and Green ICT Systems (SMARTGREENS 2016)*, 32–43. Rome. https://www.scitepress.org/papers/2016/57619/57619.pdf.

Van Heek, Julia, Katrin Arning, and Martina Ziefle. 2017. "Where, Wherefore, and How? Contrasting Two Surveillance Contexts According to Acceptance." In *International Conference on Smart Cities and Green ICT Systems (SMARTGREENS)*, 87–98. Porto. https://doi.org/10.5220/0006362400870098.

Väyrynen, Pekka. 2021. "Thick Ethical Concepts." In *The Stanford Encyclopedia of Philosophy*, edited by Edward N. Zalta, Spring 2021. Stanford: Metaphysics Research Lab, Stanford University.

Vélez, María Alejandra, Carlos Andres Trujillo, Lina Moros, and Clemente Forero. 2016. "Prosocial Behavior and Subjective Insecurity in Violent Contexts: Field Experiments." *PLOS ONE* 11 (7): e0158878.

Verbrauchs- und Medienanalyse. 2022. "Den Markt Im Blick. Basisinformationen Für Fundierte Mediaentscheidungen. VuMa Touchpoints 2022." Frankfurt. https://www.vuma.de/fileadmin/user_upload/PDF/berichtsbaende/VuMA_Berichtsband_2022.pdf.

Vermeersch, Hans, and Evelien de Pauw. 2017. "The Acceptance of New Security Oriented Technologies: A 'Framing' Experiment." In *Surveillance, Privacy and Security: Citizens' Perspectives*, edited by Michael Friedewald, J. Peter Burgess, Johann Cas, Walter Peissl, and Rocco Bellanova, 52–70. London; New York: Routledge.

Vermeule, Adrian. 2014. "Security and Liberty. Critiques of the Trade-Off Thesis." In *The Long Decade: How 9/11 Changed the Law*, edited by David Jenkins, Amanda Jacobsen, and Anders Henriksen, 31–44. New York: Oxford University Press.

Vermeulen, Matthias. 2014. "SURVEILLE Deliverable D4.7 The Scope of the Right to Private Life in Public Places." https://surveille.eui.eu/wp-content/uploads/sites/19/2015/04/D4.7-The-scope-of-the-right-to-privacy-in-public-places.pdf.

Vieno, Alessio, Michele Roccato, and Silvia Russo. 2013. "Is Fear of Crime Mainly Social and Economic Insecurity in Disguise? A Multilevel Multinational Analysis." *Journal of Community & Applied Social Psychology* 23 (6): 519–35.

Viscusi, W. Kip, and Richard J. Zeckhauser. 2003. "Sacrificing Civil Liberties to Reduce Terrorism Risks." *Journal of Risk and Uncertainty* 26 (2/3): 99–120.

Volkens, Andrea, Tobias Burst, Werner Krause, Pola Lehmann, Theres Matthieß, Nicolas Merz, Sven Regel, and Bernhard Weßels. 2020. "Manifesto Data Collection. Manifesto Project (MRG/CMP/MARPOR)." Berlin: Wissenschaftszentrum Berlin für Sozialforschung (WZB). https://doi.org/10.25522/manifesto.mpds.2020b.

Vultee, Fred. 2010a. "Securitization. A New Approach to Framing of the 'War on Terror.'" *Journalism Practice* 4 (1): 33–47.

Vultee, Fred. 2010b. "Securitization as Media Frame." In *Securitization Theory. How Security Problems Emerge and Dissolve*, edited by Thierry Balzacq, 77–93. London: Routledge.

Wadle, Lisa-Marie, Noemi Martin, and Daniel Ziegler. 2019. "Privacy and Personalization: The Trade-off between Data Disclosure and Personalization Benefit." In *Adjunct Publication of the 27th Conference on User Modeling, Adaptation and Personalization*, 319–24. UMAP'19 Adjunct. New York, NY, USA: Association for Computing Machinery. https://doi.org/10.1145/3314183.3323672.

Wæver, Ole. 1995. "Securitization and Desecuritization." In *On Security*, edited by Ronnie Lipschutz, 46–86. New York: Columbia University Press.

Wakefield, Robin. 2013. "The Influence of User Affect in Online Information Disclosure." *The Journal of Strategic Information Systems* 22 (2): 157–74.

Waldron, Jeremy. 1987. "Theoretical Foundations of Liberalism." *The Philosophical Quarterly* 37 (147): 127–50.

Waldron, Jeremy. 2003. "Security and Liberty: The Image of Balance." *Journal of Political Philosophy* 11 (2): 191–210.

Waldron, Jeremy. 2006. "Safety and Security." *Nebraska Law Review* 85 (2): 454–508.

Wall, David S. 2005. "Surveillant Internet Technologies and the Growth of Information Capitalism: Spams and Public Trust in the Information Society." In *The New Politics of*

Surveillance and Visibility, edited by Kevin D. Haggerty and Richard Ericson, 340–62. Toronto: University of Toronto Press.

Warren, Samuel D., and Louis D. Brandeis. 1890. "The Right to Privacy." *Harvard Law Review* 4 (5): 193–220.

Watson, Hayley, Rachel L. Finn, and David Barnard-Wills. 2017. "A Gap in the Market: The Conceptualisation of Surveillance, Security, Privacy and Trust in Public Opinion Surveys." *Surveillance & Society* 15 (2): 269–85.

Watson, Scott D. 2012. "'Framing' the Copenhagen School: Integrating the Literature on Threat Construction." *Millennium* 40 (2): 279–301.

Weber, Max. 1946. "Politics as a Vocation." In *From Max Weber: Essays in Sociology*, edited by Hans H. Gerth and C. Wright Mills, 77–128. New York: Oxford University Press.

Weller, Toni. 2012. "The Information State: A Historical Perspective on Surveillance." In *Routledge Handbook of Surveillance Studies*, edited by Kirstie Ball, Kevin D. Haggerty, and David Lyon, 57–63. Routledge.

Welsh, Brandon C., and David P. Farrington. 2002. "Crime Prevention Effects of Closed Circuit Television: A Systematic Review." Home Office Research Study 252. London: Home Office. https://popcenter.asu.edu/sites/default/files/Responses/video_surveillance/PDFs/Welsh&Farrington_2002.pdf.

Welsh, Brandon C., and David P. Farrington. 2009. "Public Area CCTV and Crime Prevention: An Updated Systematic Review and Meta-Analysis." *Justice Quarterly* 26 (4): 716–45.

Welzel, Christian. 2013. *Freedom Rising*. Cambridge: Cambridge University Press.

Wenzelburger, Georg, and Helge Staff. 2016. "German Exceptionalism? An Empirical Analysis of 20 Years of Law and Order Legislation." *Politics & Policy* 44 (2): 319–50.

Wester, Misse, and Johan Giesecke. 2019. "Accepting Surveillance—An Increased Sense of Security after Terror Strikes?" *Safety Science* 120: 383–87.

Westin, Alan F. 1967. *Privacy and Freedom*. New York: Atheneum.

Westin, Alan F. 1996. "Privacy in the Workplace: How Well Does American Law Reflect American Values?" *Chicago-Kent Law Review* 72 (1): 271.

Whitaker, Reginald. 1999. *The End of Privacy: How Total Surveillance Is Becoming a Reality*. New York: New Press.

Whitman, James Q. 2004. "The Two Western Cultures of Privacy: Dignity versus Liberty." *The Yale Law Journal* 113 (6): 1151–1221.

Wigan, Marcus, and Roger Clarke. 2006. "Social Impacts of Transport Surveillance." *Prometheus* 24 (4): 389–403.

Wilcoxon, Frank. 1945. "Individual Comparisons by Ranking Methods." *Biometrics Bulletin* 1 (6): 80–83.

Williams, Dave, and Jobuda Ahmed. 2009. "The Relationship between Antisocial Stereotypes and Public CCTV Systems: Exploring Fear of Crime in the Modern Surveillance Society." *Psychology, Crime & Law* 15 (8): 743–58.

Williams, Michael C. 2010. "The Continuing Evolution of Securitization Theory." In *Securitization Theory. How Security Problems Emerge and Dissolve*, edited by Thierry Balzacq, 212–22. London: Routledge.

Williams, Richard. 2012. "Using the Margins Command to Estimate and Interpret Adjusted Predictions and Marginal Effects." *The Stata Journal: Promoting Communications on Statistics and Stata* 12 (2): 308–31.

Willison, Donald J., Valerie Steeves, Cathy Charles, Lisa Schwartz, Jennifer Ranford, Gina Agarwal, Ji Cheng, and Lehana Thabane. 2009. "Consent for Use of Personal Information for Health Research: Do People with Potentially Stigmatizing Health Conditions and the General Public Differ in Their Opinions?" *BMC Medical Ethics* 10 (1): 10.

Wilson, Dave, and Joseph S. Valacich. 2012. "Unpacking the Privacy Paradox: Irrational Decision-Making within the Privacy Calculus." In *33rd International Conference on Information Systems (ICIS)*, 101. Orlando: Citeseer. https://aisel.aisnet.org/icis2012/proceedings/ResearchInProgress/101.

Wilson, Theodore, David Maimon, Bertrand Sobesto, and Michel Cukier. 2015. "The Effect of a Surveillance Banner in an Attacked Computer System: Additional Evidence for the Relevance of Restrictive Deterrence in Cyberspace." *Journal of Research in Crime and Delinquency* 52 (6): 829–55.

Wirth, Jakob. 2018. "Dependent Variables in the Privacy-Related Field: A Descriptive Literature Review." In *Proceedings of the 51st Hawaii International Conference on System Sciences*, edited by Tung Bui, 3658–67. Waikoloa Village, Hawaii. https://aisel.aisnet.org/cgi/viewcontent.cgi?article=1476&context=hicss-51.

Wirth, Jakob, Christian Maier, and Sven Laumer. 2019. "Justification of Mass Surveillance: A Quantitative Study." In *14th International Conference on Wirtschaftsinformatik*, 1337–51. Siegen.

Wittgenstein, Ludwig. 1958. *Philosophical Investigations*. Translated by G.E.M. Anscombe. 2nd ed. Oxford: Basil Blackwell.

Wolfendale, Jessica. 2007. "Terrorism, Security, and the Threat of Counterterrorism." *Studies in Conflict & Terrorism* 30 (1): 75–92.

Wolfers, Arnold. 1952. "'National Security' as an Ambiguous Symbol." *Political Science Quarterly* 67 (4): 481–502.

Wolfers, Arnold. 1962. *Discord and Collaboration: Essays on International Politics: Essays in International Politics*. Baltimore: Johns Hopkins University Press.

Wonderly, Monique. 2019. "On the Affect of Security." *Philosophical Topics* 47 (2): 165–82.

Wood, David Murakami, David Lyon, and Kiyoshi Abe. 2007. "Surveillance in Urban Japan: A Critical Introduction." *Urban Studies* 44 (3): 551–68.

Woodruff, Allison, Vasyl Pihur, Sunny Consolvo, Laura Brandimarte, and Alessandro Acquisti. 2014. "Would a Privacy Fundamentalist Sell Their DNA for $1000...If Nothing Bad Happened as a Result? The Westin Categories, Behavioral Intentions, and Consequences." In *10th Symposium On Usable Privacy and Security (SOUPS 2014)*, 1–18. Menlo Park, California. https://www.usenix.org/conference/soups2014/proceedings/presentation/woodruff.

World Health Organization. 2023. "Cancer." 2023. https://www.who.int/health-topics/cancer.

Wottrich, Verena M., Eva A. van Reijmersdal, and Edith G. Smit. 2018. "The Privacy Trade-off for Mobile App Downloads: The Roles of App Value, Intrusiveness, and Privacy Concerns." *Decision Support Systems* 106: 44–52.

Wright, David, Michael Friedewald, Serge Gutwirth, Marc Langheinrich, Emilio Mordini, Rocco Bellanova, Paul De Hert, Kush Wadhwa, and Didier Bigo. 2010. "Sorting out Smart Surveillance." *Computer Law & Security Review* 26 (4): 343–54.

Wuttke, Alexander, Christian Schimpf, and Harald Schoen. 2020. "When the Whole Is Greater than the Sum of Its Parts: On the Conceptualization and Measurement of Populist

Attitudes and Other Multidimensional Constructs." *American Political Science Review* 114 (2): 356–74.

Wyszynski, Marc, and Adele Diederich. 2023. "Individual Differences Moderate Effects in an Unusual Disease Paradigm: A Psychophysical Data Collection Lab Approach and an Online Experiment." *Frontiers in Psychology* 14: 1086699.

Xu, Heng, and Tamara Dinev. 2012. "The Security-Liberty Balance: Individuals' Attitudes towards Internet Government Surveillance." *Electronic Government, an International Journal* 9 (1): 46–63.

Xu, Heng, Tamara Dinev, H. Jeff Smith, and Paul Hart. 2008. "Examining the Formation of Individual's Privacy Concerns: Toward an Integrative View." In *ICIS 2008 Proceedings*. Paris. https://aisel.aisnet.org/icis2008/6/.

Yu, Lu, He Li, Wu He, Feng-Kwei Wang, and Shiqiao Jiao. 2020. "A Meta-Analysis to Explore Privacy Cognition and Information Disclosure of Internet Users." *International Journal of Information Management* 51: 102015.

Yun, Haejung, Gwanhoo Lee, and Dan J. Kim. 2019. "A Chronological Review of Empirical Research on Personal Information Privacy Concerns: An Analysis of Contexts and Research Constructs." *Information & Management* 56 (4): 570–601.

Zachary, Iris, Suzanne A Boren, Eduardo Simoes, Jeannette Jackson-Thompson, J Wade Davis, and Lanis Hicks. 2015. "Information Management in Cancer Registries: Evaluating the Needs for Cancer Data Collection and Cancer Research." *Online Journal of Public Health Informatics* 7 (2): e213.

Zafeiropoulou, Aristea M., David E. Millard, Craig Webber, and Kieron O'Hara. 2013. "Unpicking the Privacy Paradox: Can Structuration Theory Help to Explain Location-Based Privacy Decisions?" In *Proceedings of the 5th Annual ACM Web Science Conference*, 463–72. WebSci '13. New York, NY, USA: Association for Computing Machinery. https://doi.org/10.1145/2464464.2464503.

Zaller, John. 1992. *The Nature and Origins of Mass Opinion*. Cambridge: Cambridge University Press.

Zedner, Lucia. 2003. "The Concept of Security: An Agenda for Comparative Analysis." *Legal Studies* 23 (1): 153–75.

Zedner, Lucia. 2006. "Policing Before and After the Police: The Historical Antecedents of Contemporary Crime Control." *The British Journal of Criminology* 46 (1): 78–96.

Zedner, Lucia. 2007. "Pre-Crime and Post-Criminology?" *Theoretical Criminology* 11 (2): 261–81.

Zedner, Lucia. 2008. "Terrorism, the Ticking Bomb, and Criminal Justice Values." *Criminal Justice Matters* 73 (1): 18–19.

Zedner, Lucia. 2009. *Security*. Key Ideas in Criminology. London ; New York: Routledge.

Ziller, Conrad, and Marc Helbling. 2021. "Public Support for State Surveillance." *European Journal of Political Research* 60 (4): 994–1006.

Zuboff, Shoshana. 2019. *The Age of Surveillance Capitalism: The Fight for a Human Future at the New Frontier of Power*. London: Profile Books Ltd.

Zurawski, Nils. 2007. "Einleitung: Surveillance Studies. Perspektiven Eines Forschungsfeldes." In *Surveillance Studies: Perspektiven Eines Forschungsfeldes*, edited by Nils Zurawski, 7–24. Leverkusen: Verlag Barbara Budrich.

Zurawski, Nils. 2015. "Technische Innovationen Und Deren Gesellschaftliche Auswirkungen Im Kontext von Überwachung." *Schriftenreihe Sicherheit (Forschungsforum Öffentliche Sicherheit)* 15.

Zureik, Elia, and L. Lynda Harling Stalker. 2010. "The Cross-Cultural Study of Privacy: Problems and Prospects." In Surveillance, Privacy, and the Globalization of Personal Information: International Comparisons, edited by Elia Zureik, L. Lynda Harling Stalker, Emily Smith, David Lyon, and Yolande E. Chan, 8–30. Montreal, Kingston, London, Ithaca: McGill-Queen's Press.

The manufacturer's authorised representative in the EU is Springer Nature Customer Service Centre GmbH, Europaplatz 3, 69115 Heidelberg, Germany. If you have any concerns regarding our products, please contact ProductSafety@springernature.com

Printed and bound by CPI Group (UK) Ltd, Croydon, CR0 4YY
01/10/2026
02225861-0004